A LIFE OF MIRACLES

A LIFE OF MIRACLES

A 365-Day Guide to Prayer and Miracles

Bill Johnson

Compiled by Jan Sherman.

Treasure House
An imprint of
Destiny Image® Publishers, Inc.
P.O. Box 310
Shippensburg, PA 17257-0310

"For where your treasure is, there will your heart be also" (Matthew 6:21).

ISBN 10: 0-7684-2612-X

ISBN 13: 978-0-7684-2612-0

For Worldwide Distribution
Printed in the U.S.A.

This book and all other Destiny Image, Revival Press, MercyPlace, Fresh Bread, Destiny Image Fiction, and Treasure House books are available at Christian bookstores and distributors worldwide.

1 2 3 4 5 6 7 8 9 10 / 12 11 10 09 08

For a U.S. bookstore nearest you, call **1-800-722-6774.**

For more information on foreign distributors, call **717-532-3040.**

Reach us on the Internet: **www.destinyimage.com.**

10/23/08

Isaiah 58:10—And if you spend yourselves in behalf of the hungry and satisfy the needs of the oppressed, then your light will rise in the darkness, and your night will become like the noonday.

BOOK QUOTE: *When Heaven Invades Earth* [Chapter 1]

O N a cold and rainy Saturday, church buses were sent to the neediest parts of our city, Redding, to find the homeless and the poor. The bride and groom eagerly anticipated their return and prepared a meal in their honor. The needy were to be the distinguished guests of their wedding.

Ralph and Colleen met while working in our ministry to the poor. They shared a passion for God and a love for the needy. Although it is common for the bride and groom to register for gifts at fine department stores, Ralph and Colleen did so at Target; and all they put on their *wish list* were coats, hats, gloves, and sleeping bags…to be given to their *guests*. This was not going to be a typical wedding.

In our pre-wedding meeting the bride and groom encouraged me to be sensitive to the Holy Spirit in case He wanted to heal people during the wedding. They had created far too great a *miracle opportunity* for God not to do something extraordinary.

Following the ceremony, the newly married couple went directly to the reception hall, got behind the serving table, and dished the food for their guests. The hungry became satisfied. God was pleased.

But before the wedding ever started two or three people came to me with excitement in their voice. "There is somebody here who only has two and a half to three years to live!" We had crossed a milestone. Miracles of healing had become more common…to the point that a life-threatening disease seemed more like a potential miracle than it did something to fear. That in itself is a dream come true for me—people in North America *expecting* something supernatural from God!

*They had created far too great a **miracle opportunity** for God not to do something extraordinary.*

Lord sometimes I'm afraid to expect because of fear of disappointment. I know that Your ways are better than mine! It just gets so hard day after day expecting You to show up & step in & meet the needs of my heart. Where are You? Why don't You come? I love You so much & I just want to be near You, so come Lord in strength & power, in gentleness & love, just come.

Mark 2:17—On hearing this, Jesus said to them, "It is not the healthy who need a doctor, but the sick. I have not come to call on the righteous, but sinners."

BOOK QUOTE: *When Heaven Invades Earth* [Chapter 1]

HIS name was Luke. Luke walked with difficulty, needing the help of a cane. He wore braces on each arm, and a large brace around his neck.

My brother Bob and I brought him into the church kitchen, asking him about the braces on each arm. He told us his problem was carpal tunnel syndrome. We laid our hands on his wrists, commanding the *tunnel* to open and all numbness and pain to be gone. He then moved his hands freely, experiencing the healing he had just received.

When we asked him about his cane and the obvious problem with his leg, he described how he had suffered a horrible accident. As a result he had an artificial shin and hip and had even lost half a lung. When the surgeons put him back together, his leg was an inch too short. We commanded the leg to grow. It did. God was at work. He replaced one inch of missing bone and removed all the pain caused by Luke's accident.

Next we asked about Luke's neck. He told me he had cancer and was given a couple of years to live. He went on to explain that the brace was necessary because of the loss of the muscles in his neck. As we began to pray, I heard a doctor from our congregation command new muscles to grow. When we were finished, Luke turned his head from side to side. All was restored. He then placed his hand on the side of his neck and exclaimed, "The lumps are gone!"

His doctor gave him a clean bill of health, and the miracles continued long past the physical healing. Within weeks Luke got a job, the first time he had worked in 17 years. Jesus heals the whole person.

Jesus heals the whole person.

Lord I believe in Your healing, miracles, & prayer. Come to me Lord & show me Your power. I believe in Your Son & Your Holy Spirit. I want to see more of You in my life. I want to sit at Your feet dear Jesus & know You more. Come in Spirit & truth & power. I want to experience You healing all of me physical, emotional, spiritual, & financial. I believe Lord, please let it be!

Romans 1:16—*I am not ashamed of the gospel, because it is the power of God for the salvation of everyone who believes.*

BOOK QUOTE: *When Heaven Invades Earth* [Chapter 1]

[TAKE time to read the first two entries. The healing that is shared in the last entry took place during the wedding in the first entry.]

Although this kind of wedding remains unusual, our church's deliberate pursuit of the poor and the miracles are common. This story is true, and it is closer to the normal Christian life than what the Church *normally* experiences. The lack of miracles isn't because it is not in God's will for us. The problem exists between our ears. As a result, a transformation—*a renewing of the mind*—is needed, and it's only possible through a work of the Holy Spirit that typically comes upon desperate people.

The aforementioned bride and groom, although noble, are ordinary people who serve an extravagant Father. There wasn't a great person involved, except for Jesus. All the rest of us simply made room for God, believing Him to be good 100 percent of the time. The risks that the bride and groom took were more than God could pass up. In the midst of this marriage celebration God invaded a home marked by hellish disease and established a testimony for His glory.

Stories of this nature are becoming the norm, and the company of people who have joined this quest for an authentic gospel—*the gospel of the Kingdom*—is increasing. Loving God and His people is an honor. We will no longer make up excuses for powerlessness because powerlessness is inexcusable. Our mandate is simple: raise up a generation that can openly display the raw power of God. This book is all about that journey…the quest for the King and His Kingdom.

The kingdom of God is not a matter of talk but of power (1 Cor. 4:20).

Seek first the kingdom of God (Matt. 6:33).

Our mandate is simple: raise up a generation that can openly display the raw power of God.

Acts 2:22—Men of Israel, listen to this: Jesus of Nazareth was a man accredited by God to you by miracles, wonders and signs, which God did among you through Him, as you yourselves know.

BOOK QUOTE: *When Heaven Invades Earth* [Chapter 2]

JESUS could not heal the sick. Neither could He deliver the tormented from demons or raise the dead. To believe otherwise is to ignore what He said about Himself, and more importantly, to miss the purpose of His self-imposed restriction to live as a man.

Jesus Christ said of Himself, "The Son can do nothing"(John 5:19). In the Greek language that word *nothing* has a unique meaning—it means "*nothing*," just like it does in English! He had NO supernatural capabilities whatsoever! While He is 100 percent God, He chose to live with the same limitations that man would face once He was redeemed. He made that point over and over again. Jesus became the model for all who would embrace the invitation to invade the impossible in His name. He performed *miracles, wonders, and signs*, as a man in right relationship to God...not as God. If He performed miracles because He was God, then they would be unattainable for us. But if He did them as a man, I am responsible to pursue His lifestyle. Recapturing this simple truth changes everything...and makes possible a full restoration of the ministry of Jesus in His Church.

What were the distinctions of His humanity?

1. He had no sin to separate Him from the Father.

2. He was completely dependent on the power of the Holy Spirit working through Him.

What are the distinctions of our humanity?

1. We are sinners cleansed by the blood of Jesus. Through His sacrifice He has successfully dealt with the power and effect of sin for all who believe. Nothing now separates us from the Father. There remains only one unsettled issue—

2. How dependent on the Holy Spirit are we willing to live?

Jesus became the model for all who would embrace the invitation to invade the impossible in His name.

Genesis 1:28—*God blessed them and said to them, "Be fruitful and increase in number; fill the earth and subdue it. Rule over the fish of the sea and the birds of the air and over every living creature that moves on the ground."*

BOOK QUOTE: *When Heaven Invades Earth* [Chapter 2]

THE backbone of Kingdom authority and power is found in the *commission*. Discovering God's original commission and purpose for mankind can help to fortify our resolve to a life of history-changing significance. To find that truth we must go back to the beginning.

Man was created in the image of God and placed into the Father's ultimate expression of beauty and peace: the Garden of Eden. Outside of that garden it was a different story. It was without the order and blessing contained within and was in great need of the touch of God's delegated one—Adam.

Adam and Eve were placed in the garden with a mission. God said, "Be fruitful and multiply; fill the earth and subdue it" (Gen. 1:28). It was God's intention that as they bore more children, who also lived under God's rule, they would be extending the boundaries of His garden (His government) through the simplicity of their devotion to Him. The greater the number of people in right relationship to God, the greater the impact of their leadership. This process was to continue until the entire earth was covered with the glorious rule of God through man.

But in Genesis 1, we discover it's not a perfect universe. Satan had rebelled and had been cast out of heaven, and with him a portion of the fallen angels took dominion of the earth. It's obvious why the rest of the planet needed to be subdued—it was under the influence of darkness (Gen. 1:2). God could have destroyed the devil and his host with a word, but instead He chose to defeat darkness through His delegated authority—those made in His image who were lovers of God by choice.

Discovering God's original commission and purpose for mankind can help to fortify our resolve to a life of history-changing significance.

Genesis 1:26—*Then God said, "Let us make man in our image, in our likeness, and let them rule over the fish of the sea and the birds of the air, over the livestock, over all the earth, and over all the creatures that move along the ground."*

God, I've lost the romance in my relationship with you. Days are a race to get things done, but I feel like doing nothing. I feel defeated, ashamed, neglected. The anxiety is too much to bear & the thought of being exposed terrifies me. I want You God! I just don't know how to get You back. Come close. I want to sit at Your feet & enjoy Your presence in this day & always.

BOOK QUOTE: *When Heaven Invades Earth* [Chapter 2]

THE Sovereign One placed us—Adam's children—in charge of planet earth. "The heaven, even the heavens, are the Lord's; but the earth He has given to the children of men" (Ps. 115:16). This highest of honors was chosen because love always chooses the best. That is the beginning of the romance of our creation…created in His image, *for intimacy,* that dominion might be expressed through love. It is from this revelation that we are to learn to walk as His ambassadors, thus defeating the "Prince of this world." The stage was set for all of darkness to fall as man exercised His godly influence over creation. But instead, man fell.

Satan didn't come into the Garden of Eden violently and take possession of Adam and Eve. He couldn't! Why? He had no dominion there. Dominion empowers. And since man was given the keys of dominion over the planet, the devil would have to get his authority from them. The suggestion to eat the forbidden fruit was simply the devil's effort to get Adam and Eve to agree with him in opposition to God, thus empowering him. Through that agreement he is enabled to *kill, steal, and destroy*. It's important to realize that even today satan is empowered through man's agreement.

Mankind's authority to rule was forfeited when Adam ate the forbidden fruit. Paul said, "You are that one's slaves whom you obey" (Rom. 6:16). In that one act mankind became the slave and possession of the Evil One. All that Adam owned, including the title deed to the planet with its corresponding position of rule, became part of the devil's spoil. God's predetermined plan of redemption immediately kicked into play, "I will put enmity between you and the woman, and between your seed and her Seed; He shall bruise your head, and you shall bruise His heel" (Gen. 3:15). Jesus would come to reclaim all that was lost.

*That is the beginning of the romance of our creation… created in His image, **for intimacy**, that dominion might be expressed through love.*

1 Corinthians 15:22—*For as in Adam all die, so in Christ all will be made alive.*

BOOK QUOTE: *When Heaven Invades Earth* [Chapter 2]

GOD'S plan of rulership for man never ceased. Jesus came to bear man's penalty for sin and recapture what had been lost. Luke 19:10 says that Jesus came "to seek and to save that which was lost." Not only was mankind lost to sin, his dominion over planet earth was also lost. Jesus came to recapture both. Satan tried to ruin that plan at the end of Jesus' 40-day fast. The devil knew he wasn't worthy of Jesus' worship, but he also knew that Jesus had come to reclaim the authority that man had given away. Satan said to Him, "All this authority I will give You, and their glory; for this has been delivered to me, and I give it to whomever I wish. Therefore, if You will worship before me, all will be Yours" (Luke 4:6-7). Notice the phrase "for this has been delivered to me." Satan could not steal it. It had been relinquished when Adam abandoned God's rule. It was as though satan was saying to Jesus, "I know what You came for. You know what I want. Worship me and I'll give You back the keys." In effect, satan offered Jesus a shortcut to His goal of recapturing the keys of authority that man lost through sin. Jesus said "no" to the shortcut and refused to give him any honor. (It was this same desire for worship that caused satan's fall from Heaven in the first place. See Isaiah 14:12.) Jesus held His course, for He had come to die.

The Father wanted satan defeated by man…one made in His image. Jesus, who would shed His blood to redeem mankind, emptied Himself of His rights as God and took upon Himself the limitations of man. Satan was defeated by a man—the Son of Man, who was rightly related to God. Now, as people receive the work of Christ on the cross for salvation, they become grafted into that victory. Jesus defeated the devil with His sinless life, defeated him in His death by paying for our sins with His blood, and again, in the resurrection, rising triumphant with the keys of death and hell.

Now, as people receive the work of Christ on the cross for salvation, they become grafted into that victory.

Romans 5:17—*For if, by the trespass of the one man, death reigned through that one man, how much ore will those who receive God's abundant provision of grace and of the gift of righteousness reign in life through the one man, Jesus Christ.*

BOOK QUOTE: *When Heaven Invades Earth* [Chapter 2]

IN redeeming man, Jesus retrieved what man had given away. From the throne of triumph He declared, "All authority has been given to Me in heaven and on earth. Go therefore…" (Matt. 28:18-19). In other words: *I got it all back. Now go use it and reclaim mankind.* In this passage Jesus fulfills the promise He made to the disciples when He said, "I will give you the keys of the kingdom of heaven" (Matt. 16:19). The original plan was never aborted; it was fully realized once and for all in the resurrection and ascension of Jesus. We were then to be completely restored to His plan of ruling as a people made in His image. And as such we would learn how to enforce the victory obtained at Calvary: "The God of peace will soon crush satan under your feet" (Rom. 16:20 NIV).

We were born to rule—rule over creation, over darkness—to plunder hell and establish the rule of Jesus wherever we go by preaching the gospel of the Kingdom. *Kingdom* means: *King's domain*. In the original purpose of God, mankind ruled over creation. Now that sin has entered the world, creation has been infected by darkness, namely: disease, sickness, afflicting spirits, poverty, natural disasters, demonic influence, etc. Our rule is still over creation, but now it is focused on exposing and undoing the works of the devil. We are to give what we have received to reach that end (Rom. 16:20 NIV). If I truly receive power from an encounter with the God of power, I am equipped to give it away. The invasion of God into impossible situations comes through a people who have received power from on high and learn to release it into the circumstances of life.

Our rule is still over creation, but now it is focused on exposing and undoing the works of the devil.

Matthew 16:19—*I will give you the keys of the kingdom of heaven; whatever you bind on earth will be bound in heaven, and whatever you loose on earth will be loosed in heaven.*

BOOK QUOTE: *When Heaven Invades Earth* [Chapter 2]

THE gospel of salvation is to touch the whole man: spirit, soul, and body. A study on the word *evil* confirms the intended reach of His redemption. That word is found in Matthew 6:13 (KJV), "Deliver us from evil." The word *evil* represents the entire curse of sin upon man. *Poneros,* the Greek word for evil, came from the word *ponos,* meaning "pain." And that word came from the root word *penes,* meaning "poor." Look at it: *evil*—sin, *pain*—sickness, and *poor*—poverty.

Jesus destroyed the power of sin, sickness, and poverty through His redemptive work on the cross. In Adam and Eve's commission to subdue the earth, they were without sickness, poverty, and sin. Now that we are restored to His original purpose, should we expect anything less? After all, this is called the better covenant!

We were given the keys to the Kingdom—which in part is the authority *to trample over all the powers of hell* (Matt. 16:19; Luke 10:19). There is a phrase *key of David,* which is mentioned in both Revelation and Isaiah (Rev. 3:7; Isa. 22:22). All that the Father has is ours through Christ. His entire treasure is at our disposal in order to fulfill His commission. But the more sobering part of this illustration is found in *controlling who gets in to see the King.* Isn't that what we do with this gospel? When we declare it, we give opportunity for people to come to the King to be saved. When we are silent, we have chosen to keep those who would hear away from eternal life. It was a costly key for Him to purchase, and it's a costly key for us to use. But, it's even more costly to *bury it and not obtain an increase for the coming King.* That price will be felt throughout eternity.

When we are silent, we have chosen
to keep those who would hear away from eternal life.

Ephesians 3:20—*Now to him who is able to do immeasurably more than all we ask or imagine, according to his power that is at work within us...*

BOOK QUOTE: *When Heaven Invades Earth* [Chapter 2]

IT's time for a revolution in our vision. When prophets tell us, *your vision is too small,* many of us think the antidote is to increase whatever numbers we're expecting. For example: if we're expecting 10 new converts, let's change it to 100. If we were praying for cities, let's pray instead for nations. With such responses, we're missing the sharp edge of the frequently repeated word. Increasing the numbers is not necessarily a sign of a larger vision from God's perspective. Vision starts with identity and purpose. Through a revolution in our identity, we can think with divine purpose. Such a change begins with a revelation of Him.

Some believe that the condition of the Church will always be getting worse; therefore, tragedy in the Church is just another sign of these being the last days. In a perverted sense, the weakness of the Church confirms to many that they are on the right course. The worsening condition of the world and the Church becomes a sign to them that all is well. This kind of thinking *requires no faith*!

Embracing a belief system that requires no faith is dangerous. It is contrary to the nature of God and all that the Scriptures declare. Since He plans to do *above all we could ask or think,* according to Ephesians 3:20, His promises by nature challenge our intellect and expectations. The result of forgetting His promises is not one we can afford.

We are often more convinced of our *unworthiness* than we are of His *worth*. Our *inability* takes on greater focus than does His *ability*. But the same One who called *fearful Gideon* a Mighty Warrior and *unstable Peter* a Rock has called us the Body of His beloved Son on earth (Judg. 6:12; Matt. s16:18). That has to count for something.

*Embracing a belief system
that requires no faith is dangerous.*

Luke 24:47—*And repentance and forgiveness of sins will be preached in his name to all nations, beginning at Jerusalem.*

BOOK QUOTE: *When Heaven Invades Earth* [Chapter 3]

ISRAEL expected their Messiah to come as the King who would rule over all other kings. And He did. But their misunderstanding of greatness in His Kingdom made it difficult for them to grasp how He could be born without earthly fanfare and become the servant of all.

They expected Him to rule with a rod of iron. In doing so they would finally have revenge on all those who had oppressed them throughout the ages. Little did they realize that His vengeance would not be aimed so much at the enemies of Israel as it would be toward the enemies of man: sin, the devil and his works, and the self-righteous attitudes fostered by religion.

Jesus the Messiah came…full of surprises. Only the contrite in heart could keep up with His constant *coloring outside the lines* and stay unoffended. His purpose was revealed in His primary message: "Repent, for the kingdom of heaven is at hand" (Matt. 4:17). Now there's something that caught them completely off guard; He brought His world with Him!

Repentance means much more than weeping over sin, or even turning from those sins to follow God. In fact, turning from sin to God is more the *result* of true repentance than it is the actual act. *Repentance* means you "change your way of thinking." And it's only in changing the way we think that we can discover the focus of Jesus' ministry—the Kingdom.

This is not just a heavenly mandate to have happy thoughts. Obeying this command is possible only for those who surrender to the grace of God. The renewed mind is the result of a surrendered heart.

Repentance *means you*
"change your way of thinking."

Hebrews 6:1—Therefore let us leave the elementary teachings about Christ and go on to maturity, not laying again the foundation of repentance from acts that lead to death, and of faith in God.

BOOK QUOTE: *When Heaven Invades Earth* [Chapter 3]

REPENTANCE is often defined as *doing an about-face*. It implies that I was pursuing one direction in life, and I change to pursue another. Scripture illustrates it like this, "Repentance from dead works…faith toward God" (Heb. 6:1). Faith then is both the crown and the enabler of repentance.

This command has been preached strongly in recent years. It has kept us from the purity that breeds boldness and great faith. Repentance is not complete until it envisions His Kingdom.

The focus of repentance is to change our way of thinking until the presence of His Kingdom fills our consciousness. The enemy's attempt to anchor our affections to the things that are visible is easily resisted when our hearts are aware of the presence of His world. Such awareness aids us in the task of being *co-laborers* with Christ—*destroying the works of the devil*. (See First Corinthians 3:9; 1 John 3:8.)

If the Kingdom is *here and now*, then we must acknowledge it's in the invisible realm. Yet being *at hand* reminds us that it's also *within reach*. Paul said that the invisible realm is eternal, while that which is seen is only temporal. (See 2 Corinthians 4:18.) Jesus told Nicodemus that he'd have to be born again to see the Kingdom. (See John 3:3.) That which is unseen can be realized only through *repentance*. It was as though He said, "If you don't change the way you perceive things, you'll live your whole life thinking that what you see in the natural is the superior reality. Without changing the way you think you'll never see the world that is right in front of you. It's My world, and it fulfills every dream you've ever had. And I brought it with Me." All that He did in life and ministry, He did by drawing from that *superior* reality.

Faith then is both the crown and the enabler of repentance.

Matthew 5:6—*Blessed are those who hunger and thirst for righteousness, for they will be filled.*

BOOK QUOTE: *When Heaven Invades Earth* [Chapter 3]

"IT is the glory of God to conceal a matter, but the glory of kings is to search out a matter" (Prov. 25:2). Some things are only discovered by the *desperate*. That highly valued Kingdom attitude (see Matt. 5:6.) is what marks the heart of true *Kingdom royalty* ["and from Jesus Christ, who is the faithful witness, the firstborn from the dead, and the ruler of the kings of the earth" (Rev. 1:5).] The God who put the gold in the rocks brought His Kingdom with Him, but left it unseen.

Paul dealt with this in his letter to the Colossians. There he informs us that God hid our abundant life *in Christ*. ["For you died, and your life is now hidden with Christ in God" (Col. 3:3).] Where is He? *Seated at the right hand of the Father, in heavenly places.* (See Ephesians 1:20.) Our abundant life is hidden in the Kingdom realm. And only faith can make the withdrawals.

Look at the word *Kingdom*—King/dom. It refers to the *King's Domain,* implying authority and lordship. Jesus came to offer the benefits of His world to all who surrender to His rule. The realm of God's dominion, that realm of all sufficiency, is the realm called the Kingdom. The benefits of His rule were illustrated through His works of forgiveness, deliverance, and healing.

The Christian life has been harnessed to this goal, verbalized in the Lord's Model Prayer: "Your kingdom come. Your will be done on earth as it is in heaven" (Matt. 6:10).

His dominion is realized when what happens here is *as it is in heaven.*

And only faith can make the withdrawals.

Matthew 5:12a—*Rejoice and be glad for great is your reward in Heaven…*

BOOK QUOTE: *When Heaven Invades Earth* [Chapter 3]

THE actual Presence of the Spirit of God upon Jesus stirred up a hunger for God in the people. That hunger brought a change in their attitudes. He could have put it this way: *This is how the repentant mind looks.*

Blessed means *happy*! The following is a personal paraphrase of *Matthew 5:3-12.*

3. You are happy if you are poor in spirit, for yours is the kingdom of Heaven.

4. You are happy if you mourn, for you shall be comforted.

5. You are happy if you are meek, for you shall inherit the earth.

6. You are happy if you hunger and thirst for righteousness, for you shall be filled.

7. You are happy if you are merciful, for you shall obtain mercy.

8. You are happy if you are pure in heart, for you shall see God.

9. You are happy if you are peacemakers, for you shall be called sons of God.

10. You are happy if you are persecuted for righteousness' sake, for yours is the kingdom of Heaven.

11. You are happy if they revile and persecute you, and say all kinds of evil against you falsely for My sake.

12. Rejoice and be exceedingly glad, for great is your reward in Heaven, for so they persecuted the prophets who were before you.

Examine the promised result of each new attitude—*receiving the Kingdom, being comforted, obtaining mercy, seeing God,* etc. This is important because many approach the teachings of Jesus as *just another form of the Law. Grace* is different from the *Law* in that the favor comes *before* the obedience. Under grace the commandments of the Lord come fully equipped with the ability to perform them…to those who hear from the heart. *Grace enables what it commands.*

Grace is different from the **Law**
in that the favor comes **before** the obedience.

Colossians 1:15-16—He is the image of the invisible God, the firstborn over all creation. For by Him all things were created: things in Heaven and on earth, visible and invisible, whether thrones or powers or rulers or authorities; all things were created by Him and for Him.

BOOK QUOTE: *When Heaven Invades Earth* [Chapter 3]

THE unseen world has influence over the visible. If the people of God will not reach for the Kingdom at hand, the realm of darkness is ready to display its ability to influence. The good news is that "*His* [the Lord's] *kingdom rules over all*" (Ps. 103:19).

Jesus illustrated this reality in Matthew 12:28, saying, "If I cast out demons by the Spirit of God, then the kingdom of God has come upon you." There are two things to notice. First, Jesus worked only through the Spirit of God; and second, the kingdom of God came upon someone in his deliverance. Jesus caused the collision between two worlds: the world of darkness and the world of light. Darkness *always* gives way to light! And in the same way, when the dominion of God was released through Jesus to that man, he became free.

That same collision between light and darkness happens when the sick are healed. Walter had experienced two strokes in the previous year, which left him without feeling on the entire right side of his body. Conviction, one of the words used to detect faith, (see Heb. 11:1 KJV) began to burn in my heart. I had become aware of the Kingdom where no numbness existed. I didn't want to become more aware of how severe his problem was. Soon after I started to pray he told me that he felt my hand on his shoulder and could even feel the fabric of my shirt with his right hand. That world began to collide with the world of numbness. Numbness lost.

Faith is the key to discovering the superior nature of the invisible realm. It is the "gift of God" within to uncover.

*Darkness **always** gives way to light!*

Matthew 6:6—But when you pray, go into your room, close the door and pray to your Father, who is unseen. Then your Father, who sees what is done in secret, will reward you.

BOOK QUOTE: *When Heaven Invades Earth* [Chapter 4]

FAITH has its anchor in the unseen realm. It lives *from* the invisible *toward* the visible. Faith actualizes what it realizes. The Scriptures contrast the life of faith with the limitations of natural sight. (See 2 Cor. 5:7.) Faith provides eyes for the heart.

Jesus expects people to see from the heart. Many of us have thought that the ability to see into the spiritual realm is more the result of a special gift than an unused potential of everyone.

We are born again by grace through faith. (See Eph. 2:8.) The born-again experience enables us to see from the heart. (See John 3:3.) A heart that doesn't see is a hard heart. (See Mark 8:17-18.) Faith was never intended only to get us *into* the family. Rather, it is the nature of life in this family. Faith sees. It brings His Kingdom into focus. All of the Father's resources, all of His benefits, are accessible through faith.

To encourage us in our capacity to see, Jesus gave specific instruction, "Seek first the kingdom of God..." (Matt. 6:33). Paul taught us, "Set your mind on things above, not on things on the earth" (Col. 3:2). He also stated, "For the things which are seen are temporary, but the things which are not seen are eternal" (2 Cor. 4:18). The Bible instructs us to turn our attention toward the invisible. This theme is repeated enough in Scripture to make those of us bound by the logic of this Western culture quite nervous.

Herein lies the secret to the supernatural realm that we want restored to the Church. Jesus told us that He only did what He *saw* His Father do. Such an insight is vital for those who want more. The power of His actions, for instance, the mud in the eye of the blind, is rooted in His ability to see.

Faith provides eyes for the heart.

John 4:24—*God is spirit, and His worshipers must worship in spirit and in truth.*

BOOK QUOTE: *When Heaven Invades Earth* [Chapter 4]

GOD is very committed to teaching us how to see. To make this possible He gave us the Holy Spirit as a tutor. The curriculum that He uses is quite varied. But the one class we all qualify for is worship. Learning *how to see* is not the purpose for our worship, but it is a wonderful by-product.

Those who worship in spirit and truth learn to follow the Holy Spirit's lead. His realm is called the kingdom of God. The throne of God, which becomes established upon the *praises of His people,* is the center of that Kingdom. (See Psalm 22:3.) It's in the environment of worship that we learn things that go way beyond what our intellect can grasp—and the greatest of these lessons is the value of His Presence. (See Ephesians 3:20.) David was so affected by this that all his other exploits pale in comparison to his abandoned heart for God. We know that he learned to see into God's realm because of statements like, "I have set the Lord always before me; because He is at my right hand I shall not be moved" (Ps. 16:8). The Presence of God affected his seeing. He would constantly practice recognizing the Presence of God. He saw God daily, not with the natural eyes, but with the eyes of faith. That priceless revelation was given to a worshiper.

The privilege of worship is a good beginning place for those unaccustomed to addressing some of these kinds of themes found in Scripture. It's in that wonderful ministry that we can learn to pay attention to this God-given gift: the ability to see with the heart. As we learn to worship with purity of heart, our eyes will continue to open. And we can expect to see what He wants us to see.

Those who worship in spirit and truth learn to follow the Holy Spirit's lead.

2 Corinthians 4:18—*So we fix our eyes not on what is seen, but on what is unseen. For what is seen is temporary, but what is unseen is eternal.*

BOOK QUOTE: *When Heaven Invades Earth* [Chapter 4]

THE invisible realm is superior to the natural. The reality of that invisible world dominates the natural world we live in…both positively and negatively. Because the invisible is superior to the natural, faith is anchored in the unseen.

Faith lives within the revealed will of God. When I have misconceptions of who He is and what He is like, my faith is restricted by those misconceptions. For example, if I believe that God allows sickness in order to build character, I'll not have confidence praying where healing is needed. If I believe that sickness is to the body what sin is to the soul, then no disease will intimidate me. Faith is much more free to develop when we truly see the heart of God as good.

These misconceptions affect those who need faith for their own miracle. A woman who needed a miracle told me that she felt God had allowed her sickness for a purpose. I told her that if I treated my children that way I'd be arrested for child abuse. After truth came into her heart, her healing came.

Unbelief is anchored in what is visible or reasonable apart from God. It honors the natural realm as superior to the invisible. The apostle Paul states that what you can see is temporal, and what you can't see is eternal. (See 2 Corinthians 4:18.) Unbelief is faith in the inferior.

The natural realm is the anchor of unbelief. But that realm is not to be considered as evil. Rather the humble of heart recognize the hand of God through what is seen. God has created all things to speak of Him—whether it is rivers and trees, or angels and heaven. The natural realm carries the witness of His greatness…for those with eyes to see and ears to hear. (See Romans 1:20-21.)

God has created all things to speak of Him—
whether it is rivers and trees, or angels and Heaven.

Colossians 3:2—*Set your minds on things above, not on earthly things.*

BOOK QUOTE: *When Heaven Invades Earth* [Chapter 4]

Most all of the people that I've known who are filled with unbelief have called themselves "realists." They believe the material world rules over the spiritual world.

Materialism is not simply the accumulation of goods. I can want nothing and be materialistic because materialism is faith in the natural as the superior reality.

We are a sensual society with a culture shaped by what is picked up through the senses. We're trained to believe only in what we see. Real faith is not living in denial of the natural realm. If the doctor says you have a tumor, it's not faith to pretend that it's not there. However, faith is founded on a reality that is superior to that tumor. I can acknowledge the existence of a tumor and still have faith in the provision of His stripes for my healing…I was provisionally healed 2,000 years ago. It is the product of the kingdom of Heaven—a superior reality. There are no tumors in Heaven, and faith brings that reality into this one.

Satan would like to inflict heaven with cancer. But he has no dominion there. He only has dominion here when and where man has come into agreement.

Fear of appearing to live in denial is what keeps many from faith. Why is what anyone thinks so important to you that you'd not be willing to risk all to trust God? The fear of man is very strongly associated with unbelief. Conversely, the fear of God and faith are very closely related.

People of faith are also realists. They just have their foundation in a superior reality.

Unbelief is actually faith in something other than God. He is jealous over our hearts. The one whose primary trust is in another grieves the Holy Spirit.

> *People of faith are also realists.*
> *They just have their foundation in a superior reality.*

2 Corinthians 3:6—*He has made us competent as ministers of a new covenant—not of the letter but of the Spirit; for the letter kills, but the Spirit gives life.*

BOOK QUOTE: *When Heaven Invades Earth* [Chapter 4]

FAITH is born of the Spirit in the hearts of mankind. Faith is neither intellectual nor anti-intellectual. It is superior to the intellect. The Bible does not say, *with the mind man believes!* Through faith, man is able to come into agreement with the mind of God.

When we submit the things of God to the mind of man, unbelief and religion are the results. (I interpret religion as form without power.) When we submit the mind of man to the things of God, we end up with faith and a renewed mind. The mind makes a wonderful servant, but a terrible master.

Much of the opposition to revival comes from soul-driven Christians. The soul is the mind, will, and emotions. Anything that doesn't make sense to their rational mind is automatically in conflict with Scripture.

The Holy Spirit lives in my spirit. That is the *place* of communion with God. As we learn to receive from our spirits we learn how to be Spirit led.

"By faith, we understand" (Heb. 11:3.) Faith is the foundation for all true intellectualism. When we *learn to learn* that way, we open ourselves up to grow in true faith because faith does not require understanding to function.

I'm sure that most of you have had this experience—you've been reading the Bible, and a verse *jumps out at you.* There is great excitement over this verse that gives so much life to you. Yet initially you couldn't teach or explain that verse if your life depended on it. What happened is this: Your spirit received the life-giving power of the word from the Holy Spirit. "The letter kills, but the Spirit gives life" (2 Cor. 3:6). When we learn to receive from our spirit, our mind becomes the student and is therefore subject to the Holy Spirit. Through the process of revelation and experience our mind eventually obtains understanding. That is biblical learning—the spirit giving influence to the mind.

Faith is neither intellectual nor anti-intellectual.
It is superior to the intellect.

Hebrews 11:1—*Now faith is being sure of what we hope for and certain of what we do not see.*

BOOK QUOTE: *When Heaven Invades Earth* [Chapter 4]

FAITH is the mirror of the heart that reflects the realities of His world into ours. It is the substance of the unseen realm. This wonderful gift from God is the initial earthly manifestation of His Kingdom. It is a testimony of an invisible realm called the Kingdom of God. Through prayer we are able to pull that reality into this one—that is how faith functions.

If I go into a pizza parlor and order a pizza, they will give me a number and a receipt. Someone may come to my table and announce that they won't give me any pizza. I'll just point to the number and tell him, *When pizza number 52 is done, it's mine!* That number is the *substance* of the pizza hoped for. If that guy tells me that my number isn't any good, I'll point to my receipt. It verifies the value of the number. When my pizza is done, the waiter will look for my number. How does the product of Heaven know where to land? He looks for the substance...the number. If a question comes up over the validity of my number, my receipt, which is contained in the Bible, verifies my right to both the number and the pizza.

Heaven is not moved simply by the needs of man. It's not that God doesn't care. It was out of His great compassion that He sent Jesus. When God is moved by human need He seldom fixes the problem outright; instead, He provides Kingdom principles that when embraced correct the problems. If God was moved solely by human need then countries like India and Haiti would become the wealthiest nations in the world. It doesn't work like that. Heaven is moved by faith. Faith is the currency of Heaven.

Faith is the currency of Heaven.

Ephesians 3:16,17—*I pray that out of His glorious riches He may strengthen you with power through His Spirit in your inner being, so that Christ may dwell in your hearts through faith...*

BOOK QUOTE: *When Heaven Invades Earth* [Chapter 4]

THE following is a summary of the affects of faith found in Hebrews 11:2-30:

By faith —the elders obtained a testimony,
　　　　　—we understand,
　　　　　—Enoch was taken away having pleased God,
　　　　　—Noah became an heir,
　　　　　—Abraham obeyed, and dwelled in a land of promise,
　　　　　—Sarah received strength to conceive, and judged God as faithful who gave her the promise.

By faith —Abraham received promises,
　　　　　—Isaac blessed his son,
　　　　　—Joseph gave a prophecy of what would follow his death.

By faith —Moses' parents preserved him, seeing he was special,
　　　　　—Moses refused to be aligned with the whole Egyptian system and chose instead to be rejected by people.

By faith —the walls of Jericho fell,
　　　　　—Rahab did not perish.

By faith —they subdued kingdoms,
　　　　　—worked righteousness,
　　　　　—obtained promises,
　　　　　—shut the mouths of lions,
　　　　　—quenched the violence of fire,
　　　　　—escaped the edge of the sword,
　　　　　—were made strong,
　　　　　—were made valiant in battle,
　　　　　—turned to fight the enemies.

"Faith comes by hearing..." (Rom. 10:17.) It does not say that it comes from *having heard*. It is the listening heart, in the present tense, that is ready for Heaven's deposit of faith.

The apostle Paul was driven by the command, "Go into all the world and preach the gospel..." (Mark 16:15). However, when he was ready to preach the gospel in Asia, God said no. (See Acts 16:6.) What God *had said* appeared to be in conflict with what

God *was saying*. God never contradicts His Word. But He *is* willing to contradict our understanding of His Word. The principle of the Great Commission (in Mark 16:15) was not nullified by the Acts 16 situation. Their application of the principle was God's target. Paul then prepared to go to Bithynia. Again, God said no. Following this Paul had a dream of a man calling out to him from Macedonia. This was recognized as the will of God, and they went.

Even though we may know the will of God from Scripture, we still need the Holy Spirit to help us with the interpretation, application, and empowerment to perform His will.

> *It is the listening heart, in the present tense,*
> *that is ready for Heaven's deposit of faith.*

Psalm 27:1—The Lord is my light and my salvation—whom shall I fear? The Lord is the stronghold of my life—of whom shall I be afraid?

BOOK QUOTE: *When Heaven Invades Earth* [Chapter 4]

THE biblical command repeated most often is: *Do not fear.* Why? Fear attacks the foundation of our relationship with God...our faith. Fear is faith in the devil; it is also called unbelief. Jesus would ask His fearful disciples, *"Why are you so faithless?"* because fearfulness is the same as faithlessness. Fear and faith cannot coexist—they work against each other.

The devil is called Beelzebub, which means, *lord of the flies.* He and his hosts are attracted to decay. We had a freezer in a building detached from our house. One Sunday, we came home from church only to be hit with a wall of smell that is unfortunately hard to forget. Our freezer had died.

From the front seat of my car I looked at the window of the shop about 40 feet away. It was black with flies...a number that is still hard to imagine these many years later. The freezer was filled with all sorts of meat. Flies found a happy breeding ground in spoiled flesh and were multiplying in unbelievable numbers. Both the meat and the freezer were taken to the dump.

Issues such as bitterness, jealousy, and hatred qualify as the decay of the heart that invites the devil to come and give influence—yes, even to Christians. (See James 3:15-16.) Remember Paul's admonition to the church of Ephesus, "Neither give place to the devil" (Eph. 4:27 KJV). Fear is also a decay of the heart. It attracts the demonic in the same way as bitterness and hatred. How did the flies know where my freezer was? Through the scent of decaying meat. Fear gives off a similar scent. Like faith, *fear* is "substance" in the spiritual realm. Satan has no power except through our agreement. Fear becomes our heart's response when we come into agreement with his intimidating suggestions.

Fear attacks the foundation of our relationship with God...our faith.

Mark 16:14—*Later Jesus appeared to the Eleven as they were eating; He rebuked them for their lack of faith and their stubborn refusal to believe those who had seen Him after he had risen.*

BOOK QUOTE: *When Heaven Invades Earth* [Chapter 4]

MANY who have feared the excesses made by others in the name of faith have ironically embraced unbelief. Reaction to error usually produces error. Some people would have no belief system were it not for the error of others. Their teachings are the antithesis of what others believe and practice. As a result those who strive for balance become anemic. The word *balance* has come to mean "middle of the road"—of no threat to people or the devil, with little risk, and above all…the best way to keep our nice image intact.

The Church warns its members about the great sin of presumption. God warns us of the sin of unbelief. Jesus *didn't* say, "When I return will I find people who are excessive and presumptuous?" He was concerned about finding people with faith, the kind He displayed. While we often huddle in groups of like-minded people, those with faith blaze a trail that threatens all of our comfort zones. Faith offends the stationary.

People of great faith are hard to live with. Their reasoning is *otherworldly*. My grandfather, a pastor, sat under the ministry of several great men and women of God of the early 1900s. He used to tell me how not everyone liked Smith Wigglesworth. His faith made other people feel uncomfortable. We either become like them or we avoid them. We find their lifestyle either contagious or offensive with little neutral ground. Smith is well loved today…but it's only because he's dead. Israel loved their dead prophets too.

There's something amazing about unbelief—it is able to fulfill its own expectations. Unbelief is safe because it takes no risk and almost always gets what it expects. Then, after a person gets the answer for their unbelief, they can say, *I told you so.*

He was concerned about finding people with faith, the kind He displayed.

Mark 9:23—*" 'If you can'?" said Jesus. "Everything is possible for him who believes."*

BOOK QUOTE: *When Heaven Invades Earth* [Chapter 4]

Y faith is not just an abiding faith; it is active. It is aggressive by nature. It has focus and purpose. Faith grabs hold of the reality of the Kingdom and forcefully and violently brings it into a collision with this natural one. An inferior kingdom cannot stand.

One of the more common things people tell me when I'm about to pray for their healing is, *I know God can do it.* So does the devil. At best that is hope…not faith. Faith knows He will.

For one who has faith, there is nothing impossible. There are no impossibilities when there is faith…and there are no exceptions.

Sheri came forward for prayer. She had suffered with Lupus for 24 years, the last four of which had gone into Pulmonary Hypertension. It had gotten so bad that she had an aluminum shunt placed into her heart. To this a pump was attached, which supplied the needed medication to keep her alive. Her doctor told her that without this medication she could live for only three minutes.

When she walked up to me, I actually felt a presence of something I had never felt in that measure before. It was faith. As she received prayer, she fell to the ground under the power of God. When she got up I asked her how she was doing. She described a heat that was on her chest. As she left I told her, "Your faith got you this one!"

That was Saturday night. At 7 A.M. that following morning, the Lord spoke to her saying she didn't need the medication any more. (When I'm asked what to do regarding medication, I tell people to do what's in their heart. It wouldn't do them any good to do what I had faith for, or to keep them from doing what could be infected by my unbelief.)

She showed up 14 hours later giving testimony of God's wonderful healing power.

She has since had the aluminum shunt removed—she doesn't need it anymore!

Faith knows He will.

Proverbs 2:2—*...turning your ear to wisdom and applying your heart to understanding.*

BOOK QUOTE: *When Heaven Invades Earth* [Chapter 4]

"So then faith comes by hearing, and hearing by the word of God" (Rom. 10:17). Notice it does not say, *faith comes from having heard.* The whole nature of faith implies a relationship with God that is current. The emphasis is on hearing...in the now!

What this world needs is for the Church to return to a *show and tell* message on the kingdom of God. They need an anchor that is greater than everything they can see. The world system has no answers to the world's increasing problems—every solution is only temporary.

Dale had deceived us out of some money and felt the need to confess in person. After I expressed both God's and my forgiveness, I asked him about his back. He had walked into my office with difficulty in great pain. He had broken his back and had been in a car accident that further aggravated his injury. He told me that God would probably like to heal him, but that he got in His way. I told him he wasn't big enough. All I could picture was the greatness of God and the puny condition of man. Although Dale didn't move into great faith, he did begin to doubt his doubt. That was all it took. I then commanded it to be healed. He left pain-free with full movement and a heart full of praise.

Faith is not the absence of doubt; it's the presence of belief. I may not always feel that I have great faith. But I can always obey, laying my hands on someone and praying. It's a mistake for me to ever examine my faith. I seldom find it. It's better for me to obey *quickly*. After it's over I can look back and see that my obedience came from faith.

It's better for me to obey **quickly**.

Deuteronomy 32:30a—How could one man chase a thousand or two put ten thousand to flight...

BOOK QUOTE: *When Heaven Invades Earth* [Chapter 4]

WHEN the corporate level of faith grows, it has what I call a *cluster bomb effect,* where innocent bystanders get touched by the miracle-working power of God.

Francis is a woman who had esophagus cancer. One Sunday morning during worship she leaned over to her husband and said, "I was just healed!" She felt the *fire* of God touch her hands and concluded that it represented God's healing touch. When she went to the doctor she told him of her experience. His response was, "This kind does not go away." After examining her he stated, "Not only do you not have cancer, you have a new esophagus!"

Corporate faith pulls on Heaven in marvelous ways. His world becomes manifest all around us.

Sharon had suffered an accident many years ago in which she had destroyed a tendon that ran down her leg. It left her with restricted movement and partial numbness in her foot. I was giving an altar call for people to get right with God during one of our Saturday night meetings. She began to make all kinds of noise. I stopped the altar call and asked her what happened. She told us of the tingling feeling that ran down her leg and the subsequent restoration of all movement and feeling to her foot. A creative miracle happened without anyone praying.

The crowd at this particular meeting was quite small. But power is not in the number of people in attendance. It's the number of people in agreement. Exponential power is the product of the *unity of faith.* (See Deut. 32:30.)

In some meetings it's easy to mistake enthusiasm for faith. In that setting I emphasize the use of testimonies to stir peoples' hearts to believe for the impossible so He might invade.

... power is not in the number of people in attendance.
It's the number of people in agreement.

Matthew 9:29—*Then he touched their eyes and said, "According to your faith will it be done to you."*

BOOK QUOTE: *When Heaven Invades Earth* [Chapter 4]

Just as fear is a tangible element in the spirit world, so faith is tangible there. In the natural a loud voice may intimidate another man. But devils know the difference between the one who is truly bold and aggressive *because of* their faith, and the one who is simply covering his fears with aggressive behavior. Christians often use this tactic when casting out devils. Many of us have yelled threats, called on angels for help, promised to make it harder on the demons on Judgment Day, and other foolish things only to try and cover immaturity and fear. Real faith is anchored in the invisible realm and is connected to the authority given in the name of the Lord Jesus Christ.

The authority to cast out demons is found in rest. Rest is the climate that faith grows in. (See Heb. 3:11; 4:11.) It comes out of the peace of God. And it is the Prince of Peace who will soon crush satan underneath our feet! (Rom. 16:20.) What is restful for us is violent to the powers of hell. That is the violent nature of faith.

This is not to be a soulish attempt at self-confidence or self-determination. Instead it is a moving of the heart into a place of surrender…a place of rest. A surrendered heart is a heart of faith. And faith must be present to please God.

"Until now the kingdom of heaven suffers violence, and the violent take it by force" (Matt. 11:12). Two blind men who sat by the road called out to Jesus. People told them to be quiet. That only hardened their determination. They became more desperate and cried out all the louder. He called them forth and healed them saying, "The kingdom has come near you." He attributed their miracle to their faith. (See Matt. 9:27.)

*Real faith is anchored in the invisible realm
and is connected to the authority given
in the name of the Lord Jesus Christ.*

Matthew 9:22—*Jesus turned and saw her. "Take heart, daughter," he said, "your faith has healed you." And the woman was healed from that moment.*

BOOK QUOTE: *When Heaven Invades Earth* [Chapter 4]

A woman who had hemorrhaged for 12 years pressed through a crowd. When she was finally able to touch the garment of Jesus, she was healed. He attributed it to her faith. (See Matt. 9:20-22.)

The stories of this kind are many, all with similar endings—they were healed or delivered because of their faith. Faith may quietly press in, or it may cry out very loudly, but it is always violent in the spirit world. It grabs hold of an invisible reality and won't let go. Taking the Kingdom by faith is the violent act that is necessary to come into what God has made available.

An automobile may have several hundred horsepower. But the car will go nowhere until the clutch is released, connecting the power contained in the running motor and transferring that power to the wheels. So it is with faith. We have all the power of heaven behind us. But it is our faith that connects what is available to the circumstances at hand. Faith takes what is available and makes it actual.

It's not illegal to try to grow in faith. It's not wrong to seek for signs and the increase of miracles. Those are all within the rights of the believer. But learning how to pray is the task at hand.

Faith takes what is available and makes it actual.

Matthew 18:18—*I tell you the truth, whatever you bind on earth will be bound in Heaven, and whatever you loose on earth will be loosed in Heaven.*

BOOK QUOTE: *When Heaven Invades Earth* [Chapter 5]

THE Fourth of July Celebration was the biggest event of the year for our wonderful community. The parade, rodeo, and demolition derby were just a few of the activities that took place during the festival that lasted nearly a week.

One year a fortune-teller tried to get in on the celebration. She pitched her tent with the others and laid out her tarot cards, crystal ball, and other psychic paraphernalia. The devil sent her to impart the gift of *demon possession* to the citizens of my city. The folks in our church began to pray.

As I walked around her tent I began to declare,

You don't exist in Heaven; you are not to exist here. This is my town. You are here illegally. I forbid you to establish roots here! God has declared that wherever the soles of my feet tread, God has given it to me. I bind you to the Word of God that declares that I have authority over you. Be gone!

I did not speak these things to the woman. I didn't even do it loud enough to draw her attention. She was not my enemy, nor was she my problem. The kingdom of darkness that empowered her was my target.

While she was doing her *sorcery* to a couple seated at her table, I stood only a few feet away. I held my hands toward them, binding the power of hell that was intent on their destruction. I left when I felt I was done. (The hands that are surrendered to God can release the power of Heaven into a situation. In the spirit world it is released like lightning. See Habakkuk 3:2-4.) Although the fair went on for many more days, she left town the next morning. The power that influenced her had been broken.

The hands that are surrendered to God can release the power of Heaven into a situation.

Isaiah 42:13—The Lord shall go forth like a mighty man; He shall stir up His zeal like a man of war. He shall cry out, yes, shout aloud; He shall prevail against His enemies. NKJV

BOOK QUOTE: *When Heaven Invades Earth* [Chapter 5]

THE Lord's Model Prayer provides the clearest instruction on how we bring the reality of His world into this one. The generals of revival speak to us from ages past saying, "If you pray, He will come!"

Jesus' model reveals the only two real priorities of prayer: First, intimacy with God that is expressed in worship—*holy is Your name*. And second, to bring His Kingdom to earth, establishing His dominion over the needs of mankind—*Your Kingdom come*.

"Our Father in Heaven, hallowed be Your name."

The title Father is a title of honor and a call to relationship. What He did to make it possible for us to call Him "Our Father" is all one needs to see to begin to become a true worshiper. *Hallowed* means "respected or revered." This too is an expression of praise. In the Book of Revelation, it is obvious that praise and worship are the primary activities of Heaven. The more we live as citizens of Heaven, the more Heaven's activities infect our lifestyles.

Worship is our number one priority in ministry. Everything else we do is to be affected by our devotion to this call. He inhabits our praise. One translation puts it this way, *But You are holy, enthroned in the praises of Israel*. God responds with a literal invasion of Heaven to earth through the worship of the believer (Ps. 22:3).

As His presence becomes manifest upon a worshiping people even unbelievers are brought into an encounter with God. My son and daughter have ministered to the Lord on troubled streets in San Francisco. As people walked by we saw many who manifested demons while others broke out in joyful laughter as they came into the presence of the Lord.

These things shouldn't surprise us. Look at how God responds to the praises of His people in Isaiah 42:13 (see above).

God responds with a literal invasion of Heaven to earth through the worship of the believer.

1 Corinthians 2:9-10—*However, as it written: "No eye has seen, no ear has heard, no mind has conceived what God has prepared for those who love Him"—but God has revealed it to us by His Spirit.*

BOOK QUOTE: *When Heaven Invades Earth* [Chapter 5]

"Your kingdom come. Your will be done on earth as it is in Heaven."

THIS is the primary focus for all prayer—if it exists in Heaven, it is to be loosed on earth. The praying Christian *looses* heaven's expression here. When the believer prays according to the revealed will of God, faith is specific and focused. Faith grabs hold *of that* reality. Enduring faith doesn't let go. Such an invasion causes the circumstances here to line up with Heaven. Everything that happens here is supposed to be a shadow of Heaven. In turn, every revelation that God gives us of heaven is to equip us with a prayer focus.

How much of heaven has God purposed to become manifest here on earth? No one knows for sure. We know through the Scripture that it's even more than has ever entered our minds. (See 1 Corinthians 2:9-10 and Ephesians 3:20-21.)

The will of God is seen in the ruling presence of God. Wherever the Spirit of the Lord is demonstrating the Lordship of Jesus, liberty is the result. *When the King of kings manifests His dominion, the fruit of that dominion is liberty.* That is the realm called *The Kingdom of God.* God, in response to our cries, brings His world into ours.

Conversely, if it is not free to exist in heaven, it must be bound here. Again, through prayer we are to exercise the authority given to us. "I will give you the keys of the kingdom of heaven; and whatever you bind on earth *shall have been* bound in heaven, and whatever you loose on earth *shall have been* loosed in heaven" (Matt. 16:19 NASB, emphasis mine.) Notice the phrase *shall have been.* The implication is that we can only bind or loose here what has already been bound or loosed there. Once again, Heaven is our model.

God, in response to our cries,
brings His world into ours.

Philippians 4:19—*And my God will meet all your needs according to His glorious riches in Christ Jesus.*

BOOK QUOTE: *When Heaven Invades Earth* [Chapter 5]

"Give us this day our daily bread."

Is anyone starving in Heaven? Of course not. This request is a practical application of how His dominion should be seen here on earth—abundant supply. The abuses of a few in the area of prosperity do not excuse the abandonment of the promises of God to provide abundantly for His children. It is His good pleasure to do so. Because there is complete and perfect provision in heaven, there must be the same here. Heaven sets the standard for a Christian's material world—enough to satisfy the desires born of God and *enough "for every good work"* (2 Cor. 9:8). Our legal basis for provision comes from the heavenly model given to us in Christ Jesus: "And my God shall supply all your need according to His riches in glory by Christ Jesus" (Phil. 4:19). According to what? *His riches.* Where? *In glory.* Heaven's resources are to affect us here and now.

"And forgive us our debts, as we forgive our debtors."

Is there any unforgiveness in Heaven? No! Heaven provides the model for our relationships here on earth. "And be kind to one another, tenderhearted, forgiving one another, even as God in Christ forgave you. Therefore be imitators of God as dear children" (Eph. 4:32-5:1). These verses make it quite clear that our model is Jesus Christ…the One ascended to the right hand of the Father…the One whose Kingdom we seek. Once again this prayer illustrates a practical way to pray for Heaven's reality to bring an effect on planet earth.

Because there is complete and perfect provision in Heaven, there must be the same here.

James 1:13—*When tempted, no one should say, "God is tempting me." For God cannot be tempted by evil, nor does He tempt anyone.*

BOOK QUOTE: *When Heaven Invades Earth* [Chapter 5]

"And do not lead us into temptation, but deliver us from the evil one."

THERE is no temptation or sin in Heaven. Neither is there any presence of evil. Keeping separate from evil is a practical evidence of our coming under our King's rule. This prayer does not imply that God wants to tempt us. We know from James 1:13 that it is impossible for God to entice us to sin. This kind of praying is important because it requires us to face our need for grace. It helps us to align our heart with Heaven—in an absolute dependency on God. God's Kingdom gives us the model for the issues of the heart. This prayer is actually a request for God not to promote us beyond what our character can handle. Sometimes our anointing and gift are ready for increase of responsibility, but our character isn't. When promotion comes too soon the impact of our gift brings a notoriety that becomes the catalyst of our downfall.

The phrase *deliver us from evil,* as it is traditionally rendered, actually means, "deliver us from the evil one." A heart modeled after heaven has great success in spiritual warfare. That's why it says, "Submit to God. Resist the devil and he will flee from you."(See James 4:7.)

Jesus was able to say, "*satan has nothing in Me.*" The believer is to be completely free from all satanic influence and attachments. That is the cry voiced in this prayer of our Lord Jesus.

Keeping separate from evil is a practical evidence of our coming under our King's rule.

Luke 12:32—*Do not be afraid, little flock, for your Father has been pleased to give you the kingdom.*

BOOK QUOTE: *When Heaven Invades Earth* [Chapter 5]

"For Yours is the kingdom and the power and the glory forever. Amen."

THE Kingdom of God is His possession, which is why He alone can give it to us. (See Luke 12:32.) When we declare that reality we move into declarations of praise! All through the Scriptures we hear the declarations of praise similar to this one contained in His model prayer declaring that *all glory and power* belong to Him.

One of the most important teachings that I have ever received came from Derek Prince about thirty years ago. It was a wonderful message on praise. In it he suggested that if we only have ten minutes to pray we should spend about eight praising God. It's amazing how much we can pray for with the two minutes we have left. That illustration helped me to reinforce the priority of worship that I was learning from my pastor—my dad.

As I have shared in previous journal entries, this prayer has two main objectives: (1) Minister to God out of an intimate personal relationship; and (2) bring the reality of His rulership (the Kingdom) to earth.

An outline of this Matthew 6:9-13 gives us the Kingdom approach to prayer:

1. Praise and worship (Our Father in Heaven, hallowed be Your name.)

2. Praying for Heaven on earth (Your kingdom come. Your will be done on earth as it is in Heaven.)

> **a.** Heaven's effect on material needs (Give us this day our daily bread.)
>
> **b.** Heaven's effect on personal relationships (And forgive us our debts, as we forgive our debtors.)
>
> **c.** Heaven's effect on our relationship to evil (And do not lead us into temptation, but deliver us from the evil one.)

3. Praise and worship (For Yours is the kingdom and the power and the glory forever. Amen.)

. . . if we only have ten minutes to pray we should spend about eight praising God.

Hebrews 12:2—*Let us fix our eyes on Jesus, the author and the perfecter of our faith, who for the joy set before Him endured the cross, scorning its shame, and sat down at the right hand of the throne of God.*

BOOK QUOTE: *When Heaven Invades Earth* [Chapter 5]

"Seek first the kingdom of God and His righteousness, and all these things shall be added to you" (Matt. 6:33).

GRANTED, the verse above is not in the prayer model that Jesus gave in Matthew 6:9-13. But it is in the context of His overall message of the Kingdom in the Sermon on the Mount. In it He establishes the priority that encompasses all Christian values and objectives. *Seek His Kingdom first!*

Understanding the "Lord's Prayer" from Matthew 6 helps us to realize the intended goal of all prayer—that the Lordship of Jesus would be seen in all circumstances of life. As the Kingdom of God confronts sin, forgiveness is given and change comes to the nature that had only known how to sin. When His rule collides with disease, people are healed. When it runs into the demonized, they are set free. The Kingdom message's nature provides salvation for the whole man—spirit, soul, and body. That is the gospel of Jesus Christ.

It has always seemed to me that the phrase "and all these things shall be added to you" meant that if my priorities were correct He'd make sure I got what I needed. After understanding the model prayer better, I'm not so sure that was His intent. He was saying that, if we seek His Kingdom first, we'll find His Kingdom comes fully equipped to meet our needs and beyond. It brings with it His answer to our material and relational needs, and our fight against evil.

The Kingdom message's nature provides salvation for the whole man—spirit, soul, and body.

Psalm 8:6—*You made him ruler over the works of your hands; you put everything under his feet….*

BOOK QUOTE: *When Heaven Invades Earth* [Chapter 5]

SUPPOSE I owned a very successful restaurant and you wanted to purchase the right to a franchise. By purchasing a franchise of my restaurant, you would obtain its name and all that goes with it—menus, unique design, management program, etc. You would be required to follow the prescribed standards established at the flagship restaurant. In essence, I would superimpose the main restaurant over each new location until all the locations looked alike.

When we pray for His Kingdom to come, we are asking Him to superimpose the rules, order, and benefits of His world over this one until this one looks like His. That's what happens when the sick are healed or the demonized are set free. His world collides with the world of darkness, and His world always wins. Our battle is always a battle for dominion—a conflict of kingdoms.

We were created for intimacy. From that intimacy comes our commission to rule. Keep in mind that He views ruling differently than most of us. We rule through service. Many have made the mistake of thinking that Christians are to be the heads of all corporations, governments, and departments. As good as that may sound, it's actually a *fruit* of the true goal. Christ-likeness—*excellence with humility* is the real goal. Promotion comes from the Lord. If we spent more time developing a *Kingdom heart,* we'd have more people in key places of leadership.

Prayer is the simplest activity of the believer. Child to Father…lover-to-lover conversation…sometimes spoken. Prayer is also one of the more complicated issues for us. Formulas don't work in this Kingdom relationship.

The honor that we have in being able to pray is beyond all comprehension. We are His representation on earth—ambassadors of His world. Our cries, all of them, touch His heart.

*Christ-likeness—**excellence with humility**
is the real goal.*

Joshua 1:3—*I will give you every place where you set your foot.*

BOOK QUOTE: *When Heaven Invades Earth* [Chapter 5]

"*For our citizenship is in heaven, from which we also eagerly wait for the Savior, the Lord Jesus Christ.*" Paul spoke these words to the church at Philippi, a Roman city in the country of Macedonia. It enjoyed a Roman culture and the rule and protection of Roman government, all while living in Macedonia. Philippians understood very well Paul's charge about being citizens of another world. Paul spoke, not about going to Heaven some day, but about living as citizens of Heaven today…specifically from *Heaven toward earth.*

We have the privilege of representing Heaven *in* this world, so that we might bring a manifestation of Heaven *to* this world.

As ambassadors we live in one world while representing another. An embassy is the headquarters of an ambassador and his or her staff. It is actually considered a part of the nation it represents. So it is with the believer/ambassador.

Just as ambassadors of the United States have an income based on the standard of living of this nation regardless of what nation they serve in, so also ambassadors of the kingdom of God live according to the economy of Heaven, though they are still on earth. All of our King's resources are at our disposal to carry out His will. That is how Jesus could speak of the carefree life—*consider the sparrow.*

As an ambassador, the military of the Kingdom I represent is at my disposal to help me carry out the King's orders. If as a representative of a nation my life is threatened, all of my government's military might is prepared to do whatever necessary to protect and deliver me. So it is with the heaven's angelic host. They *render service for those who would inherit salvation.*

We have the privilege of representing Heaven in this world, so that we might bring a manifestation of Heaven to this world.

John 8:28—*So Jesus said, "When you have lifted up the Son of Man, then you will know that I am the one I claim to be and that I do nothing on my own but speak just what the Father has taught me.*

BOOK QUOTE: *When Heaven Invades Earth* [Chapter 5]

ONE of the best reasons to not pray comes from watching some who do. Many who call themselves intercessors live depressed lives. I don't want to minimize the genuine effect of the burden of the Lord that comes upon us when we are praying effectively. It is real and necessary. But an unstable lifestyle has been promoted by those who claim to be intercessors, but have not learned to *release things* in prayer. The burden of the Lord takes us somewhere! I learned this the hard way.

My focus in prayer often turned to my own spirituality...or should I say, the lack of it. I would rise early and pray late into the night. God honored the sacrifice I made, but my personal victories did not coincide with my elaborate prayer times. Instead, they seemed more linked to my acts of faith. Because my focus was still on me, there was little victory I actually could trace back to my prayers.

Travailing in prayer is not always a sign of true intercession. Many are not yet able to distinguish the difference between *the burden of their own unbelief and the burden of the Lord.* I now pray until I come into a place of faith for that situation. When that happens, my perspective on the problem changes. I begin to see it from heaven's view. My role also changes. Instead of asking God to invade my circumstances, I begin to command the *mountains to be removed* in His name. It is from this place of faith (or rest) that I discover my role as the pray-er.

Pray until there's a breakthrough. Then exercise the authority given to execute His will over the circumstances at hand.

I now pray until I come into a place of faith for that situation.

Matthew 11:11—*I tell you the truth, among those born of women there has not risen one greater than John the Baptist; yet he who is least in the kingdom of Heaven is greater than he.*

BOOK QUOTE: *When Heaven Invades Earth* [Chapter 6]

JOHN the Baptist was the *high water mark* for all under the Old Covenant. But the least in this new era were born to surpass him through their relationship with the Holy Spirit.

The members of our church and the students of the Bethel School of Supernatural Ministry often embrace this privilege.

One student named Jason was ordering a meal inside a fast-food restaurant. Not content to share Christ only with those behind the counter, he began to speak past the cashier to three men in a car at the drive up window! After receiving his food, Jason left noticing they had parked to eat. He renewed his conversation with them and saw that the man in the back seat had a broken leg. So he climbed into the car with them and invited the Holy Spirit to come…and He came. The man began to curse. He had no understanding about the holy *fire* on his leg. They all jumped out of the car, and the injured man removed his brace and stomped his leg. He was completely healed! The three were so moved by God's goodness that they opened the trunk of their car, which was filled with illegal drugs. They dumped the narcotics onto the pavement, dancing on them and destroying them! Jason brought the three men to the Alabaster House, our 24-hour prayer house, and led them to Christ. The kindness of God led them to repentance. This is the normal Christian life.

The Holy Spirit is the agent of Heaven who makes these kinds of encounters possible. Not only that, He makes them the norm for those who would follow.

But the least in this new era were born to surpass Him through their relationship with the Holy Spirit.

Matthew 11:13-14—*For all the Prophets and the Law prophesied until John. And if you are willing to accept it, he is the Elijah who was to come.*

BOOK QUOTE: *When Heaven Invades Earth* [Chapter 6]

JESUS sets a standard saying John the Baptist was the greatest of all Old Testament Prophets. (See John 11:11.) He didn't do any miracles that we know of. His ministry was gloriously necessary, but not one we'd normally compare to some of the more spectacular prophets like Elijah or Daniel. Yet the One who knows all says he's the greatest. There is a truth contained in this passage that helps us to see our potential from Heaven's perspective. It is such a wonderful truth that all of hell has made a priority of trying to keep us from its simplicity.

With that in mind, a more startling bit of news comes next— *He who is least in the kingdom of Heaven is greater than he* (John 11:11). He wasn't saying that the people in heaven were greater than John. There's no purpose for such a statement. He was talking about a realm of living that was soon to become available to every believer. John prophesied of Christ's coming, and went so far as to confess his personal need of it. "He who is coming after me is mightier than I…He will baptize you with the Holy Spirit and fire" (Matt. 3:11).

Jesus came to be baptized; John tried to prevent Him: "I need to be baptized by You…" (Matt. 3:14).

John confessed his personal need of Jesus' baptism. Not one of the Old Testament prophets, not even John, had what was about to be offered to the *least of all saints*. It is the baptism in the Holy Spirit that became God's goal for mankind.

The baptism in the Holy Spirit makes a lifestyle available to us to which not even John had access. Jesus whetted our appetite for this lifestyle through His example; then He gave us the promise of its availability.

The baptism in the Holy Spirit
makes a lifestyle available to us…

Matthew 3:11—*I baptize you with water for repentance. But after me will come one who is more powerful than I, whose sandals I am not fit to carry. He will baptize you with the Holy Spirit and with fire.*

BOOK QUOTE: *When Heaven Invades Earth* [Chapter 6]

THERE is a difference between immediate and ultimate goals. Success with an immediate goal makes it possible to reach an ultimate goal. But failure in the immediate prevents us from reaching our final goal.

Bowlers know this. Each lane not only has ten pins at the far end, it also has markers on the lane itself. A good bowler knows how his or her ball rotates as it is released from a hand. Bowlers will aim at a marker in the lane as an initial target. Yet they receive no points for hitting it. Points are only given when the ultimate target is hit—the pins at the end of the lane.

Likewise, salvation was not the ultimate goal of Christ's coming. It was the immediate target…the marker in the lane. Without accomplishing redemption, there was no hope for the ultimate goal—which was to fill each born again person with the Holy Spirit. God's desire is for the believer to overflow with Himself, that we might "… *be filled with all the fullness of God*" (Eph. 3:19).The resulting fullness of the Spirit was different than anyone had ever before experienced. For that reason, the greatest of all Old Testament prophets could confess: "I need to be baptized by you," meaning, "I need your baptism…the one I was assigned to announce!"

The baptism in the Holy Spirit makes a lifestyle available to us that not even John had access to. Consider this: we could travel off of this planet in any direction at the speed of light, 186,000 miles a second, for billions of years, and never begin to exhaust what we already know to exist. All of that rests in the palm of His hand. And it's *this* God who wants to fill us with His fullness.

Success with an immediate goal
makes it possible to reach an ultimate goal.

Mark 1:8—I baptize you with water, but He will baptize you with the Holy Spirit.

BOOK QUOTE: *When Heaven Invades Earth* [Chapter 6]

ISRAEL left Egypt when the blood of a lamb was shed and applied to the doorposts of their homes. In the same way, we were set free from sin when the blood of Jesus was applied to our lives. Going through the Red Sea is referred to as *the baptism of Moses* (1 Cor. 10:2). Similarly, we face the waters of baptism after our conversion. When the Jews finally entered the Promised Land, they entered through a river—another baptism.

This new baptism would take them into a different way of life. For example: once they crossed the Jordan River, wars would be fought differently. He makes the Promised Land possible, and we pay the price to live there. He'll give us His baptism of fire if we'll give Him something worth burning.

This baptism in the Holy Spirit is the fulfillment of the Old Testament picture of entering the Promised Land. Suppose the children of Israel had chosen to cross the Jordan but became content to live on the banks of the river. They would have missed the purpose for crossing the river in the first place. There were nations to destroy and cities to possess. Contentment short of God's purposes would mean having to learn to live with the enemy. That is what it is like when a believer is baptized in the Holy Spirit but never goes beyond speaking in tongues. When we become satisfied apart from God's ultimate purpose of dominion, we learn to tolerate the devil in some area of our life. As glorious as the gift of tongues is, it is an entrance point to a lifestyle of power. That power has been given to us that we might dispossess the strongholds of hell and take possession for the glory of God.

As glorious as the gift of tongues is,
it is an entrance point to a lifestyle of power.

Mark 9:1—*There are some of you standing here who will not taste of death until you see the Kingdom of God come with power.*

BOOK QUOTE: *When Heaven Invades Earth* [Chapter 6]

EACH time the above statement is mentioned in the Gospels it is followed by the incident on the Mount of Transfiguration. Some have considered this to mean that what happened to Jesus on that mountain was the Kingdom coming in power. However, if that were so then why would Jesus need to emphasize that some there would not die until they saw the Kingdom come with power? Jesus was speaking of a much grander event. He spoke of the coming *promise of the Father*…the event that would clothe us with power from on high—the baptism in the Holy Spirit.

The baptism in the Holy Spirit is not a one-time event. Acts 2, we find 120 being baptized in the Spirit in the upper room. Yet, in Acts 4 we find some of the same crowd being *refilled*. Some have put it this way: one baptism, many fillings. Why? We leak.

Over the past decade, people travel from around the world to different *watering holes* because of an instinctive hunger for more. In some places they stand in lines, waiting for prayer. In others they crowd around the front of a sanctuary waiting for someone to be used by God to lay hands on them and bless them. Personally, because of my passion for the blessing of God I have little problem with those who return time after time to receive another blessing. I *need* His blessing. The problem is not in receiving more of the blessing of God. It's the refusal to give it away to others once we have received it ourselves.

The time spent receiving prayer has become a tool God has used to fill His people with more of Himself. It has become a method for this wonderful time of impartation.

The time spent receiving prayer has become a tool God has used to fill His people with more of Himself.

Matthew 12:28— *But if I cast out demons by the Spirit of God, surely the kingdom of God has come upon you. NKJV*

BOOK QUOTE: *When Heaven Invades Earth* [Chapter 6]

Look at this phrase, "by the Spirit of God…the kingdom." The Holy Spirit encompasses the Kingdom. While they are not the same, they are inseparable. The Holy Spirit enforces the lordship of Jesus, marking His territory with liberty (2 Cor. 3:17). *The king's domain* becomes evident through His work.

The second part of this verse reveals the nature of ministry. Anointed ministry causes the collision of two worlds—the world of darkness with the world of light. This passage shows the nature of deliverance. When the Kingdom of God comes upon someone, powers of darkness are forced to leave. Light is so superior to darkness that its triumph is immediate.

The Holy Spirit has no battle wounds. He bears no teeth marks from the demonic realm fighting for preeminence. Those who learn how to work with the Holy Spirit actually cause the reality of His world, (His dominion), to collide with the powers of darkness that have influence over a person or situation. The greater the manifestation of His Presence, the quicker the victory.

Those who discover the value of His presence enter realms of intimacy with God never previously considered possible. Out of this vital relationship arises a ministry of power that formerly was only a dream. The incomprehensible becomes possible because He is with us.

I will be with you is a promise made by God to all His servants. It comes when God has required something of us that is humanly impossible. It's the Presence of God that links us to the impossible. His presence makes anything possible!

God doesn't have to try to do supernatural things. He is supernatural. He would have to try to not be. If He is invited to a situation, we should expect nothing but supernatural invasion.

It's the Presence of God that links us to the impossible.

Acts 5:15—*As a result, people brought the sick into the streets and laid them on beds and mats so that at least Peter's shadow might fall on some of them as he passed by.*

BOOK QUOTE: *When Heaven Invades Earth* [Chapter 6]

PART of the privilege of ministry is learning how to release the Holy Spirit in a location. When I pastored in Weaverville, California, our church offices were downtown, located directly across from one bar and right next to another. This downtown area was the commercial center for the entire county—a perfect place for a church office.

It's not good when Christians try to do business only with other Christians. We are salt and light. We shine best in dark places! I love business and business people and have genuine interest in their success. Before entering a store, I often pray for the Holy Spirit to be released through me. If I need something on one side of the store, I'll enter on the opposite end in order to walk through the entire store. Many opportunities for ministry have developed as I've learned how to release His presence in the marketplace.

People laid the sick in the streets hoping that Peter's shadow would fall on them and they'd be healed (Acts 5:15). Nevertheless, it wasn't Peter's shadow that brought healing. There is no substance to a shadow. Peter was *overshadowed* by the Holy Spirit, and it was that presence that brought the miracles. The anointing is an expression of the person of the Holy Spirit. He is tangible. There were times in Jesus' ministry when everyone who touched Christ's clothing was healed or delivered (Mark 6:56). The anointing is substance. It is the actual presence of the Holy Spirit, and He can be released into our surroundings.

The anointing is an expression of the person of the Holy Spirit. He is tangible.

Matthew 4:18-19—As Jesus was walking beside the Sea of Galilee, He saw two brothers, Simon called Peter and his brother Andrew. They were casting a net into the lake, for they were fishermen. "Come, follow Me," Jesus said...

BOOK QUOTE: *When Heaven Invades Earth* [Chapter 6]

ALEXANDER the Great led his armies in victory after victory, and his desire for ever greater conquest finally brought him to the foot of the Himalayas. He wanted to go beyond these intimidating mountains. Yet, no one knew what was on the other side. Senior officers were troubled by his new vision. Why? They had gone to the edge of their map—there was no map for the new territory that Alexander wanted to possess. These officers had a decision to make: would they be willing to follow their leader off the map, or would they be content to live within its boundaries? They chose to follow Alexander.

Following the leading of the Holy Spirit can present us with the same dilemma. While he never contradicts His Word, He is very comfortable contradicting our understanding of it. Those who feel safe because of their intellectual grasp of Scriptures enjoy a false sense of security. None of us has a full grasp of Scripture, but we all have the Holy Spirit. He is our common denominator who will always lead us into truth. But to follow Him, we must be willing to follow off the map—to go beyond what we know. To do so successfully we must recognize His presence above all.

There is a great difference between the way Jesus did ministry and the way it typically is done today. He was completely dependent on what the Father was doing and saying. He illustrated this lifestyle after His Holy Spirit baptism. He followed the Holy Spirit's leading, even when it seemed unreasonable, which it often did.

When our focus is not the presence of God, we end up doing the best we can for God. Our intentions may be noble, but they are powerless in effect

. . . we must be willing to follow off the map—
to go beyond what we know.

Luke 4:18—The Spirit of the Lord is on Me, because he has anointed Me to preach good news to the poor. He has sent Me to proclaim freedom for the prisoners and recovery of sight for the blind, to release the oppressed.

BOOK QUOTE: *When Heaven Invades Earth* [Chapter 7]

THE word *anointing* means "to smear." The Holy Spirit is the oil of God that was smeared all over Jesus at His water baptism (Luke 3:21-22). The name *Jesus Christ* implies that "Jesus is the One smeared with the Holy Spirit."

But there is another spirit that works to ambush the church in every age. This power was identified by the apostle John when he said, "Even now many antichrists have come" (1 John 2:18). The nature of the antichrist spirit is found in its name: *anti*, "against"; *Christ*, "Anointed One."

Jesus lived His earthly life with human limitations. He laid His divinity aside as He sought to fulfill the assignment given to Him by the Father: to live life as a man without sin, and then die in the place of mankind for sin (Phil. 2:5-7). This would be essential in His plan to redeem mankind. The sacrifice that could atone for sin had to be a lamb, (powerless), and had to be spotless, (without sin).

The anointing Jesus received was the equipment necessary, given by the Father to make it possible for Him to live beyond human limitations. For He was not only to redeem man, He was to reveal the Father. In doing so, He was to unveil the Father's realm called Heaven. That would include doing supernatural things. The anointing is what linked Jesus, the man, to the divine, enabling Him to destroy the works of the devil. These miraculous ways helped to set something in motion that mankind could inherit once we were redeemed. Heaven—that supernatural realm—was to become mankind's daily bread.

Its "present tense" existence was explained in Jesus' statement, "The kingdom of Heaven is at hand." That means Heaven is not just our eternal destination, but also is a present reality, and it's within arms reach.

The anointing is what linked Jesus, the man, to the divine, enabling Him to destroy the works of the devil.

Matthew 12:32—*Anyone who speaks a word against the Son of Man, it will be forgiven him; but whoever speaks against the Holy Spirit, it will not be forgiven him, either in this age or in the age to come. NKJV*

BOOK QUOTE: *When Heaven Invades Earth* [Chapter 7]

To fulfill His mission, Jesus needed the Holy Spirit; and that mission, with all its objectives, was to finish the Father's work (John 4:34). If the Son of God was that reliant upon the anointing, His behavior should clarify our need for the Holy Spirit's presence upon us to do what the Father has assigned. For now, it's vital to understand that we must be clothed with the Holy Spirit for supernatural ministry. In the Old Testament, it was the anointing that qualified a priest for ministry (Exod. 40:15). According to Jesus' example, New Testament ministry is the same—anointing brings supernatural results.

This anointing is what enabled Jesus to *do only what He saw His Father do.* (See John 5:19.) It was the Holy Spirit that revealed the Father to Jesus.

It would seem that with all the significance attached to the name "Jesus," anyone desiring to undermine His work of redemption might be referred to as "Anti-Jesus," not "Anti-Christ." Even religious cults recognize and value Jesus, the man. At the very least, cults consider Him to be a teacher or a prophet and possibly "a" son of God. This horrendous error provides us with an understanding of why *antichrist* was the name given to this spirit of opposition. The spirits of hell are at war against the anointing, for without the anointing mankind is no threat to their dominion.

Jesus' concern for mankind was applauded. His humility was revered, but it was the anointing that released the supernatural. And it was the supernatural invasion of God Himself that was rejected by the religious leaders. This anointing is actually the person of the Holy Spirit upon someone to equip them for supernatural endeavors.

*According to Jesus' example. . .
anointing brings supernatural results.*

Romans 15:19—...by the power of signs and miracles, through the power of the Spirit. So from Jerusalem all the way to Illyricum, I have fully proclaimed the gospel of Christ.

BOOK QUOTE: *When Heaven Invades Earth* [Chapter 7]

IT was Holy Spirit empowered ministry that caused people to forsake all to follow Jesus. The anointing of the Holy Spirit forever changed the lives of the humble. But it was also Holy Spirit empowered ministry that caused great offense to the proud and brought about His crucifixion. The same sun that melts the ice hardens the clay. Similarly, a work of God can bring about two completely different responses, depending on the condition of the hearts of people.

God is our Father, and we inherit His genetic code. Every believer has written into his or her spiritual DNA the desire for the supernatural. It is our predetermined sense of destiny. This God-born passion dissipates when it has been reasoned away, when it's not exercised, or when it's buried under disappointment. "Hope deferred makes the heart sick" (Prov. 13:12).

The spirit of the antichrist attempts to influence believers to reject everything that has to do with the Holy Spirit's anointing. This rejection takes on many religious forms, but basically it boils down to this: we reject what we can't control. The spirit of control works against one of God's favorite elements in man: faith. Trust is misplaced as it becomes anchored in man's ability to reason.

It is the antichrist spirit that has given rise to religious spirits. A religious spirit works to get us to substitute being led by our intellect instead of the Spirit of God. Being led by the Holy Spirit is an ongoing God encounter. Religion idolizes concepts and avoids personal experience. It works to get us to worship past accomplishments at the expense of any present activity of God in our life. Sounds like idolatry, doesn't it? Anything that takes the place of dependence upon the Holy Spirit and His empowering work can be traced back to this spirit of opposition.

... a work of God can bring about two completely different responses, depending on the condition of the hearts of people.

Zechariah 4:6—*So He said to me, "This is the word of the Lord to Zerubbabel: 'Not by might nor by power, but by My Spirit,'" says the Lord Almighty.*

BOOK QUOTE: *When Heaven Invades Earth* [Chapter 7]

FOLLOWING the anointing, (the Holy Spirit), is very similar to Israel following the cloud of the Lord's presence in the wilderness. The Israelites had no control over Him. He led, and the people followed. Wherever He went, supernatural activities took place. If they departed from the cloud, the miracles that sustained them would be gone.

In New Testament terms, being a people focused on His presence means that we are willing to live beyond reason. Not impulsively or foolishly, for these are poor imitations for real faith. The realm beyond reason is the world of obedience to God. Obedience is the expression of faith, and faith is our claim ticket to the God realm. Strangely, this focus on His presence causes us to become like wind, which is also the nature of the Holy Spirit (John 3:8). His nature is powerful and righteous, but His ways cannot be controlled. He is unpredictable.

As church leaders, this hits us at our weakest point. Billy Graham is credited with saying, "Ninety-five percent of today's church activities would continue if the Holy Spirit were removed from us. In the early Church, ninety-five percent of all her activities would have stopped if the Holy Spirit were removed."

We plan our services, and call it diligence. We plan our year, and call it vision. (Planning is biblical. But our diligence and vision must never include usurping the authority of the Holy Spirit. The Lordship of Jesus is seen in our willingness to follow the Holy Spirit's leading. He wants His Church back!) But how can we follow Him if we don't recognize His presence?

The more pronounced His presence, the more unique the manifestations of our God encounters become. Although the manifestations we experience while encountering Him are important, it's God Himself we long for.

The more pronounced His presence, the more unique the manifestations of our God encounters become.

John 14:21—*And he who loves Me will be loved by My Father, and I will love him and manifest Myself to him.*

BOOK QUOTE: *When Heaven Invades Earth* [Chapter 7]

FEAR of deception has opened the door for a tragic movement among believers. It states that because we have the Bible we are emotionally unbalanced and in danger of deception if we seek for an actual "felt" experience with God. Jesus made a frightening statement regarding those who hold to Bible study vs. experience, "You search the Scriptures, for in them you think you have eternal life; and these are they which testify of Me" (John 5:39).

If our study of the Bible doesn't lead us to a deeper relationship, (an encounter), with God, then it simply is adding to our tendency towards spiritual pride. In John 10:16 Jesus did not say, "My sheep will know my book." It is His *voice* that we are to know. We must diligently study the Scriptures, remembering that it is in knowing Him that the greatest truths of Scripture will be understood.

In this present outpouring, we are being saturated with His presence in order that we might learn His voice. As He opens up His Word to us, we become more dependent upon Him. People are once again turning their focus on the greatest gift ever received—God Himself. While the anointing is often referred to as an it, it is more accurately *Him*.

As the Holy Spirit receives back the reigns over His people, He works to reset a more biblical parameter for the Christian life. We can and must know the God of the Bible by experience. The apostle Paul put it this way, "To know the love of Christ which passes knowledge; that you may be filled with all the fullness of God" (Eph. 3:19). Do you *know* what *surpasses knowledge*? It is His promise. Consider the result: "That you may be filled with all the fullness of God." What a reward!

Jesus did not say, "My sheep will know My book."
It is His voice that we are to know.

Matthew 9:35—*Then Jesus went about all the cities and villages, teaching in their synagogues, preaching the gospel of the kingdom, and healing every sickness and every disease among the people.* NKJV

BOOK QUOTE: *When Heaven Invades Earth* [Chapter 8]

JESUS, the model teacher, never separated teaching from doing. He is the pattern for this gift. God's revealed Word, declared through the lips of an anointed teacher, ought to lead to demonstrations of power.

Nicodemus said to Jesus, "Rabbi, we know that You are a teacher come from God; for no one can do these signs that You do unless God is with him" (John 3:2). It was understood that God's kind of teachers don't just talk—they do.

Jesus established the ultimate example in ministry by combining the proclamation of the gospel with signs and wonders. Matthew records: "And Jesus went about all Galilee, teaching in their synagogues, preaching the gospel of the kingdom, and healing all kinds of sickness and all kinds of disease among the people" (Matt. 4:23).

He then commanded His disciples to minister with the same focus. John records how this combination of words and supernatural works takes place, "The words that I speak to you I do not speak on My own authority; but the Father who dwells in Me does the works" (John 14:10). It's apparent that we speak the *word*, and the Father *does the works*—miracles!

As men and women of God who teach, we must require from ourselves *doing, with power*! And this *doing* must include a breaking into the impossible—through signs and wonders.

Bible teachers are to instruct in order to explain *what they just did*, or *are about to do*. Those who restrict themselves to mere words limit their gift, and may unintentionally lead believers to pride by increasing knowledge without an increased awareness of God's presence and power. It's in the trenches of Christ-like ministry that we learn to become totally dependent upon God. Moving in the impossible through relying on God short-circuits the development of pride.

Jesus established the ultimate example in ministry by combining the proclamation of the gospel with signs and wonders.

John 15:16—*You did not choose Me, but I chose you and appointed you to go and bear fruit—fruit that will last. Then the Father will give you whatever you ask in My name.*

BOOK QUOTE: *When Heaven Invades Earth* [Chapter 8]

IN 1987, I attended one of John Wimber's conferences on signs and wonders in Anaheim, California. I left discouraged. Everything that was taught, including many of the illustrations, I had taught. The reason for my discouragement was the fact that they had fruit for what they believed. All I had was good doctrine.

There comes a time when simply knowing truth will no longer satisfy. If it does not change circumstances for good, what good is it? A serious reexamination of personal priorities began. It was apparent that I could no longer expect good things to happen simply because I believed they could...or even should. There was a risk factor I had failed to enter into—Wimber called it *faith*. Teaching *must* be followed with *action* that makes room for God to move. (Making room for God doesn't mean He can't move without our approval. It simply means He delights in our invitation.)

Things changed immediately. We prayed for people, and we saw many miracles. It was glorious, but it didn't take long to discover that there were many also that weren't healed. Discouragement set in, and the pursuit with risks decreased.

On my first trip to Toronto in March of 1995, I promised God if He would touch me again, I would never back off. I would never again *change the subject*. My promise meant that I would make the outpouring of the Holy Spirit, with the full manifestations of His gifts—the sole purpose for my existence. And I would never stray from that call—no matter what! He touched me, and I have pursued without fail.

*Teaching **must** be followed with **action** that makes room for God to move.*

Hebrews 10:22—Let us draw near to God with a sincere heart in full assurance of faith, having our hearts sprinkled to cleanse us from a guilty conscience and having our bodies washed with pure water.

BOOK QUOTE: *When Heaven Invades Earth* [Chapter 8]

IT is possible to attend college, get a business degree, and never have received any teaching by someone who ever owned a business. We value concepts and ideas above experience with results. I wish that pertained only to secular schools—but the culture, which values ideas above experience, has shaped most of our Bible schools, seminaries, and denominations. Many present day movements have made a virtue out of *staying the course* without a God experience.

To make matters worse, those who speak subjectively of an experience are often considered suspect, and even dangerous. But God cannot be known apart from experience. Randy Clark puts it this way: "Anyone who doesn't have an experience with God, doesn't know God." He is a person, not a philosophy or a concept. It's time for those who have encountered God to stop pandering to fear by watering down their story. We must whet the appetites of the people of God for more of the supernatural. Testimony has the ability to stir up that kind of hunger.

As our ministry teams travel around the world, we have come to expect certain things. Healing, deliverance, and conversions are the fruits of our labors. While healing is seldom the subject we teach on, it is one of the most common results. As we proclaim the message of the Kingdom of God, people get well. The Father seems to say, "Amen!" to His own message by confirming the word with power. (See Mark 16:20.)

Peter knew this when he prayed for boldness in his preaching, expecting that God would respond by "extending His hand to heal, and signs and wonders would be done in the name of His holy servant Jesus" (Acts 4:29-30 NASB). God has promised to back up our message with power if our message is the gospel of His kingdom.

...God cannot be known apart from experience.

1 Corinthians 4:14-15—I do not write these things to shame you, but as My beloved children I warn you. For though you might have ten thousand instructors in Christ, yet you do not have many fathers; for in Christ Jesus I have begotten you through the gospel. Therefore I urge you, imitate Me. NKJV

BOOK QUOTE: *When Heaven Invades Earth* [Chapter 8]

THE problems we face today are not new. The apostle Paul had great concern for the Corinthian church, for they were being enticed by a gospel without power. "For this reason I have sent Timothy to you, who is my beloved and faithful son in the Lord, who will remind you of my ways in Christ, as I teach everywhere in every church" (1 Cor. 4:16-17).

Paul begins by contrasting teachers and fathers. The teachers mentioned were different from the kind that Jesus intended the church to have. Paul concedes they may be believers, saying these instructors are "in Christ." But he later refers to them as being "puffed up." (See 1 Cor. 4:18.)

In this post-denominational era we are seeing an unprecedented movement of believers gathering around spiritual fathers (not gender specific). In times past we gathered around certain truths, which led to the formation of denominations. The strength of such a gathering is the obvious agreement in doctrine, and usually practice. The weakness is it doesn't allow for much variety or change. At the turn of the Twentieth Century, the people who received the baptism in the Holy Spirit with speaking in tongues were no longer welcome in many of these churches, because most denominations held statements of faith cast in stone.

But now this gravitational pull toward fathers is happening even within denominations. Such a gathering of believers allows for differences in nonessential doctrines without causing division. Many consider this movement to be a restoration of the apostolic order of God.

In this post-denominational era we are seeing an unprecedented movement of believers gathering around spiritual fathers...

1 Corinthians 4:18-20—*Now some are puffed up, as though I were not coming to you. But I will come to you shortly, if the Lord wills, and I will know, not the word of those who are puffed up, but the power. For the kingdom of God is not in word but in power.*

BOOK QUOTE: *When Heaven Invades Earth* [Chapter 8]

PAUL'S is concerned about the puffed-up condition of his spiritual children. He makes his point by contrasting faithfulness and *pride*, which he defined as "puffed up." Paul does not want them to be tricked by the theories of good public speakers. Personal charisma is often valued more by the church than either anointing or truth. People of little character can often have positions of leadership in the church if they have personality. Paul found this particularly troubling.

He had worked hard to bring the Corinthians into the faith. He had chosen not to "wow" them with what he knew. In fact, he led them to an encounter with the God of all power who would become the anchor of their faith. (See 1 Cor. 2:1-5.) But now the sermonizers had come on the scene. Paul's answer was to send them someone just like himself—Timothy. They needed a reminder of what their spiritual father was like. This would help them to recalibrate their value system to imitate people of substance, who are also people of power!

Paul makes a stunning statement clarifying the right choice. He said, "The Kingdom of God is not in word but in power" (1 Cor. 4:20). The original language puts it like this—"The Kingdom of God is not in *logos* but in *dunamis*." Apparently they had a lot of teachers who were good at speaking many words, but displayed little power. They did not follow the pattern that Jesus set for them. *Dunamis* is "the power of God displayed and imparted in a Holy Spirit outpouring." That is the kingdom!

Fathers	Instructors
Lifestyle—Imitate fathers	Lifestyle—Gather around ideas (divisive)
Attitude—Humility	Attitude—Pride (puffed-up)
Ministry—Power	Ministry—Many words
Focus—The Kingdom	Focus—Teachings

Dunamis is "the power of God displayed and imparted in a Holy Spirit outpouring."

Matthew 22:29—*You are wrong because you know neither the Scriptures nor God's power. NLT*

BOOK QUOTE: *When Heaven Invades Earth* [Chapter 8]

IN the passage above, Jesus rebukes the Pharisees for their ignorance of the Scriptures *and* God's power. His rebuke comes within the context of *marriage* and *resurrection*, but is aimed at the ignorance infecting every area of their lives.

They didn't allow the Scriptures to lead them to God. They didn't understand…not really understand. The word *know* in this passage speaks of "personal experience." They tried to learn apart from such an experience. They were the champions of those who spent time studying God's Word. But their study didn't lead them to an encounter with God. It became an end in itself.

The Holy Spirit is the *dunamis* of Heaven. An encounter with God is often a power encounter. Such encounters vary from person to person according to God's design. And it's the lack of power encounters that lead to a misunderstanding of God and His Word. Experience is necessary in building a true knowledge of the Word.

God does as He pleases. While true to His Word, He does not avoid acting outside of our understanding of it. For example, He's the One who has been respectfully called a gentleman, yet who knocked Saul off of his donkey. (See Acts 9:4.) This uncomfortable tension is designed to keep us honest and truly dependent on the Holy Spirit for understanding who God is and what He is saying to us through His book. God is so foreign to our natural ways of thinking that we only truly see what He shows us—and we can only understand Him through relationship.

The Bible is the absolute Word of God. It reveals God; the obvious, the unexplainable, the mysterious, and sometimes offensive. It all reveals the greatness of our God. Yet it does not contain Him. God is bigger than His book.

God is so foreign to our natural ways of thinking that we only truly see what He shows us—and we can only understand Him through relationship.

Proverbs 25:2—It is the glory of God to conceal a matter, but the glory of kings is to search out a matter.

BOOK QUOTE: *When Heaven Invades Earth* [Chapter 8]

THERE are many concepts that the Church has held dear desiring to maintain a devotion to Scripture. But some of these actually work against the true value of God's Word. For example: many who reject the move of the Holy Spirit have claimed that the Church doesn't need signs and wonders because we have the Bible. That teaching contradicts the Word it tries to exalt. If you assign ten new believers the task of studying the Bible to find God's heart for this generation, not one of them would conclude that spiritual gifts are not for today. You have to be taught that stuff! The doctrine stating "signs and wonders are no longer needed because we have the Bible" was created by people who hadn't seen God's power and needed an explanation to justify their own powerless churches.

Revelation that doesn't lead to a God encounter only serves to make me more religious. Unless Scripture leads me to Him, I only become equipped to debate with those who disagree with my way of thinking.

"Knowledge puffs up..." (1 Cor. 8:1). Notice: Paul didn't say *unbiblical* knowledge, or *carnal* knowledge. Knowledge, including that which comes from Scripture, has the potential to make me proud.

The pride that comes from mere Bible knowledge is divisive. "He who speaks from himself seeks his own glory; but He who seeks the glory of the One who sent Him is true, and no unrighteousness is in Him" (John 7:18). Those trained without a revelation that takes us to Him are trained to speak from themselves, for their own glory. Knowledge without an encounter with God wars against true righteousness.

The heart that fears God only—the one that seeks first His Kingdom and desires God to receive all honor and glory—that heart is the heart where faith is born.

Revelation that doesn't lead to a God encounter only serves to make me more religious.

John 10:37—*If I do not do the works of the Father, do not believe me.* NKJV

BOOK QUOTE: *When Heaven Invades Earth* [Chapter 9]

"For this purpose the Son of God was manifested, that He might destroy the works of the devil" (1 John 3:8).

THE verses mentioned above deal with two subjects—*doing the works of the Father*, and *destroying the works of the devil.* These two things are inseparable. They help to clarify the purpose for Christ's coming. He was driven by one overwhelming passion: *pleasing His heavenly Father.*

The unveiling of His priorities started long before His ministry began. He was only 12. The realization that Jesus was missing came after Mary and Joseph had traveled several days from Jerusalem. They returned to search for their son.

We can only imagine what might have been going through their minds during their three days of separation. He was their miracle child…the promised One. Did they lose Him through carelessness? Was their job of raising Him finished? Had they failed?

They finally found Him in the temple discussing the Scriptures with adults. There's no doubt they were very happy and relieved. But realistically, they were probably also a bit upset. To make matters worse, Jesus didn't seem the least bit concerned about their anxiety. In fact, He seems a little surprised that they didn't know where He'd be. We hear no apology; we find no explanations, just a statement about His priorities: "Did you not know that I must be about My Father's business?" (Luke 2:49). Here the revelation of purpose began. Even at a young age, He seemed to show no concern for the probability that He caused an offense in His attempt to obey His heavenly Father. Think about it, any fear of what people might think of Him was nonexistent at the age of 12. He refused to allow the possibility of misunderstanding and conflict to keep Him from the Father's purposes.

The first and only recorded words of Jesus in His youth were all about His purpose. Obeying the Father was His whole ambition. Those words were sufficient. Later in adulthood He confessed that obeying the Father remained His priority. It actually brought Him *nourishment*—"My food is to do the will of Him who sent Me" (John 4:34).

Obeying the Father was His whole ambition.

1 John 3:8—For this purpose the Son of God was manifested, that He might destroy the works of the devil.

BOOK QUOTE: *When Heaven Invades Earth* [Chapter 9]

It was the custom of a Jewish father to take his son to the city square when he had reached manhood. He would announce to the city that his son was equal to himself in all business affairs, meaning when they dealt with the son they were dealing with the father. In doing so, he would announce to the whole city, "This is my much loved son, in whom I am well pleased."

At the water baptism of Jesus, when He was 30 years old, the prophet John the Baptist pronounced that Jesus was "The Lamb of God who takes away the sin of the world" (John 1:29). The Holy Spirit came upon Him, clothing Him in power, enabling Him to carry out His purpose. Then the Father spoke from Heaven, "This is My much loved Son, in whom I am well pleased" (Matt. 3:17).

In that moment, both the Father and the Holy Spirit affirmed the primary purpose embraced by the Son of God was to reveal and carry on the Father's business. Jesus declared the specifics of that role in His first sermon: "The Spirit of the Lord is upon Me, because He has anointed Me to preach the gospel to the poor; He has sent Me to heal the brokenhearted, to proclaim liberty to the captives and recovery of sight to the blind, to set at liberty those who are oppressed; to proclaim the acceptable year of the Lord." (Luke 4:18-19). Jesus' life illustrated what that pronouncement was all about—bringing salvation to the spirit, soul, and body of man, thus destroying the works of the devil. (See 1 John 3:8.) This was an expression of a kingdom that is ever increasing and continually unfolding. (See Isa. 9:7.)

Jesus' life illustrated what that pronouncement was all about—bringing salvation to the spirit, soul, and body of man, thus destroying the works of the devil.

Hebrews 1:3—The Son is the radiance of God's glory and the exact representation of His being, sustaining all things by His powerful word. After He had provided purification for sins, He sat down at the right hand of the Majesty in Heaven.

BOOK QUOTE: *When Heaven Invades Earth* [Chapter 9]

THE secret of Jesus' ministry is seen in His statements: "The Son can do nothing of Himself, but what He sees the Father do...the Son also does in like manner." (John 5:19). It was His dependence on the Father that brought forth the reality of the Kingdom into this world. It's what enabled Him to say, "The Kingdom of Heaven is at hand!"

Jesus displayed the Father's heart. All His actions were earthly expressions of His Father in Heaven. Jesus said, "If you've seen Me you've seen My Father." (See John 14:9.) The life of Jesus is a revelation of the Father and His business.

Jesus continues to point the way to the Father. It has now become our job, by means of the Holy Spirit, to discover and display the Father's heart: giving life, and destroying the works of the devil.

Understanding that the Father's business has to do with signs and wonders is no guarantee that we will truly fulfill God's purpose for our lives. It is much more than doing miracles, or even getting conversions. The supernatural interventions of God were done to reveal the extravagant heart of the Father for people. Every miracle is a revelation of His nature. And in that revelation is embedded an invitation for relationship.

The Pharisee's error is a very easy one for us to repeat. They had no understanding of the Father's heart. Much Christian activity has no relationship to that supreme value. We need much more than to learn how to identify our personal gifts or discover ways to be more successful in ministry. We need the Father Himself. We need His presence—His alone. The gospel is the story of the Father wooing the hearts of mankind through His love. All the other stuff we do overflows from that discovery.

The gospel is the story of the Father wooing the hearts of mankind through His love.

John 14:12—*I tell you the truth, anyone who has faith in Me will do what I have been doing. He will do even greater things than these, because I am going to the Father.*

BOOK QUOTE: *When Heaven Invades Earth* [Chapter 9]

WE can travel the globe and preach the gospel, but without a personal revelation of the Father's heart we're carrying around secondhand news—a story without a relationship. It might save people because it is truth, but there is so much more.

Most of the Pharisees spent their lives serving God without ever discovering the Father's heart. Jesus offended these religious leaders. While the Pharisees thought God was concerned about the Sabbath, Jesus worked to help the ones the Sabbath was created for. These leaders were accustomed to the miracles of the Scriptures remaining in the past. Jesus broke into their comfort zones by ushering in the supernatural. With every miracle He showed the *Father's business*. For them to adapt, everything would have to be overhauled. It was easier to brand Him a liar, and eventually kill this One who reminded them of what had to be changed.

Jesus, at the age of 12, taught us the lesson: we must be about our Father's business. And the Father's business flows from His heart. When we discover this, we find both the joy and the power of all ministry—we will find His presence.

The renewal that started in Toronto has both the Father's heart and the presence of the Holy Spirit as major focal points. In a sense, they are the same, or should we say they are *different sides of the same coin*. His presence always reveals His heart.

In the same way that Jesus revealed the Father's heart to Israel, so the Church is to *be a manifestation* of the Father's heart to the world. We are the carriers of His presence, doers of his will. Giving what we have received releases Him into situations previously held in the grip of darkness. That is our responsibility and privilege.

*In the same way that Jesus revealed the Father's heart to Israel, so the Church is to **be a manifestation** of the Father's heart to the world.*

John 14:10—*Don't you believe that I am in the Father, and that the Father is in Me? The words I say to you are not just My own. Rather, it is the Father, living in Me, who is doing His work.*

BOOK QUOTE: *When Heaven Invades Earth* [Chapter 9]

Everyone in our community is a target for God's love. The testimonies of radical transformation come from every sector of society and every conceivable place. There is a growing company of people who have the Father's business in mind.

When Jason, one of our students, was asked to come to the courthouse to serve on a jury, he went with the Father's business in mind. As he walked from the parking lot to the jurors' building, he saw two young men who looked troubled. The Lord began to talk to Jason about the older of the two. As Jason ministered to him, he addressed specific problems he had with his father. He realized that Jason couldn't have known this information without God showing it to him. (That is what we call a "word of knowledge." This is when a believer knows something that they could not know apart from God revealing it to them. God often uses this gift to let a person know that He cares. It stirs their faith to be able to receive the miracle that is to follow.) Therefore, the young man received Christ.

Jason finally made it to the jury selection building. He noticed a man on the other side of the room seated in a wheelchair. It was the electric type that moved by a toggle switch on the armrest. After a brief conversation with him, he found out he was a believer. Jason encouraged him with God's promises. They held hands and prayed. Strength came into the man's body as the pain left. Jason told him to stand.

The gentleman asked, "What if I fall?"

Jason responded, "What if you don't?"

In plain sight of all the others in the room, this man stood to his feet, waving his arms about. It had been years since he was able to stand. Jason turned to the crowd and declared, "God is here to heal!"

Before the day was over, two others had received the healing touch of Jesus. That is the Father's business, and every believer has a part to play in carrying out this privileged assignment.

There is a growing company of people who have the Father's business in mind.

Romans 8:29—*For those God foreknew He also predestined to be conformed to the likeness of His Son, that he might be the firstborn among many brothers.*

BOOK QUOTE: *When Heaven Invades Earth* [Chapter 9]

JOB 33:14-15, *"for this must pursue Him with reckless abandon."* The following is a list of things to do to help make your pursuit practical:

1. **Prayer**—Be specific and be relentless in praying for miracles in every part of your life. Bring the promises of God before Him in your pursuit. He hasn't forgotten what He has said and does not need our reminder. However, He enjoys seeing us standing on His covenant when we pray. Prayer with fasting is to be an integral part of this quest, as He revealed this to be an important way to get a breakthrough. (See Mark 9:29.)

2. **Study**—The most obvious place for study is in the scriptures. Spend months reading and rereading the Gospels. Look for models to follow. Look especially at all references to the Kingdom, and ask God to open the mysteries of the Kingdom to you. (See Matt. 13:11.) The right to understand such things belongs to the saints who are willing to obey. Another great place for study is to find all references to "reformation," those periods of transformation that Israel went through under different leaders, or revivalists. (One likely will not find the word reformation in scripture. Find passages that deal with the lives of these individuals and look for descriptions of spiritual renewal or reformation in Israel's history.) Good places to begin are with David, Hezekiah, Ezra, and Nehemiah. Their lives become prophetic messages for us. All true study is driven by hunger. If you don't have questions, you won't recognize the answers.

3. **Read**—Find the books that have been written by the generals of God's army—those who truly do the stuff. There is a great storehouse of information for those willing to pursue. Don't forget the leaders of the great healing revival of the 1950s. *God's Generals,* by Roberts Liardon, is a great place to start.

Prayer—be specific and be relentless…

2 Timothy 1:6—*For this reason I remind you to fan into flame the gift of God, which is in you through the laying on of my hands.*

BOOK QUOTE: *When Heaven Invades Earth* [Chapter 9]

WE are continuing to look at how we can rediscover God's original purpose for His people. Here is the rest of the list of practical ways to follow Him with abandonment:

4. **Laying on of hands**—Pursue the men and women of God who carry an anointing in their lives for the miraculous. Such an anointing can be transferred to others through the laying on of hands. (See 2 Tim. 1:6.) Occasionally there are ministry times when such an individual is willing to pray for those who desire an increase of anointing.

5. **Associations**—King David was known for killing Goliath in His youth. There are at least four other giants killed in Scripture—killed by the men who followed David, the giant killer. If you want to kill giants, hang around a giant killer. It rubs off.

Grace is that which enables us is in part. It is received by how we respond to the gifts of Christ: apostles, prophets, evangelists, pastors, and teachers. We actually receive the *grace to function* from these gifts. If you hang around an evangelist, you will think evangelistically. The same happens when we associate with those who regularly experience signs and wonders in their lives.

6. **Obedience**—No matter how much preparation is done to increase the anointing for miracles in a life, it never comes to fruition without radical obedience. I must look for the sick and tormented in order to pray for them. And if they are healed, I give God the praise. If they aren't, I still give God the praise and *continue* to look for people to pray for. I have learned that more people are healed when we pray for more people! Until we act on what we know, our knowledge is nothing more than a theory. Real learning comes through doing.

If you want to kill giants,
hang around a giant killer. It rubs off.

Luke 9:1—When Jesus had called the Twelve together, He gave them power and authority to drive out all demons and cure diseases.

BOOK QUOTE: *When Heaven Invades Earth* [Chapter 10]

MANY believers have made it their primary goal in life to be well-respected citizens of their communities. Good character enables us to be solid contributors to society, but most of what is recognized as a Christian lifestyle can be accomplished by people who don't even know God. Every believer should be highly respected *and more*. It's the "and more" part that we're often lacking.

While character must be at the heart of our ministries, power revolutionizes the world around us. Until the Church returns to Jesus' model for true revolutionaries, we will continue to be recognized by the world merely as nice people—while it is overcome with disease and torment, on its way to hell.

Some Christians actually have considered it to be more noble to choose *character* over *power*. But we must not separate the two. It is an unjustifiable, illegitimate choice. Together they bring us to the only real issue—obedience.

Once, while I was teaching a group of students about the importance of signs and wonders in the ministry of the gospel, a young man spoke up saying, "I'll pursue signs and wonders when I know I have more of the character of Christ in me." As good as that may sound, it comes from a religious mindset, not a heart abandoned to the gospel of Jesus Christ.

In response to this student's comment, I opened to the Gospel of Matthew and read the Lord's charge: "Go therefore and make disciples of all nations...teaching them to observe all things that I have commanded you" (Matt. 28:19). I then asked him, Who gave you the right to determine when you are ready to obey His command?

While character must be at the heart of our ministries, power revolutionizes the world around us.

Matthew 10:8—*Heal the sick, raise the dead, cleanse those who have leprosy, drive our demons. Freely you have received, freely give.*

BOOK QUOTE: *When Heaven Invades Earth* [Chapter 10]

DOES anyone think that God is impressed with us when we tell Him, "I'll obey You when I have more character"? Character is shaped through obedience.

Jesus commanded His disciples to go, and in going they were to teach all that they had been taught. And part of what they were taught was specific training on how to live and operate in the miraculous. (See Matthew 10:1; 5-8,17 and Luke 9:1-6.) And now they were responsible to teach this requirement as the lifestyle for all who were to become followers of Jesus Christ. In this way, *His* standard could remain *the* standard—the norm for all who call upon the name of the Lord for salvation.

Many consider themselves unworthy of God using them in the miraculous, and therefore never pursue that realm. Isn't it ironic that Christians will disobey God by not diligently seeking after spiritual gifts—they won't lay hands on the sick or seek to deliver the demonized—because they realize their need for more character? In none of the commissions of Jesus to His disciples did He deal specifically with character.

Is it possible the reason there are so few miracles in North America is because too many before us thought they had to become better Christians before God could use them? Yes! That single lie has kept us in perpetual immaturity because it protects us from the power-encounter that transforms us. The result is we have converts trained and over trained until they have no life, vision, or ingenuity left. This next generation of converts must be handled differently. We must help them by giving them their identity as world changers, provide them with a model for character, passion, and power, and open up opportunities to serve.

Character is shaped through obedience.

1 John 2:20—*But you have an anointing from the Holy One, and all of you know the truth.*

BOOK QUOTE: *When Heaven Invades Earth* [Chapter 10]

CHRIST-LIKE character can never be fully developed without serving under the anointing. Anointed ministry brings us into contact with the power needed for personal transformation.

Both the Old and New Testaments are filled with great examples of *empowering for supernatural endeavors*. For example, God spoke saying that the Spirit of the Lord would come upon King Saul and turn him into another man. (See First Samuel 10:6.) The anointing transforms as it flows through the vessel. Two key phrases follow this promise:

1. "God gave him another heart."

2. "Then the Spirit of the Lord came upon him, and He prophesied among them [the prophets]" (1 Sam. 10:9-10).

Saul was given an opportunity to become all that Israel needed him to be, (a king with a new heart), and learn to do all he needed to do (hear from God and declare His words—or prophesy).

I have a dear friend who had a huge character flaw that spiritually crippled him, yet he still had a very strong prophetic anointing. (He was not the first person to think that his successful ministry was a sign of God's approval of his private life.) When I confronted him about his secret sin, he wept with deep sorrow.

Because of his place of influence in the church, I brought him under discipline. (Discipline can bring an individual into personal victory, but punishment bridles with shame.)

Part of my restriction was to keep him from giving prophetic words for a season.

After several months, I became increasingly troubled over the statement regarding King Saul and its relationship to my friend. I realized if I didn't allow him to minister (under the anointing) I'd be limiting his exposure to the very thing that would establish his victory. When I released him to prophesy again, there was a new purity and power. It was his personal encounter with the anointing in ministry that "turned him into another man." (This illustration is not to take away from the importance of discipline. Biblical discipline is not punishment. It is choosing, in love, restrictions that are best for that person and the entire church family. The length of his discipline was nearing the point at which it would have become punishment and would have kept him from the very thing he needed.)

Anointed ministry brings us into contact with the power needed for personal transformation.

Luke 18:8—*I tell you, he will see that they get justice, and quickly. However, when the Son of Man comes, will he find faith on the earth?*

BOOK QUOTE: *When Heaven Invades Earth* [Chapter 10]

A counterfeit hundred dollar bill does not nullify the value of the real thing. Likewise, a counterfeit, abused, or abandoned gift does not invalidate our need for the Holy Spirit's power to live as Jesus did.

Pennies are not counterfeited because they're not worth the effort. In the same way, the devil only works to copy or distort those things in the Christian life that have the greatest potential effect. When I see others who have pursued great things in God but have failed, I get motivated to *pick up where they left off.* It tells me there's a treasure in that field, and I'm ready to look for it with reckless abandon. (Reckless abandon is not the same as spiritual carelessness. Most of the failures in the past have come because leaders became too detached from the people that God put in their lives. I pursue dangerous things, but I keep accountable, and I work to protect my relationships on all levels. I believe this is the realm of safety that many have abandoned in their pursuit of their "treasure in the field.") The abuses of one person never justify the neglect of another.

The eyes of the critics quickly move to the ones who tried and failed, the countless millions who confess salvation in Jesus, but never *pursue the gifts* as commanded. But the eyes of Jesus quickly look to see if there is faith on the earth. For every charlatan there are a thousand good citizens who accomplish little or nothing for the Kingdom.

Many believe His power exists only to help us overcome sin. This understanding stops short of the Father's intent for us to *become witnesses* of another world. Doesn't it seem strange that our whole Christian life should be focused on overcoming something that has already been defeated? Sin and its nature have been yanked out by the roots. Many constantly call out to God for more power to live in victory. If His death wasn't enough, what else is there? That battle has already been fought and won! Is it possible that the process of constantly bringing up issues dealt with by the blood is what has actually given life to those issues?

The abuses of one person never justify the neglect of another.

Romans 6:11—*Likewise you also, reckon yourselves to be dead indeed to sin, but alive to God in Christ Jesus our Lord. NKJV*

BOOK QUOTE: *When Heaven Invades Earth* [Chapter 10]

THE word *reckon* above points to "our need to change our minds." I don't need power to overcome something if I'm dead to it. But I do need power for boldness for the miraculous and for the impossible. (See Acts 4:28-29.)

Part of our problem is this: we are accustomed only to doing things for God that are not impossible. If God doesn't show up and help us, we can still succeed. There must be an aspect of the Christian life that is impossible without divine intervention. That keeps us on the edge and puts us in contact with our true calling.

Make no mistake; character is a supreme issue with God. But His approach is much different than ours. His righteousness and character is not built into us by our own efforts. It is developed when we quit striving and learn to abandon ourselves completely to His will.

So great was the disciple's need for power to become witnesses that they were not to leave Jerusalem until they had it. That word *power*, or "dunamis," speaks of the miracle realm. It comes from *dunamai*, which means "ability." Think about it—we get to be clothed with *God's ability*!

The remaining eleven disciples were already the most trained people in signs and wonders in all of history. No one had seen or done more. And it was those eleven who had to stay until they were clothed with "power from on high." When they got it—they knew it. This power came through an encounter with God. (See Acts 4:28-29.)

Will you bury your gifts and tell the Master when He comes that you were afraid of being wrong? Power and character are so closely aligned in Scripture that you cannot be weak in one without undermining the other.

His righteousness and character
is not built into us by our own efforts.

Galatians 5:25—Since we live by the Spirit, let us keep in step with the Spirit.

BOOK QUOTE: *When Heaven Invades Earth* [Chapter 10]

AROUND 25 years ago, I heard someone mention that if we would learn what it meant to "not grieve" and "not quench" the Holy Spirit, we would know the secret to being full of the Spirit. While that may be overly simplistic, this individual tapped into two very important truths that deal directly with the "character vs. power" trap.

The command, "Do not grieve the Holy Spirit" from Ephesians 4:30 explains how our sin affects God. It causes Him grief. This command is character centered. *Sin* is defined in two ways: "doing wrong things and a failure to do right things."

"To him who knows to do good and does not do it, to him it is sin." (See James 4:17.) Departing from the character of Christ in either of these ways brings grief to the Holy Spirit.

Continuing with this theme we have the command in First Thessalonians 5:19 (NKJV), "Do not quench the Spirit." This mandate is focused on our need to follow His leading. To *quench* means to "stop the flow" of something. As the Holy Spirit is ready to bring salvation, healing, and deliverance, we are to *flow* with Him. Failure to do so hinders His efforts to bring us into the supernatural.

If He is to be free to move in our lives, we will constantly be involved in impossibilities. The supernatural is His natural realm. The more important the Holy Spirit becomes to us, the more these issues will be paramount in our hearts.

If He is to be free to move in our lives,
we will constantly be involved in impossibilities.

1 Corinthians 14:1—*Follow the way of love and eagerly desire the spiritual gifts, especially the gift of prophecy.*

BOOK QUOTE: *When Heaven Invades Earth* [Chapter 10]

At some point we must believe in a God who is big enough to keep us safe in our quest for more of Him. Practically speaking, many Christian's devil is bigger than their God. How could a created, fallen being ever be compared with the infinite Lord of glory? It's an issue of trust. If I focus on my need to protect myself from deception, I will always be overwhelmingly aware of the power of the devil. If my heart is completely turned to the One who is "able to keep me from falling." (See Jude 24-25.) He is the only One I become impressed with. My life reflects what I see with my heart.

So how do we walk in the power of God? First, we must pursue Him. The life of power is a life of abiding in Christ, (staying plugged into our power source). The hunger for the demonstration of power must not be separated from our passion for Him. But realize this, our hunger for Him in part must be seen in our lustful pursuit of spiritual gifts (1 Cor. 14:1). That is His command!

In this endeavor I must passionately desire life-changing encounters with God, over and over again. I must cry out day and night for them…and be specific. I must be willing to travel to get what I need. If God is moving somewhere I must go! If He is using someone more than He is using me, I must humbly go to them and ask them to pray for me with the laying on of hands.

Some may ask, "Why can't God touch me where I am?" He can. But He usually moves in ways that emphasize our need for others, rather than adding to our independence. Wise men have always been willing to travel.

The hunger for the demonstration of power must not be separated from our passion for Him.

Genesis 32:28—*Then the man said, "Your name will no longer be Jacob, but Israel, because you have struggles with God and with men and have overcome."*

BOOK QUOTE: *When Heaven Invades Earth* [Chapter 10]

ONCE in the middle of the night, God came in answer to my prayer for more of Him, yet not in a way I had expected. I went from a dead sleep to being wide-awake in a moment. Unexplainable power began to pulsate through my body, seemingly just shy of electrocution. My arms and legs shot out in silent explosions as if something was released through my hands and feet. The more I tried to stop it, the worse it got.

I soon discovered that this was not a wrestling match I was going to win. This was simply the most overwhelming experience of my life. It was raw power...*it* was God. He came in response to a prayer I had been praying for months, "God, I must have more of you at any cost."

This divine moment was glorious, but not pleasant. At first I was embarrassed, even though I was the only one who knew I was in that condition.

I recalled Jacob and his encounter with the angel of the Lord. He limped for the rest of His life. And then there was Mary, the mother of Jesus. My request for more of God carried a price (Gen. 32:24-32).

At the forefront was the realization that God wanted to make an exchange—His increased presence for my dignity. You know His purpose so clearly that every other reality fades into the shadows, as God puts His finger on the one thing that matters to Him.

In the midst of the tears came a point of no return. I gladly yielded, crying, "More, God. More! I must have more of You at any cost! If I lose respectability and get You in the exchange, I'll gladly make that trade. Just give me more of You!"

You know His purpose so clearly that every other reality
fades into the shadows, as God puts His finger on
the one thing that matters to Him.

Proverbs 21:21—*He who pursues righteousness and love, finds life, prosperity, and honor.*

BOOK QUOTE: *When Heaven Invades Earth* [Chapter 10]

BIBLICAL passion is a mysterious mixture of humility, supernatural hunger, and faith. I pursue because I have been pursued. Lethargy must not be found in me. And if the average Christian life around me falls short of the biblical standard, I must pursue against the grain. If people are not being healed, I will not supply a rationale so that all those around me remain comfortable with the void. Instead, I will pursue the healing until it comes or the individual goes to be with the Lord. (At this point the prayer for resurrection is appropriate!) I will not lower the standard of the Bible to my level of experience.

Jesus healed everyone who came to Him (Matt. 8:16). To accept any other standard is to bring the *Bible down to our level of experience*, and deny the nature of the One who changes not.

As for the ministry of power, whatever I receive from God I must give away. You only get to keep what you give away. If you want to see people healed, look for those who are sick and offer to pray for them. While I am not the healer, I do have control over my willingness to serve those in need. If I minister to the needy, I give Him an opportunity to show His extravagant love for people. The ministry of signs and wonders will go nowhere if we are afraid of failure. As Randy Clark puts it, "I must be willing to fail to succeed."

As for the ministry of power,
whatever I receive from God I must give away.

Matthew 7:20—*Thus, by their fruit you will recognize them.*

BOOK QUOTE: *When Heaven Invades Earth* [Chapter 10]

JESUS said that we must receive the Kingdom like a child. The life of power is at home in the heart of a child. A child has an insatiable appetite to learn. Be childlike and read the works of those who have succeeded in the healing ministry. Stay away from the books and tapes of those who say it shouldn't or can't be done. If the author doesn't walk in power, don't listen, no matter how proficient they may be in another field. An expert in biblical finances is not necessarily proficient in signs and wonders. Maintain respect for that individual's place in God and his or her area of expertise, but never waste precious time reading the stuff of those who do not do what they teach. We have grown fat on the theories of classroom Christians. We must learn from those who *just do it!*

Someone once brought a book to my office that was critical of the revival that started in Toronto in January of 1994. I refused to read it and threw it away. You might say, "You're not very open minded." You're right. I am responsible to protect what God has given me. No one else has that assignment. Burning within my soul is a piece of the original flame from the day of Pentecost. It's been handed down generation after generation. That fire burns deep inside, and because of it I'll never be the same again. My passion for Jesus is growing continually. And the signs and wonders He promised are happening as a regular part of life.

I have no time for critics, but I do welcome the "wounds of a friend." (See Prov. 27:6.)

The corrections offered through meaningful relationships keep us from deception.

I am responsible to protect what God has given me.

1 Peter 1:3—*His divine power has given us everything we need for life and godliness through our knowledge of Him who called us by His own glory and goodness.*

BOOK QUOTE: *When Heaven Invades Earth* [Chapter 10]

WHENEVER I have taken time to seek God about the need for power to back up His message, He always comes through with an increase.

I learned something very helpful from Randy Clark. When he notices there are certain kinds of healings that are not taking place, he cries to God mentioning specific diseases in his prayers. He was having very few miracles having to do with the brain—such as dyslexia. After crying out for these kinds of miracle manifestations, he started to experience a breakthrough. I have followed his lead and have never seen God fail. Specific requests are good because they are measurable. Some of our prayers are too general. God could answer them, and we would never know it.

After learning this principle, I began to pray for disorders in the brain. One such miracle came to a woman named Cindy. She was told that a third of her brain was shut down. As a result, she had 23 learning disorders. She could do nothing with memorization, numbers, or maps. On one of our Friday night services, she stood in line for prayer for the blessing of God. When she was prayed for, she fell under the weight of His glory. During the time in which she lay there overcome by God's power, she had a vision in which Jesus asked her if she would like for Him to heal her. She, of course, said yes. At His command, she jumped up off of the floor and ran to get her Bible. For the first time in her life everything was where it was supposed to be on the page. When she testified of the miracle a couple of weeks later, she quoted many verses she had put to memory in that short time.

Whenever I have taken time to seek God about the need for power to back up His message, He always comes through with an increase.

1 Corinthians 2:4-5—*My message and my preaching were not with wise and persuasive words, but with a demonstration of the Spirit's power, so that your faith might not rest on men's wisdom, but on God's power.*

BOOK QUOTE: *When Heaven Invades Earth* [Chapter 11]

REVIVAL is the atmosphere in which Christ's power is most likely to be manifested. It touches every part of human life, breaking into society with sparks of revolution. Such glory is costly, and it is not to be taken lightly. Nevertheless, a powerless Church is far more costly in terms of human suffering and lost souls. During revival, hell is plundered and Heaven is populated. Without revival, hell is populated...period.

A primary purpose of the miracle realm is to reveal the nature of God. The lack of miracles works like a thief, stealing precious revelation that is within the grasp of every man, woman, and child. Our debt to mankind is to give them answers for the impossible, and a personal encounter with God. And that encounter must include great power. (That encounter is to include other things too. For example: the love of God must be evident through us, as should character, etc. The purpose of this book however is to fill a literary gap to help in our much needed return to a gospel of power, as well as one of love and character.)

We are to be a witness for God. To give *witness* is to "represent." This actually means to "re-present Him." Therefore, to re-present Him without power is a major shortcoming. It is impossible to give an adequate witness of God without demonstrating His supernatural power. The supernatural is His natural realm. Jesus was an exact representation of the Father's nature. (Heb. 1:3 NASB). His re-presentation of the Father is to be a model for us as we learn how to re-present Him.

The miracle realm of God is always with purpose. He doesn't come upon people with power to show off or entertain. Demonstrations of power are redemptive in nature. Even the cataclysmic activities of the Old Testament were designed to bring people to repentance.

Healing is never only one-dimensional. While a miracle may change one's physical health, it also sparks a revolution deep within the human heart. Both reveal the nature of God, which must never be compromised through powerless Christianity.

The miracle realm of God is always with purpose.

_____

_____

_____

_____

_____

_____

_____

_____

_____

_____

_____

_____

_____

_____

Luke 5:8—*When Simon Peter saw it* [the miraculous catch of fish], *he fell down at Jesus' knees, saying, "Depart from me, for I am a sinful man, O Lord!" NKJV*

BOOK QUOTE: *When Heaven Invades Earth* [Chapter 11]

PETER had been fishing all night with no success. Jesus told him to cast nets to the other side of the boat, which doubtless he had already done many times. When he did it at the bidding of the Master, the catch of fish was so great it nearly sank the boat. Peter called for help from the other boats. His response to this miracle was, "I am a sinful man."

Who told him that he was a sinner? There is no record of sermons, rebukes, or any such thing in the boat that day—just good fishing. So, how did he come under such conviction for sin? It was in the miracle. Power exposes. It draws a line in the sand and forces people to a decision.

Demonstrations of power are no guarantee that people will repent. One only needs to look at Moses to realize that sometimes the miraculous only causes our Pharaohs to become more resolved to destroy us when they see power. Without acts of power, the Pharisees might have forgotten about the Church that was born from the blood of Jesus poured out at the cross. Power stirred up the zeal of opposition in them. We must be soberminded about this: power often causes people to decide what they're for or against. Power removes the middle ground.

Mercy ministries are absolutely essential in the ministry of the gospel. They are one of the ways the love of God can and must be seen. Yet they are not complete without demonstrations of power. We must realize the sad truth—it is common for people to acknowledge the kindness of the Church and still not be brought to repentance. But power forces the issue because of its inherent ability to humble mankind.

. . . power often causes people to decide what they're for or against.

Psalm 78:9-11—*The children of Ephraim, **being** armed and **carrying** bows, turned back in the day of battle. They did not keep the covenant of God; They refused to walk in His law, And forgot His works and His wonders that He had shown them.*

BOOK QUOTE: *When Heaven Invades Earth* [Chapter 11]

A very profound part of the Jewish culture was shaped by the command to "keep the testimonies of the Lord" (Exod. 15:26). The family itself was driven by the ongoing revelation of God contained in His commandments. They were to talk about the Law of God and what God had done when they went to bed at night, rose up in the morning, walked along, etc. Just about any time of the day was a perfect time to talk about God's wondrous works.

To insure they didn't forget, they were to build monuments that would help them to remember the invasion of God into their lives. For example: They piled stones to mark the place where Israel crossed the Jordan River. (See Josh. 3:1-17.) That was so that when their young ones would ask, *Hey Dad...why is that pile of stones there?* They could respond with the story of how God worked among them.

The testimony of God creates an appetite for more of the activities of God. Expectation grows wherever people are mindful of His supernatural nature and covenant. When the expectation grows, miracles increase and testimonies increase as well. The act of sharing a testimony about God can stir up others until they expect and see God work in their day.

The reverse is also true. Where they decrease, miracles are expected less. If there is less expectation for miracles, they happen even less. As you can see, there is also a possible downward spiral. Forgetting what God has done by removing the testimony from our lips causes us to become fearful in the day of battle. The story of the children of Ephraim is tragic because they were thoroughly equipped to win. They just lacked courage. Their courage was to come from their memory of who God had been to them.

The testimony of God creates an appetite for more of the activities of God.

Matthew 11:20-22—*Then He began to rebuke the cities in which most of His mighty works had been done, because they did not repent: "Woe to you, Chorazin! Woe to you Bethsaida! For if the mighty works which were done in you had been done in Tyre and Sidon, they would have repented long ago in sackcloth and ashes. But I say to you, it will be more tolerable for Tyre and Sidon in the day of judgment than for you.*

BOOK QUOTE: *When Heaven Invades Earth* [Chapter 11]

THIS passage of Scripture makes a distinction between religious cities and those known for sin. The religious city had a numbed awareness of its need for God, while the sinful city was conscious that something was missing. Religion is even more cruel than sin.

The cities that Jesus addresses here saw more signs and wonders than all the rest combined. The miracles Jesus performed were so great in number that apostle John said you could not record them if you filled all of the books in the world. (See John 21:25.) This gives us perspective on the rebuke of Jesus upon the hard-hearted cities.

Jesus was limited in what He could do in Nazareth because of their unbelief. (See Mark 6:1-6.) Yet in Chorazin and Bethsaida, His miracles appear to be limitless, which suggests these cities had a measure of faith. His stern rebuke didn't appear to come because they didn't appreciate His working of miracles. They must have. Their problem was that they added such a move to what they were already doing, instead of making Him the focal point of their lives. That's what religion does. Like Jesus said, they failed to repent and change their way of thinking, (alter their perspective on life itself).

Many enjoy the move of God, but don't genuinely repent, (change their life's perspective, making His activities the focus and ambition of their lives). The revelation that came to them through the miraculous increased their responsibility, thus requiring change. It never came.

Powerlessness cancels that possibility, and in its place comes God's judgment.

Many enjoy the move of God, but don't genuinely repent...

John 2:11—*This beginning of signs Jesus did in Cana of Galilee, and manifested His glory; and His disciples believed in Him. NKJV*

BOOK QUOTE: *When Heaven Invades Earth* [Chapter 11]

JESUS attended a wedding where they ran out of wine. As yet He hadn't performed any of the wonders for which He would later become known. Mary knew who her son was and what was possible, so she turned to Him and said, "They have no wine." Jesus responded to her saying, "Woman, what does your concern have to do with Me? My hour has not yet come." But then Mary did something amazing—she turned to the servants and said, "Whatever He says to you, do it!" (John 2:4-5). Her faith just made room for the extravagance of God! Jesus followed this with the miracle of turning the water into wine.

It's important to remember that Jesus only did what He saw His Father do, and He only said what He heard His Father say. When Mary first mentioned the need for wine to Jesus, it is safe to say He noticed that the Father was not involved in doing any miracles for that wedding.

Then Jesus again looked to see what the Father was doing and now noticed that He was turning water into wine. So Jesus followed His lead and did the miracle. Her faith so touched the heart of the Father that He apparently changed the chosen time to unveil Jesus as the miracle-worker. Faith moves Heaven, so that Heaven will move earth.

This demonstration of God's power released the glory of God into that location. Signs and wonders do that. They release the glory of God into our cities. The miracle displaces darkness and replaces it with light—glory. When miracles are absent, so is the glory of God, which is the manifested presence of Jesus.

Faith moves Heaven, so that Heaven will move earth.

Matthew 9:8—*Now when the multitudes saw it, they marveled and glorified God, who had given such power to men. NKJV*

BOOK QUOTE: *When Heaven Invades Earth* [Chapter 11]

As glory is released, it displaces the powers of darkness and replaces it with the actually ruling presence of God. The house is *clean and swept* and becomes filled with the furnishings of Heaven. (See Luke 11:25.) As the powers of darkness are removed they must be replaced with right things, or the enemy has legal access to return, making the last state of the man worse than the first. Miracles do both—they remove the ruling influence of hell while establishing the ruling presence of God.

How will the glory of God cover the earth? I believe that, at least in part, it will be through a people who walk in power, bringing the testimony of Jesus to the nations of the world. There will be a generation that will catch this and will invade the world system with this living testimony of who Jesus is.

I talk about the miracle-working power of God in almost every meeting I lead, whether it be a traditional church service, a conference, even a board or staff meeting. When I'm speaking away from home, I will often do this to stir up faith and help listeners to direct their hearts to God. When I'm through, I ask them this question: *How many of you gave praise and glory to God when I shared those testimonies?* Most every hand goes up. Then I remind them this one important thing—*If there were no power and corresponding testimony, God would have never received that glory. Without power, we rob God of the glory He is due!*

Miracles. . . remove the ruling influence of hell while establishing the ruling presence of God.

Joshua 4:5-7—*Each of you is to take up a stone on his shoulder, according to the number of the tribes of the Israelites, to serve as a sign among you. In the future, when your children ask you, 'What do these stones mean?' tell them that the flow of the Jordan was cut off before the ark of the covenant of the Lord...these stones are to be a memorial to the people of Israel forever.*

BOOK QUOTE: *When Heaven Invades Earth* [Chapter 11]

"One generation shall praise Your works to another,
And shall declare Your mighty acts" (Psalms 145:4 NKJV).

"We will not hide them from their children,
Telling to the generation to come the praises of the Lord,
And His strength and His wonderful works that He has done.
For He established a testimony in Jacob,
And appointed a law in Israel,
Which He commanded our fathers,
That they should make them known to their children;
That the generation to come might know them,
The children who would be born,
That they may arise and declare them to their children,
That they may set their hope in God..." (Psalms 78:4-8 NKJV).

ISRAEL was to build monuments in memory of the activities of God. The reason? So that in their everyday existence there would be a reminder to coming generations of who God is, and what His covenant with His people looks like.

The testimony was to be both a record of God's activity with His people and an invitation for others to know Him in that way. One generation would speak of God's testimony to another. It doesn't say that the older generation would speak to the younger. While that is what is most often thought of in this verse, it is equally true that a younger generation would experience God, and the older could benefit. Encounters with the almighty God become a unifying factor for generations!

... in their everyday existence there would be a reminder to coming generations of who God is, and what His covenant with His people looks like.

Psalm 148:13—Let them praise the name of the Lord, for His name alone is exalted; His splendor is above the earth and Heaven. NKJV

BOOK QUOTE: *When Heaven Invades Earth* [Chapter 11]

"Bless the Lord, all His works, in all places of His dominion. Bless the Lord, O my soul!" (Psalm 103:22 NKJV).

"All Your works shall praise You, O Lord, And Your saints shall bless You" (Psalm 145:10 NKJV).

Not only do miracles stir the hearts of men to give glory to God, but miracles give Him glory on their own. I'm not sure how this works, but somehow an act of God has a life of it's own and contains the ability to actually give God glory without the assistance of mankind. The absence of miracles robs God of the glory that He is to receive from the life released in His own works.

"If I do not do the works of My Father, do not believe Me; but if I do, though you do not believe Me, believe the works, that you may know and believe that the Father is in Me, and I in Him" (John 10:37-38 NKJV).

If the Jews struggled with believing in Jesus as their Messiah, He simply told them to look at the miracles and believe them. Why? A sign always leads you somewhere. He was not afraid of where His signs would lead them. Somehow that simple step of believing in what they saw eventually could enable them to believe in Jesus Himself—as in the case of Nicodemus (John 10:37-38). Every miracle testified of Jesus' identity. Without miracles, there can never be a full revelation of Jesus.

A sign always leads you somewhere.

Romans 15:18-19—For I will not dare to speak of any of those things which Christ has not accomplished through me, in word and deed, to make the Gentiles obedient—in mighty signs and wonders, by the power of the Spirit of God.... NKJV

BOOK QUOTE: *When Heaven Invades Earth* [Chapter 11]

"And the multitudes with one accord heeded the things spoken by Philip, hearing and seeing the miracles which he did" (Acts 8:6).

PHILIP was the messenger of God for the city of Samaria. They were able to hear his words as being from God, because of the miracles. Acts of power help people to tune their hearts to the things of God. It helps to break them loose from the rationale that this material world is the ultimate reality. Such a shift in perspective is essential to the most basic response to God. In essence, that is what the word *repentance* means. Miracles provide the grace for repentance.

The desperation that miracles cause is in part responsible for this phenomenon. As our interests turn from all that is natural, we direct our attention to Him. This change of heart opens both the eyes and ears of the hearts. As a result we see what has been right in front of us all this time, and we hear what God has been saying throughout our lives.

Miracles cause a shift in priorities. They are an important aid in helping us to hear more clearly. Without them we are more inclined to be directed by our own minds and call it spirituality.

In Romans 15:18-19, Paul demonstrates how the Gentiles were brought into obedience through the power of the Spirit of God, expressed in signs and wonders. This was what he considered as *fully* preaching the gospel. It wasn't a complete message without a demonstration of the power of God. It's how God says "amen" to His own declared word!

Nothing thrills the heart more than knowing God. He is limitless in power. He is for us and not against us, and is big enough to make up for our smallness. Conversely, being raised where there is little or no evidence of power disillusions a generation created for great exploits.

Nothing thrills the heart more than knowing God.

John 3:2— *This man came to Jesus by night and said to Him, "Rabbi, we know that You are a teacher come from God; for no one can do these signs that You do unless God is with him."*

BOOK QUOTE: *When Heaven Invades Earth* [Chapter 11]

THE promise, "I will be with you," was given many times throughout the Scriptures. It was always given to one who would be brought into impossible circumstances—circumstances that would need a miracle. (Look at Moses in Exodus 3:12, Joshua in Joshua 1:9, and Gideon in Judges 6:12 for further study on this subject.) While His presence is comforting, while His sweet fellowship is what draws me into an intimate relationship with Him, His presence also is a provision from heaven designed to bring me into a place of great courage for signs and wonders.

Jesus commanded the most highly trained individuals in the supernatural to ever walk the earth to "wait in Jerusalem for what the Father has promised." (See Acts 1:4.) Even though they had been with Him, even though they had experienced His power through their own ministry, they were to wait for *Dunamis*—the ability to perform miracles.

It is as if they had been working under the umbrella of His anointing. The time had come for them to get an anointing of their own through an encounter with God. The baptism of fire would give them their own ongoing encounter that would help to keep them at the center of God's will *when* persecution came.

The baptism of the Holy Spirit is an immersion into the *dunamis* of heaven. The ability to pray in tongues is a wonderful gift given through this baptism. The fullness of God ought to do more for me than give me a supernatural language. It's a glorious gift from God. But His purposes bring us into more, to a divine partnership in which we become co-laborers with Christ. Power came to make us witnesses. When the Spirit of God came upon the people in the Scriptures, all of nature bowed before them. Power was displayed, and impossibilities gave way to the full expression of God's presence.

Power came to make us witnesses.

Acts 4:30—*Stretch our your hand to heal and perform miraculous signs and wonders through the name of your holy servant Jesus.*

BOOK QUOTE: *When Heaven Invades Earth* [Chapter 11]

MANY fear signs and wonders because of the possibility of deception. So, in order to prevent any opportunity of being deceived they replace displays of power with religious traditions or Christian activities. They often become satisfied with knowledge. But, when this happens who is deceived?

Signs have a purpose. They are not an end in themselves. They point to a greater reality. When we exit a building, we don't go out through the exit sign. The sign is real. But it points to a reality greater than itself.

A sign along a highway can confirm we are on the right road. Without signs we have no way of knowing we are where we think we are. Signs aren't needed when I travel familiar roads. But I do need them when I'm going where I've never been. So it is in this present move of God. We've gone as far as we can with our present understanding of Scripture. It's time to let signs have their place. They illustrate Scripture, all the while pointing to Jesus, the Son of God. Yet they also confirm to a people who have embraced an authentic gospel that they are going in the right direction.

Not one of us understood salvation until we were saved. It was the miracle—an experience—which gave us understanding. So it is with signs. They point us to the person. In this hour the *experience* will help to open up those portions of Scripture that have been closed to us. (Strong relationships and accountability are what helps us to stay safe and undeceived.)

No one in their right mind would claim to understand all that is contained in the Bible for us today. Yet to suggest that more is coming causes many to fear. Get over it, so you don't miss it!

We've gone as far as we can with our present understanding of Scripture. It's time to let signs have their place.

Matthew 28:20—And surely I am with you always, to the very end of the age.

BOOK QUOTE: *When Heaven Invades Earth* [Chapter 12]

God's covenant promise, "I will be with you," has always been linked to mankind's need for courage to face the impossible. There is no question that the presence of God is what brings us great comfort and peace. But the presence of God was always promised to His chosen ones to give them assurance in the face of less than favorable circumstances.

He is the great treasure of mankind. He always will be. It is this revelation that enabled the revolutionary exploits of the apostle Paul. It's what strengthened a king named David to risk his life in order to transform the system of sacrifice and worship. Moses needed this assurance as the man who was sent to face Pharaoh and his demon possessed magicians. They all needed incredible confidence to fulfill their callings.

The Great Commission provides more interesting reading for those who remember what kind of men God was giving His charge to—greedy, prideful, angry, and self-centered. Yet Jesus called them to change the world. What was the one word of assurance that He gave them before departing from sight? "I will be with you always…." (See Matt. 28:19-21.)

We know that such a promise is given to everyone who calls on the name of the Lord for salvation. But why do some walk with a greater sense of God's presence than others? Some people place high value on the presence of God, and others don't. The ones who do enjoy fellowship throughout their day with the Holy Spirit are extremely conscious of how He feels about their words, attitudes, and activities. The thought of grieving Him brings great sorrow. It's their passion to give Him preeminence in everything. That passion brings that believer into a supernatural life—one with the constant activity of the Holy Spirit working through them.

The ones who do enjoy fellowship throughout their day with the Holy Spirit are extremely conscious of how He feels about their words, attitudes, and activities.

2 Corinthians 5:5—*Now it is God who has made us for this very purpose and has given us the Spirit as a deposit, guaranteeing what is to come.*

BOOK QUOTE: *When Heaven Invades Earth* [Chapter 12]

THE presence of God is to be realized in the anointing. Remember, *anointing* means "smeared"—it is God covering us with His power-filled presence. Supernatural things happen when we walk in the anointing!

For the most part, the anointing has been hoarded by the Church for the Church. Many have misunderstood why God has covered us with Himself, thinking it is for our enjoyment only. In the Kingdom of God we only get to keep what we give away. This wonderful presence of God is to be taken to the world. If it isn't, our effectiveness decreases. Perhaps this phrase will help to clarify this point: *He is in me for my sake, but He's upon me for yours!*

Not only is all ministry to be Spirit empowered, it is to have a gathering element to it. Either we take what God has given us and give it to the world, or what we have received will bring division. It's our perspective on the world that keeps us in the center of His purposes.

The anointing equips us to bring the world into an encounter with God. That encounter is what we owe them. For that reason, every caring evangelist should cry out for a greater anointing; every believer should cry for the same. When we are smeared with God, it rubs off on all we come into contact with—and it's that anointing that breaks the yokes of darkness (Isa. 10:27).

The most common understanding of our need for the anointing is in the preaching of the Word or praying for the sick. These are just two of the very common ways of bringing this encounter to people. While these are true, it's the person with the continual anointing that opens up many more opportunities for ministry.

The anointing equips us to bring the world into an encounter with God.

Ephesians 4:12—...to prepare God's people for works of service, so that the body of Christ may be built up.

BOOK QUOTE: *When Heaven Invades Earth* [Chapter 12]

WHEN we minister in the anointing, we actually give away the presence of God—we impart Him to others. Jesus went on to teach His disciples what it meant to *give it away*. It included the obvious things, such as: healing the sick, casting out demons, etc. But it also included one often forgotten aspect: "When you go into a house...let your peace come upon it." There is an actual impartation of His presence that we are able to make in these situations. This is how we bring the lost into an encounter with God. We learn to recognize His presence, cooperate with His passion for people, and invite them to receive *salvation*. (*Salvation* or *sozo* means "salvation, healing, and deliverance.")

He has made us stewards of the presence of God. It is not as though we can manipulate and use His presence for our own religious purposes. We are moved upon by the Holy Spirit, thereby becoming co-laborers with Christ. In that position we invite Him to invade the circumstances that arise before us.

Jesus said, "If I do not do the works of My Father, do not believe Me" (John 10:37). The works of the Father are miracles. Even the Son of God stated it was the miraculous that validated His ministry on earth. In that context He said, "...he who believes in Me...greater works than these he will do, because I go to My Father" (John 14:12). The miraculous is a large part of the plan of God for this world. And it is to come through the Church.

I look forward to the day when the Church stands up and says, "Don't believe us unless we are doing the works that Jesus did!" The Bible says that we are to pursue earnestly, (lustfully), spiritual gifts, and that those gifts make us *established*. Which ones? All of them (1 Cor. 14:1. and Rom. 1:11).

When we minister in the anointing, we actually give away the presence of God—we impart Him to others.

Genesis 28:16—When Jacob awoke from his sleep, he thought, "Surely the Lord is in this place, and I was not aware of it."

BOOK QUOTE: *When Heaven Invades Earth* [Chapter 12]

I owe the world a Spirit filled-life, for I owe them an encounter with God. Without the fullness of the Holy Spirit in and upon me, I do not give God a surrendered vessel to flow through.

The fullness of the Spirit was the goal of God throughout the law and prophets. Salvation was the immediate goal, but the ultimate goal on earth was the fullness of the Spirit in the believer. Getting us to heaven is not near as great a challenge as it is to get heaven into us. This is accomplished through the *fullness of the Spirit* in us.

Jacob, an Old Testament patriarch, was sleeping in the great outdoors when he had a dream that contained one of the more startling revelations ever received by man. He saw an open heaven with a ladder coming down to earth. On the ladder were angels ascending and descending. He was frightened and said, "*God is here and I didn't even know it.*" (See Genesis 28:16.) That statement describes much of what we've been witnessing in this revival for the past several years—God is present, yet many remain unaware of His presence.

I have witnessed God's touch upon thousands of people in this present outpouring—conversions, healings, restored marriages, addictions broken, and the demonized set free. The list of *how lives have been changed* is gloriously long, and increasing daily. Yet as these have been changed, there have always been those in the same meeting who can hardly wait for the service to end and get out the door. One person recognizes God's presence and is forever changed; the other never realized what could have been.

I owe the world a Spirit-filled life,
for I owe them an encounter with God.

Matthew 5:14—*You are the light of the world. A city on a hill cannot be hidden.*

BOOK QUOTE: *When Heaven Invades Earth* [Chapter 12]

FOR us to become all that God intended, we must remember that Jesus' life was a model of what mankind could become if it were in right relationship with the Father. Through the shedding of His blood, it would be possible for everyone who believed on His name to do as He did and become as He was. This meant then that every true believer would have access to the realm of life that Jesus lived in.

Jesus came as the light of the world. He then passed the baton to us announcing that we are the light of the world. Jesus came as the miracle worker. He said that we would do "greater works" than He did (John 14:12). He then pulled the greatest surprise of all, saying, "right now the Holy Spirit is with you, but He's going to be in you." (See John 14:17, my paraphrase.) Jesus, who illustrates to us what is possible for those who are *right with God*, now says that His people are to be the tabernacle of God on planet earth. Paul affirms this revelation with statements such as, "Do you not know that you are the temple of God?" (1 Cor. 3:16). "…and you are a dwelling place of God." (See Ephesians 2:22.)

What was the initial revelation of the house of God? It has the presence of God, a gate to heaven, and a ladder with angels ascending and descending upon it. Why is this important to understand? This revelation shows the resources that are at our disposal to carry out the Master's plan.

This principle of being the stewards of the heavenly realm then becomes more than the assignment of the individual, and becomes the privilege of an entire Church for the sake of their entire city.

Jesus came as the light of the world. He then passed the baton to us announcing that we are the light of the world.

Hebrews 1:7—*In speaking of the angels He says, "He makes His angels winds, His servants flames of fire."*

BOOK QUOTE: *When Heaven Invades Earth* [Chapter 12]

ANGELS are impressive beings. They are glorious and powerful. So much so that when they showed up in Scripture, people often fell to worship them. While it is foolish to worship them, it is equally foolish to ignore them. Angels are assigned to serve wherever we serve, *if the supernatural element is needed.* "Are not all angels ministering spirits sent to serve those who will inherit salvation?" (Heb. 1:14).

I believe angels have been bored because we live the kind of lifestyle that doesn't require much of their help. Their assignment is to assist us in supernatural endeavors. If we are not people of risk, then there is little room for the supernatural. Risks must be taken to pursue solutions to impossible situations. When the Church regains its appetite for the impossible, the angels will increase their activities among men.

As the fires of revival intensify, so do the supernatural activities around us. If angels are assigned to assist us in supernatural endeavors, then there must be need for the supernatural. Risk must be taken to pursue solutions to impossible situations. The gospel of power is the answer to the tragic condition of humankind. John Wimber said, "Faith is spelled R-I-S-K." If we really want more of God then we must change our lifestyle so that His manifested presence will increase upon us. This is not an act on our part to somehow manipulate God. Instead it is the bold attempt to take Him at His Word, so that as we radically obey His charge, He says "Amen" with the miraculous (Mark 16:20). I challenge you to pursue God passionately! And in your pursuit, insist on a supernatural lifestyle—one that keeps the hosts of Heaven busy, ushering in the King and His Kingdom!

As the fires of revival intensify, so do the supernatural activities around us.

Exodus 23:20—*See, I am sending an angel ahead of you to guard you along the way and to bring you to the place I have prepared.*

BOOK QUOTE: *When Heaven Invades Earth* [Chapter 12]

WHILE God has provided angels to assist us in our commission, I don't take the posture that we are to command angels. Some feel they have that liberty. However, I believe it is a dangerous proposition. There is reason to believe that they are to be commissioned by God Himself in response to our prayers.

Daniel needed an answer from God. He prayed for 21 days. An angel finally showed up with his answer. He said to Daniel, "Do not fear, Daniel, for from the first day that you set your heart to understand, and to humble yourself before your God, your words were heard; and I have come because of your words. But the prince of the kingdom of Persia withstood me 21 days; and behold, Michael, one of the chief princes, came to help me, for I had been left alone there with the kings of Persia" (Dan. 10:12-13). When Daniel prayed, God responded by sending an angel with the answer. The angel ran into interference. Daniel continued to pray, which appears to have helped to release the archangel Michael to fight and release the first angel to deliver the message.

There are many other times angels came in response to the prayers of the saints. Each time they were sent out for service by the Father. I think it's best to pray much and leave commanding angels to God.

I contain a gate to Heaven, with a ladder providing angelic activities according to the need of the moment. Simply put, *I am an open Heaven!* This does not apply to a select few. On the contrary, this revelation is about the house of God and the principles of the house apply to all believers. But few realize or implement this *potential* blessing.

Simply put, **I am an open Heaven!**

Psalm 34:7—*The angel of the Lord encamps around those who fear Him, and He delivers them.*

BOOK QUOTE: *When Heaven Invades Earth* [Chapter 12]

WITH an open Heaven I become a vehicle in the hand of God to release the resources of Heaven into the calamities of mankind. Angels are commissioned to carry out the will of God. "Bless the Lord, you His angels, who excel in strength, who do His word, heeding the voice of His word" (Ps. 103:20). He is more eager to invade this world than we are to receive the invasion. And angels play an integral part.

They respond to His command and enforce His Word. But the *voice of His Word* is heard when the Father speaks to the hearts of His people. Angels await the people of God speaking His Word. I believe angels pick up the fragrance of the throne room through the word spoken by people. They can tell when a word has its origins in the heart of the Father. And, in turn, they recognize that word as their assignment.

I recently saw this happen at a meeting in Germany. Before the meeting, I was praying with some of the leaders that had sponsored the meetings. As we were praying, I saw a woman sitting to my right with an arthritic spine. It was a brief picture of the mind, which is the visual equivalent of the *still small voice*—as easy to miss as it is to get. In this picture, I had her stand and declared over her, "The Lord Jesus heals you!"

When it came time for the meeting, I asked if there was anyone there with arthritis in the spine. A woman to my right waved her hand. I had her stand and declared over her, "The Lord Jesus heals you!" I then asked her where she had pain.

She wept saying, "It is impossible, but it is gone!" Angels enforced a word that originated in the heart of the Father. But for that moment, I was the *voice of His Word*.

Angels await the people of God speaking His Word.

John 10:25—*Jesus answered, "I did tell you, but you do not believe. The miracles I do in my Father's name speak for Me...."*

BOOK QUOTE: *When Heaven Invades Earth* [Chapter 12]

His world has been breaking into ours with regularity in salvations, healings, and deliverances. The manifestations of that invasion vary. They are quite fascinating, and too numerous to catalog. While some are difficult to understand at first glance, we know that God always works redemptively.

On many occasions laughter has filled a room, bringing healing to broken hearts. Gold dust sometimes covers people's faces, hands, or clothing. Oil sometimes appears on the hands of His people; and it especially happens among children. A wind has come into a room with no open windows, doors, vents, etc. Believers have seen an actual cloud of His presence appearing over the heads of worshiping people. We've also had the fragrance of heaven fill a room.

These phenomena seem to offend many that fully embrace this move of God. Jerrel Miller, editor of *The Remnant*, a newspaper whose purpose is to record the events surrounding this revival, took a lot of heat when he reported the unusual manifestation we experienced of feathers falling in our meetings. Like the generations before us, those who criticized his report are dangerously close to regulating God's work by a *list of acceptable manifestations*. No longer is it just tears during a special song or a time of repentance following a moving sermon. Our list may include falling, shaking, laughter, etc. The problem is—it is still a list. And God will violate it. We must learn to recognize His move by recognizing His presence. Our lists are only good for revealing our present understanding or experience. While I don't seek to promote strange manifestations, or go after *novelty*, I refuse to be embarrassed over what God is doing. The list that keeps us from certain types of errors also keeps us from certain types of victories.

I refuse to be embarrassed over what God is doing.

Psalm 63:2—*I have seen You in the sanctuary and beheld Your power and Your glory.*

BOOK QUOTE: *When Heaven Invades Earth* [Chapter 12]

SIGNS are realities that point to a greater reality. If He is giving us signs, who are we to say they are unimportant? Many react to this because they fear *sign worship*. While their reasoning may be noble in intent, it is foolish to think I can carry out my assignment from God and ignore God's *personal notes* along the way. In the natural, we use signs to help us find a city, a particular restaurant, or a place of business. In the same way, signs and wonders are a natural part of the Kingdom of God. They are the normal way to get us from where we are to where we need to be. That is their purpose. Had the wise men not followed the star they would have had to be content reading about the experiences of others. I am not. There's a difference between *worshiping signs* and *following signs*. The first is forbidden; the latter is essential. When we follow His signs to the greater depths in God, His signs follow us in greater measure for the sake of mankind.

Power has little pleasure if there is no intimate relationship with God. But that comment is often religious in nature. Someone who has a passion for the power and glory of God intimidates those who don't. My hunger for His power is only surpassed by my desire for Him. It's been my pursuit of Him that has led me to this passion for an authentic gospel.

Something happened in me that won't let me accept a gospel that isn't backed with signs and wonders. Is it because I have caught a revelation of miracles on the earth? No! It caught me. I have discovered there isn't any lasting satisfaction in life apart from expressions of faith.

Power has little pleasure if there is no intimate relationship with God.

2 Corinthians 4:6—*For God, who said, "Let light shine out of darkness," made His light shine in our hearts to give us the light of the knowledge of the glory of God in the face of Christ.*

BOOK QUOTE: *When Heaven Invades Earth* [Chapter 13]

JESUS was the suffering servant, headed for the cross. But Jesus is triumphantly resurrected, ascended, and glorified. In the Revelation of Jesus Christ, John described Him in this way: "His head and hair were white like wool, as white as snow, and His eyes like a flame of fire; His feet were like fine brass, as if refined in a furnace, and His voice as the sound of many waters" (Rev. 1:14-15).

The "as He is, so are we" declaration is far beyond what any of us could have imagined; especially in light of the glorified description of Jesus in Revelation 1. Yet, the Holy Spirit was sent specifically for this purpose that we might attain…"to the measure of the stature of the fullness of Christ" (Eph. 4:13).

The Holy Spirit came with the ultimate assignment at the perfect time. During Jesus' ministry, it was said, "The Holy Spirit was not yet given, because Jesus was not yet glorified (John 7:39). The Holy Spirit comforts us, gives us gifts, reminds us of what Jesus has said, and clothes us with power. But He does all this to *make us like Jesus.* That is His primary mission. So why didn't the Father send Him until Jesus was glorified? Because without Jesus in His glorified state there was no *heavenly model of what we were to become!* As a sculptor looks at a model and fashions the clay into its likeness, so the Holy Spirit looks to the glorified Son and shapes us into His image. *As He is, so are we in this world.*

> *The Holy Spirit . . .*
> *does all this to make us like Jesus.*

Ephesians 1:22-23—And appointed Him to be head over everything for the Church, which is His body, the fullness of Him who fills everything in every way.

BOOK QUOTE: *When Heaven Invades Earth* [Chapter 13]

THE Christian life is not found *on* the Cross. It is found *because* of the Cross. It is His resurrection power that energizes the believer. The shed blood of the spotless Lamb wiped out the power and presence of sin in our lives. *We have nothing without the Cross!* Yet, the Cross is not the end—it is the beginning, the entrance to the Christian Life. Even for Jesus the cross was something to be endured in order to obtain the joy on the other side! (See Heb. 12:2.)

Suppose I had been forgiven a financial debt. It could be said I have been brought *out of the red*. Yet, after my debts are forgiven, I still am *not in the black*. I have nothing unless the one who forgave my debt gives me money to call my own, and that's what Christ did. His blood wiped out my debt of sin. But it was His resurrection that brought me *into the black*. (See John 10:10.)

Why is this important? *Because it profoundly changes our sense of identity and purpose.*

Jesus became poor so that I could become rich. He suffered with stripes to free me from affliction, and He became sin so I might become the righteousness of God. (See 2 Cor. 5:21.) Why then should I try to become *as He was*, when He suffered so I could become *as He is*? At some point, the reality of the resurrection must come into play in our lives—we must discover the power of the resurrection for all who believe. (See Eph.1:21 and 3:20.)

*The Christian life is not found on the Cross.
It is found because of the Cross.*

Matthew 16:24—*Then Jesus said to his disciples, "If anyone desires to come after Me, he must deny himself, and take up his cross, and follow Me."*

BOOK QUOTE: *When Heaven Invades Earth* [Chapter 13]

A misunderstanding of this call has led many to follow His life of self-denial, but to stop short of His life of power. For them the cross-walk involves trying to crucify their sin nature by embracing joyless brokenness as an evidence of the Cross. But, we must *follow Him all the way*—to a lifestyle empowered by the resurrection!

Most every religion has a copy of the *cross-walk*. Self-denial, self-abasement, and the like are all easily copied by the sects of this world. People admire those who have religious disciplines. But show them a life filled with joy because of the transforming power of God, and they will not only applaud but will want to be like you. Religion is unable to mimic the life of resurrection with its victory over sin and hell.

One who embraces an inferior cross is constantly filled with introspection and self-induced suffering. But the Cross is not self-applied—Jesus did not nail Himself to the cross. Christians who are trapped by this counterfeit are constantly talking about their weaknesses.

I often became preoccupied with my faults and weakness was humility. It's not! If I'm the main subject, talking incessantly about my weaknesses, I have entered into the most subtle form of pride. Repeated phrases such as, "I'm so unworthy," become a nauseating replacement for the declarations of the worthiness of God. By being *sold* on my own unrighteousness, the enemy has disengaged me from effective service. It's a perversion of true holiness when introspection causes my spiritual self-esteem to increase, but my effectiveness in demonstrating the power of the gospel to decrease.

True brokenness causes complete dependency on God, moving us to radical obedience that releases the power of the gospel to the world around us.

*...we must **follow Him all the way**—to a lifestyle empowered by the resurrection!*

1 Chronicles 28:9—*And you, my son Solomon, acknowledge the God of your father, and serve Him with wholehearted devotion and with a willing mind, for the Lord searches every heart and understands every motive behind the thoughts. If you seek Him, He will be found by you; but if you forsake Him, He will reject you forever.*

BOOK QUOTE: *When Heaven Invades Earth* [Chapter 13]

I struggled for many years with self-evaluation. The main problem was that I never found anything good in me. It always led to discouragement, which led to doubt, and eventually took me to unbelief. Somehow I had developed the notion that this was how I could become holy—by showing tremendous concern for my own motives.

Today, I don't examine my motives anymore. That's not my job. I work hard to obey God in everything that I am and do. If I am *out to lunch* on a matter, it is His job to point that out to me. After many years of trying to do what only He could do, I discovered I was not the Holy Spirit. I cannot convict and deliver myself of sin. Does that mean that I never deal with impure motives? No. He has shown Himself to be very eager to point out my constant need for repentance and change. But He's the one with the spotlight, and He alone can give the grace to change.

There is a major difference between the believer who is being dealt with by God, and the one who has become introspective. When God searches the heart, He finds things in us that He wants to change. He brings conviction because of His commitment to deliver us. Such a revelation brought me to pray in the following manner:

Father, you know that I don't do so well when I look inward, so I'm going to stop. I am relying on You to point out to me the things that I need to see. I promise to stay in Your Word. By Your grace I am a new creation. I want that reality to be seen that the name of Jesus would be held in highest honor.

... He's the one with the spotlight, and He alone can give the grace to change.

Romans 6:14—*For sin shall not be your master because you are not under the law, but under grace.*

BOOK QUOTE: *When Heaven Invades Earth* [Chapter 13]

I believe that for the most part this counterfeit cross-walk is embraced because it requires no faith. It's easy to see my weakness, my propensity toward sin, and my inability to be like Jesus. Confessing this truth requires no faith at all. On the contrary, to do as Paul commanded in Romans 6:13, to consider myself dead to sin, I must believe God.

Therefore, in your weakest state declare, *"I am strong!"* Agree with God regardless of how you feel and discover the power of resurrection. Without faith it is impossible to please Him. The first place that faith must be exercised is in our own standing with God.

Jesus paid the ultimate price to make it possible for us to have a change in our identity. Isn't it time we believe it and receive the benefits? If we don't, we'll break down in our confidence as we stand before the world in these final days. The boldness we need is not self-confidence, but the confidence that the Father has in the work of His Son in us. It's no longer a question of Heaven or hell. It's only a question of how much of hell's thinking I will allow into this heavenly mind of mine.

Doesn't it honor Him more when His children no longer see themselves only as *sinners saved by grace*, but now as *heirs of God*? Isn't it a greater form of humility to believe Him when He says we are precious in His sight when we don't feel very precious? We must rise up to the high call of God and stop saying things about ourselves that are no longer true. Maturity comes from faith in the sufficiency of God's redemptive work that establishes us as sons and daughters of the Most High.

Jesus paid the ultimate price to make it possible for us to have a change in our identity.

2 Corinthians 10:3—*For though we live in the world, we do not wage war as the world does.*

BOOK QUOTE: *When Heaven Invades Earth* [Chapter 13]

*A*s *He is, so are we in this world.* The revelation of Jesus in His glorified state has at least four overwhelming characteristics that directly affect the coming transformation of the Church; these must be embraced as a part of God's plan in these final hours. Here is the first one:

1. Glory—This is the manifested presence of Jesus. Revival history is filled with stories of His manifest presence resting upon His people. He lives in all believers, but the glory of His presence comes to rest on only a few. It is sometimes seen and frequently felt. He is returning for a glorious Church. It is not an option.

Tongues of fire were seen on the heads of the apostles on the day of Pentecost. In more modern times, fire has been seen blazing from the top of church buildings when the people of God are gathered together in His name. At the Azuza Street revival, the fire department was called to extinguish a blaze, only to discover that the people inside were worshiping Jesus. Water couldn't put it out as it was not a natural fire. All the powers of hell cannot put it out. The only ones capable of such a thing are those to whom that fire has been entrusted. Well meaning believers will often use control as a means to bring this fire into order, thinking they are serving God. On the other hand, some will turn to hype to fan an emotional flame when the fire is no longer there. Both are expressions of the carnal man—and when the carnal man is in charge, the glory of God must lift.

If the Father filled the Old Testament houses with His glory, though they were built by human hands, how much more will He fill the place that He builds with His own hands! He is building us into His eternal dwelling place.

Well meaning believers will often use control as a means to bring this fire into order, thinking they are serving God.

Hebrews 10:10—*And by that will, we have been made holy, through the sacrifice of the body of Jesus Christ once for all.*

BOOK QUOTE: *When Heaven Invades Earth* [Chapter 13]

THE revelation of Jesus in His glorified state has four characteristics that directly affect the coming transformation of the Church. Here are the next three:

2. Power—To be *as He is* involves being a continuous expression of power. The baptism in the Holy Spirit clothes us with this heavenly element. As clothing is on the outside of the body, so that power is to be the most visible part of the believing Church.

The power vacuum in the Church allows cults and false prophetic gifts to flourish. But there will be no contest when such counterfeits go up against this Elijah generation that becomes clothed with Heaven's power on the Mount Carmel of human reasoning.

3. Triumph—Jesus conquered all things: the power of hell, the grave, sin, and the devil. The attitude of those who live *from* the triumph of Christ is different than those who live under the influence of their past. The only part of the past that we have legal access to is the *testimony of the Lord*.[11] The rest is dead, buried, forgotten, and covered under the blood. Living from the victory of Christ is the privilege for every believer. This realization is at the foundation of a Church that will triumph even as He has triumphed.

4. Holiness—Jesus is perfectly holy—separate *from* all that is evil, *unto* all that is good. Holiness in the Church reveals the beauty of God. Our understanding of holiness has often been centered around our behavior—what we can and cannot do. Soon this will become the greatest revelation of God the world has ever seen. Whereas power demonstrates the heart of God, holiness reveals the beauty of His nature. This is the hour of the great unveiling of the beauty of holiness.

Holiness in the Church reveals the beauty of God.

Hebrews 12:1—*Therefore, since we are surrounded by such a great cloud of witnesses, let us throw off everything that hinders and the sin that so easily entangles, and let us run with perseverance the race marked out for us.*

BOOK QUOTE: *When Heaven Invades Earth* [Chapter 14]

For too long the Church has played defense in the battle for souls. We hear of what some cult or political party is planning to do, and we react by creating strategies to counter the enemies' plans. Committees are formed, boards discuss, and pastors preach against whatever it is the devil is doing or about to do. I don't care what the devil plans to do. The Great Commission puts me on the offensive.

Picture a football team in a huddle on the playing field. The coach sends in the play, and the quarterback communicates with his offensive teammates. On the sidelines is the opposing team's offense. Their quarterback lines up out-of-bounds with his offensive team, but they don't have the game ball, nor are they on the actual playing field. Now imagine the real offense getting distracted by the intimidating actions of the other offense. Caught up in their antics, the quarterback runs off the field in a panic, informing the coach that they better put the defense on the field because the other team is about to use a surprise play.

This is the condition of much of the Church in this hour. Satan reveals his plans to put us on the defensive. The devil roars, and we act as if we got bit. Let's stop this foolishness and quit praising the devil with endless discussions of *what's wrong in the world because of him*. We have the ball. The alumni from the ages past watch with excitement as the *two-minute offense* has been put on the field. The superior potential of this generation has nothing to do with our goodness, but it does have everything to do with the Master's plan of placing us at this point in history. We are to be the devil's worst nightmare.

*The alumni from the ages past watch with excitement as the **two-minute offense** has been put on the field.*

2 Chronicles 20:15—*He said: "Listen, King Jehoshaphat and all who live in Judah and Jerusalem! This is what the Lord says to you: 'Do not be afraid or discouraged because of this vast army. For the battle is not yours, but God's.'"*

BOOK QUOTE: *When Heaven Invades Earth* [Chapter 14]

SPIRITUAL warfare is unavoidable, and ignoring this subject won't make it go away. Therefore, we must learn to battle with supernatural authority! The following principles are often overlooked insights:

1. "Then it came to pass, when Pharaoh had let the people go, that God did not lead them by way of the land of the Philistines, although that was near; for God said, "Lest perhaps the people change their minds when they see war, and return to Egypt" (Exod. 13:17).

God is mindful of what we can handle in our present state. He leads us only into a battle we are prepared to win.

The safest place in this war is obedience. In the center of His will, we face only the situations we are equipped to win. Outside of the center is where many Christians fall, facing undue pressures that are self-inflicted.

2. "You prepare a table before me in the presence of my enemies" (Ps. 23:5).

God is in no way intimidated by the devil's antics. In fact, God wants fellowship with us right before the devil's eyes. Intimacy with God is our strong suit. Never allow anything to distract you from this point of strength. Choosing a *warfare intense* mentality causes us to depart from joy and intimacy with God.

3. "…in no way alarmed by your opponents—which is a sign of destruction for them, but of salvation for you, and that too, from God" (Phil. 1:28 NASB).

When we refuse fear, the enemy becomes terrified. A confident heart is a sure sign of his ultimate destruction and our present victory! Do not fear—ever. Return to the promises of God, spend time with people of faith, and encourage one another with the testimonies of the Lord. Praise God for who He is until fear no longer knocks at the door.

He leads us only into a battle we are prepared to win.

Psalm 149:9—*to carry out the sentence written against them, This is the glory of all His saints. Praise the Lord.*

BOOK QUOTE: *When Heaven Invades Earth* [Chapter 14]

THE following principles are often overlooked insights in the area of spiritual warfare:

4. "Therefore submit to God. Resist the devil and he will flee from you" (James 4:7).

Submission is the key to personal triumph. Our main battle in spiritual warfare is not against the devil. It is against the flesh. Coming into subjection puts the resources of heaven at our disposal for enduring victory.

5. "... and the *gates of hell* shall not prevail against it" [the Church] (Matt. 16:18 KJV).

The Church is on the attack. That's why it's the gates of hell, the place of demonic government and strength, will not prevail against the Church.

6. "He increased His people greatly, and made them stronger than their enemies. He turned their heart to hate His people, to deal craftily with His servants" (Ps. 105:24-25).

God makes us strong, and then He stirs up the devil's hatred towards us. Why? It's because He likes to see the devil defeated by those who are made in His image.

7. "...let the inhabitants of Sela sing aloud. He will arouse His zeal like a man of war. He will shout, yes, He will raise a war cry. He will prevail against His enemies" (Isa. 42:11,13 NASB).

Praise honors God. But it also edifies us and destroys the powers of hell!

It's amazing to think that I can praise Him and have Him say that I am a mighty man of valor. He destroyed the powers of hell on my behalf and gave me the 'points' for the victory.

We were born in a war. There are no time outs, no vacations, no leaves of absence. The safest place is in the center of God's will, which is the place of deep intimacy. There He allows only the battles to come our way that we are equipped to win.

We were born in a war. There are no time outs, no vacations, no leaves of absence.

John 4:48—*"Unless you people see miraculous signs and wonders," Jesus told him, "You will never believe."*

BOOK QUOTE: *When Heaven Invades Earth* [Chapter 15]

REVIVAL is central to the message of the Kingdom, for it is in revival that we more clearly see what His dominion looks like and how it is to affect society. Revival at its best is, "Thy Kingdom come" (Matt. 6:10).

In a way, revival illustrates the normal Christian life.

Before the Messiah came, the religious leaders prayed for and taught about His coming. There was a worldwide stirring, even in a secular society, about something wonderful that was about to happen. And then in a manger in Bethlehem, Jesus was born.

The stargazers knew who He was and traveled a great distance to worship and give Him gifts. The devil also knew, and moved Herod to kill the first-born males in an attempt to stop Jesus' plan to redeem mankind. After he failed, he tried to lure Jesus to sin with temptation in the wilderness. What is even more startling is that this visitation of God did not escape the notice of the demon-possessed. *Such was the man at the Gadarenes* (Matt. 8:28-34). When he saw Jesus, he fell down before Him in worship and was soon set free from his life of torment. Yet the religious leaders that prayed for His coming didn't recognize Him when He came.

Paul and Silas preached the gospel throughout Asia Minor. The religious leaders said they were of the devil. But a demon-possessed fortune-teller girl said they were of God. How is it that those who are thought to be spiritually blind are able to see, and those who were known for their insight didn't recognize what God was doing?

History is filled with people who prayed for a visitation of God and missed it when it came. And this happened even though some had a strong relationship with God.

History is filled with people who prayed for a visitation of God and missed it when it came.

2 Corinthians 3:14—*But their minds were made dull, for to this day the same veil remains when the old covenant is read. It has not been removed, because only in Christ is it taken away.*

BOOK QUOTE: *When Heaven Invades Earth* [Chapter 15]

MANY believers have a blindness that the world doesn't have. The world knows its need. But for many Christians, once they are born again they gradually stop recognizing their need. There is something about desperation for God that enables a person to recognize whether or not something is from God. Jesus spoke of this phenomenon saying, "For judgment I have come into this world, that those who do not see may see, and that those who see may be made blind" (John 9:39).

The testimony of history and the record of Scripture warn us of the possibility of this error. "Therefore let him who thinks he stands take heed lest he fall." (See Matt. 13:15.)

Matthew says it's the *dull of heart* who can't see (1 Cor. 10:12). A dull knife is one that has been used. The implication is that the dull of heart had a history in God, but did not keep current in what God was doing. We maintain our *sharp edge* as we recognize our need and passionately pursue Jesus. This *first love* somehow keeps us safely in the center of God's activities on earth.

The church of Ephesus received a letter from God. In it Jesus addressed the fact that they had left their first love. First love is passionate by nature and dominates all other issues in one's life. If they didn't correct this problem, God said He would remove their "lampstand." While theologians don't all agree on what that lampstand is, one thing is for certain: a lamp enables us to see. Without it the church in Ephesus would lose their perceptive abilities. The above mentioned blindness or dullness doesn't lead us to the fullness of what God has intended for us while here on earth. When passion dies, the lamp of perception is eventually removed.

*We maintain our **sharp edge** as we recognize our need and passionately pursue Jesus.*

Matthew 5:3—*Blessed are the poor in spirit, for theirs is the kingdom of Heaven.*

BOOK QUOTE: *When Heaven Invades Earth* [Chapter 15]

THOSE who reject a move of God are generally those who were the last to experience one. This is not true of everyone, as there are always those whose hunger for God only increases throughout their years. But many form the attitude that *they have arrived*, not to perfection, but to where God intended. They paid a price to experience *the* move of God.

They wonder, "Why would God do something new, without showing it to us first?" God is a God of new things. Hungering for Him requires us to embrace the change brought on by His *new things*. Passion for God keeps us fresh and equips us to recognize the hand of God, even when others reject it. The fear of deception gets swallowed up by confidence that God is able to keep us from falling. (See Jude 24.)

In His wisdom, God created things in such a way that when He is on the move the world often takes notice first. I look for the response of the demonized. It's the drug addict, the ex-con, and the prostitute that I want to hear from. When God moves in revival power, these people look on, not as critics, but as people in great need of God. And we are hearing from them in great numbers. They are being transformed, saying, "Only God could make this change in my life. This is God!"

Being in a place of great need enables a person to detect when God is doing something new. That *place of great need* doesn't have to be drug addiction or prostitution. Every Christian is supposed to maintain a desperate heart for God. Remaining poor in spirit, combined with a *first love passion for Jesus* are the keys God created to anchor us to the center of His work.

. . . God created things in such a way that when He is on the move the world often takes notice first.

Isaiah 51:7— *Hear me, you who know what is right, you people who have my law in your hearts. Do not fear the reproach of men or be terrified by their insults.*

BOOK QUOTE: *When Heaven Invades Earth* [Chapter 15]

MARY received the most shocking announcement ever given to a person. She was to give birth to the Christ child. She was chosen by God, being called "highly favored of the Lord."

This favor started with a visitation from an angel. That experience was quite frightening! Then she was given news that was incomprehensible and impossible to explain. The initial shock was followed by the duty of having to tell Joseph, her husband to be. His response was to "put her away secretly." (See Matt. 1:19.) In other words he didn't believe it was God, and didn't want to go through with their wedding plans. After all, where is the chapter and verse for this manifestation of how God works with his people? It's never happened before. There was no biblical precedent of a virgin giving birth to a child.

On top of this obvious conflict with Joseph, Mary would have to bear the stigma of being the mother of an illegitimate child all the days of her life. Favor from Heaven's perspective is not always so pleasant from ours.

Like Mary, those who experience revival have spiritual encounters that are beyond reason. We seldom have immediate understanding of what God is doing and why. Sometimes our dearest friends want to *put us away*, declaring the move to be from the devil. And then we can be looked at as a *fringe element* by the rest of the Body of Christ. The willingness to bear reproach from our brothers and sisters is part of the cost we pay for the move of the Spirit.

"Therefore Jesus…suffered outside the gate. Therefore let us go forth to Him, outside the camp, bearing His reproach" (Heb. 13:12-13). Revival usually takes us outside the camp—the religious community. That is often where He is—*outside the camp!*

The willingness to bear reproach from our brothers and sisters is part of the cost we pay for the move of the Spirit.

Matthew 6:10—*Your kingdom come, Your will be done on earth as it is in Heaven.*

BOOK QUOTE: *When Heaven Invades Earth* [Chapter 15]

QUENCHING the Spirit is probably responsible for the end of more revivals than any other single cause. Even those who have embraced the move of God often come to a place where their comfort zone is stretched about as far as they are willing to go. They then begin to look for a place to settle—a place of understanding and control.

The second greatest reason for a revival's end is when the Church begins to look for the return of the Lord instead of pursuing a greater breakthrough in the Great Commission. *That kind* of hunger for Heaven is not encouraged in Scripture. It turns the blessed hope into the blessed escape. To want Jesus to come back now is to sentence billions of people to hell forever. It's not that we shouldn't long for Heaven. Paul said that longing was to be a comfort for the Christian. But to seek for the end of all things is to pronounce judgment on all of mankind outside of Christ. Is Jesus, the One who paid for all sin, eager to return without that final great harvest? I think not.

There's a difference between crying for *Heaven now* and *Heaven here!* If a revival has brought us to the *end* of our dreams, does that mean we have reached the end of His? A revival must go beyond all we could imagine. Anything less falls short.

Many revivalists had such significant breakthroughs that they viewed the Lord's return to be at hand. They failed to equip the Church to do what they were gifted to do. As a result, they touched multitudes instead of nations and generations.

We must plan as though we have a lifetime to live, but work and pray as though we have very little time left.

We must plan as though we have a lifetime to live, but work and pray as though we have very little time left.

Acts 2:17—In the last days, God says, "I will pour out my Spirit on all people."

BOOK QUOTE: *When Heaven Invades Earth* [Chapter 15]

THE disciples, who were accustomed to Jesus surprising them at every turn in the road, found themselves in yet another unusual situation: waiting for the promise of the Father—whatever that was.

Ten days had passed, Pentecost had come, and they were still praying as they did the other nine days. "And suddenly..." (Acts 2:2). A room with 120 people was now filled with the sound of wind, fire, and ecstatic expressions of praise uttered through known and unknown languages (Acts 2:4-11).

No matter how people interpret Paul's instruction on the use of spiritual gifts, one thing must be agreed upon: this meeting was entirely directed by the Holy Spirit. This infant Church hadn't learned enough to try and control God. They had no biblical or experiential grid for what was happening. Notice the elements of this Spirit directed service:

1. They were praying.
2. They were in unity.
3. They all spoke in tongues.
4. Unbelievers heard those tongues.
5. People were saved.

Is it possible that Paul's instructions on the proper use of the gifts have been used to define Acts 2 instead of Acts 2 illustrating the proper interpretation of Paul's instruction in First Corinthians 12 and 14?

Consider the Acts 2 company's predicament: they just had an encounter with God without a chapter and verse to explain what just happened. Peter, under the direction of the Holy Spirit, chose to use Joel 2 as the proof-text to give the needed backbone to their experience. Joel 2 declares there would be an outpouring of the Holy Spirit involving prophecy, dreams, and visions. The outpouring happened as promised in Acts 2, but it had none of the things mentioned by Joel. Instead it had the sound of wind, fire, and tongues. It was God who used this passage to support this new experience.

The Word does not contain God—it reveals Him. Joel 2 revealed the nature of God's work among man. Acts 2 was an illustration of what God intended by that prophecy.

The Word does not contain God—it reveals Him.

Matthew 18:3—*And He said: "I tell you the truth, unless you change and become like little children, you will never enter the kingdom of Heaven."*

BOOK QUOTE: *When Heaven Invades Earth* [Chapter 15]

THE Church has an unhealthy addiction to perfection: the kind that makes no allowances for messes. This standard can only be met by restricting or rejecting the use of the gifts of the Spirit. Messes are necessary for increase.

How important is increase to God? Jesus once cursed a fig tree for not bearing fruit out of season! (See Mark 11:13-14.) A man in one of his parables was cast into outer darkness for burying his money and not obtaining an increase for his master. (See Matt. 25:24-30.)

There is a big difference between graveyards and nurseries. One has perfect order; the other has life. The childless person may walk into the church nursery with all the joyous activities of the children and mistakenly call the place out of order. Compared to their living room, it is. But when a parent walks in and sees her little one playing with other youngsters, she thinks it is perfect! It's all a matter of perspective. Order is for the purpose of promoting life. Beyond that it works against the things we say we value.

We miss God when we live as though we have Him figured out. We have the habit of making Him look like us. In fact, if we think we understand Him we have probably conformed Him into our image. There must remain mystery in our relationship with this One who has purposed to work beyond our capacity to imagine. (See Eph. 3:20.)

To endeavor to know Him is to embark on an adventure in which questions increase.

Our God-born desire for revival must keep us desperate enough to recognize Him when He comes. Without such desperation, we get satisfied with our present status and become our own worst enemies at changing history.

History cannot be changed effectively until we are willing to get our hands *dirty*.

There is a big difference between graveyards and nurseries.

Luke 13:20-21—To what shall I liken the kingdom of God? It is like leaven, which a woman took and hid in three measures of meal till it was all leavened.

BOOK QUOTE: *When Heaven Invades Earth* [Chapter 16]

I once taught on this passage in a small pastor's conference in a European country. My subject was: *The Infiltrating Power of the Kingdom of God.* I spoke about some of the practical strategies we had taken as a church to infiltrate the social system in our area for the cause of Christ.

We had a young man in our church who committed a crime before his conversion. Both the judge and the prosecuting attorney admitted this young man's life had been transformed by God. They wanted some measure of justice so they sentenced him to six months in a short-term prison. We laid our hands on him, sending him out as a missionary to a mission field that none of us could get into. As a result of this infiltration, over 60 of the approximate 110 prisoners confessed Christ within a year.

Following my message, several leaders discussed the concepts I had presented. They informed me that I was in error. "Leaven always refers to sin" they said, "and this parable shows how the Church will be filled with sin and compromise in the last days." They saw it as a warning, not a promise.

The mistake my brothers made is twofold:

1. They mistook the Church for the Kingdom. The Church is to live in the realm of the *King's domain*, but it in itself is not the Kingdom. While sin does infect the Church, the Kingdom is the realm of God's rule. Sin cannot penetrate and influence that realm.

2. Their predisposition to see a weak, struggling Church in the last days has made it difficult to see the promise of God for revival. It is impossible to have faith where you have no hope. Such approaches to understanding Scripture have crippled the Church.

*The Church is to live in the realm of the **King's domain**, but it in itself is not the Kingdom.*

1 John 2:13—*I write to you, fathers, because you have known him who is from the beginning. I write to you, young men, because you have overcome the evil one. I write to you, dear children, because you have known the Father.*

BOOK QUOTE: *When Heaven Invades Earth* [Chapter 16]

WITHOUT a revelation of what God intends to do with His Church, we cannot move in overcoming faith. When the main goal of our faith is keeping us safe from the devil, our faith becomes inferior to what God expects. Jesus had in mind more for us than survival. We are destined to overcome.

Every conversion plunders hell. Every miracle destroys the works of the devil. Every God encounter is an *invasion of the Almighty* into our desperate condition. This is our joy.

The original flame of Pentecost, the Holy Spirit Himself, burns within my soul. I have a promise from God. I am a part of a company of people destined to do greater works than Jesus did in His earthly ministry. Why is it so hard to see the Church with significant influence in the last days? It was God who determined that the bride should be spotless and without wrinkle. It was God who declared, "Behold darkness will cover the earth, but His glory will appear upon you" (Isa. 60:2 NASB). It was God who calls us, His Church, overcomers. (See Rev. 12:11.)

The parable about leaven illustrates the subtle but overwhelming influence of the Kingdom in any setting into which it is placed. In these days, God has planned to put us into the darkest of situations to demonstrate His dominion.

A jeweler often places a diamond on a piece of black velvet. The brilliance of the gem is clearer against that background. So it is with the Church. The dark condition of world's circumstances becomes the backdrop upon which He displays His glorious Church! "Where sin abounded, grace abounded much more" (Rom. 5:20).

Without a revelation of what God intends to do with His Church, we cannot move in overcoming faith.

Daniel 1:20—*In every matter of wisdom and understanding about which the king questioned them, he found them ten times better than all the magicians and enchanters in his whole kingdom.*

BOOK QUOTE: *When Heaven Invades Earth* [Chapter 16]

DANIEL started as a trainee in Nebuchadnezzar's court, but later was promoted to an advisor of foreign kings. He grew above all others in wisdom, becoming a counselor to the king. Because of his excellence in service and power, the king considered him 10 times better than all the others. (See Dan. 1:20.)

To more accurately understand, remember that Daniel is now a part of one of the most demonically inspired kingdoms to ever rule the earth. He is deeply embedded into that system. He is numbered with the magicians, astrologers, and sorcerers. While God considered him to be His man, he was just another spiritualist to the king…at least for a season. What a strange group of people to be associated with, especially when you consider that we're talking about Daniel, a prophet without blemish. His unwillingness to be defiled is legendary, raising the high water mark for generations of prophets to follow.

Babylon was a sophisticated society, with enough distractions to keep any Hebrew in the constant tension between devotion to God and an unhealthy love for this world. When you add strong idolatrous worship and the demonic presence it brings, you have a deadly combination that would undermine the faith of any casual Christian. Daniel, on the other hand, was absolute in His devotion to God, and uncompromising in his purpose. He sought for excellence in his position as *leaven*. If you want to find someone with a reason for bitterness, you've just found him—taken away from his family, made into a eunuch, and forced to serve among the cultists. Greatness in God is often on the other side of injustice and offense. Daniel made it over this hurdle, but not because he was great. He was victorious because of His devotion to the One who is great!

Greatness in God is often on the other side of injustice and offense.

Matthew 20:26—*Not so with you. Instead, whoever wants to become great among you must be your servant.*

BOOK QUOTE: *When Heaven Invades Earth* [Chapter 16]

DANIEL discovered early on, the power of holiness. He was unwilling to eat the king's delicacies. Separation to God is demonstrated in personal lifestyle, not associations. He could not control his surroundings. But it's a Spirit-empowered life that has the affect of leaven in a dark world.

The ultimate challenge came to all the king's wise men when he asked them not only to interpret a dream he just had, but also tell him what the dream was! When they couldn't, he ordered all the wise men killed. In the process, they sought to kill Daniel and his friends. Daniel asked for an audience with the king. He believed God would enable him to bring the Word of the Lord. Before he told the king the dream and it's interpretation, he taught him a virtue of the kingdom of God called humility. Daniel stated, "This secret has not been revealed to me because I have more wisdom than anyone living, but for our sakes who make known the interpretation to the king, and that you may know the thoughts of your heart" (Dan. 2:30).

In other words, it's not because I am great or gifted; it's because God wants us to live, and He wants you to have this message. He then interprets the dream as a servant.

So much of today's Kingdom theology is focused on us ruling, in the sense of believers becoming the heads of corporations and governments. And, in measure, it is true. But our strong suit has been, and always will be, service. If in serving we get promoted to positions of rulership, we must remember that *what got us there, will keep us useful.* In the kingdom, the greatest is the servant of all. Use every position to serve with more power.

. . . it's a Spirit-empowered life that has the affect of leaven in a dark world.

Matthew 5:11-12—*Blessed are you when people insult you, persecute you and falsely say all kinds of evil against you because of me. Rejoice and be glad, because great is your reward in Heaven, for in the same way they persecuted the prophets who were before you.*

BOOK QUOTE: *When Heaven Invades Earth* [Chapter 16]

THERE is no mention of Daniel operating in the gift of interpreting dreams before the king's crisis. Something similar happened to an evangelist friend of mine while still in his youth. He was invited to speak in a church. When he got off the plane, the pastor met him with a surprised look on his face, saying, "You're not Morris Cerullo!" The Pastor had a great hunger for signs and wonders to be restored to his church, and thought he had booked with Morris Cerullo. The shocked pastor asked the young man if he had a signs and wonders ministry.

He answered, "No."

The pastor, looking at his watch said, "You've got four hours to get one." Out of desperation, the young evangelist cried out to God, and God honored his cry. That night was the beginning of the signs and wonders ministry that has marked his life to this day. God orchestrated these circumstances so that both Daniel and this young evangelist would earnestly pursue spiritual gifts.

Infiltrating the system often involves our willingness to bring spiritual gifts into our world. These gifts actually work better in the world than in the confines of church meetings. When we practice the gifts only in the church, they lose their sharp edge. Invading the world system with His dominion keeps us sharp and gets them saved.

Promotion does not go unchallenged. Just when you think you have been placed into a position of influence, something will happen to totally rock your boat. Nebuchadnezzar ordered everyone to worship a golden image that stood 90 feet tall. But the Hebrew children would not. There is a distinction between submission and obedience. Sometimes we are to go against the command of our leaders—but even then, only with submissive hearts.

Infiltrating the system *often involves our willingness to bring spiritual gifts into our world.*

Daniel 4:35—*All the peoples of the earth are regarded as nothing. He does as he pleases with the powers of Heaven and the peoples of the earth. No one can hold back his hand or say to him: "What have you done?"*

BOOK QUOTE: *When Heaven Invades Earth* [Chapter 16]

THERE is an additional lesson from Daniel's life as leaven is found in Chapter 4. He has been given the interpretation to another dream. It is about the judgment of God against Nebuchadnezzar. Remember, this is the leader of a demonically-inspired kingdom—one that required idolatry! Men of lesser character would have rejoiced in God's judgment. Not Daniel. His response to his master was: "My lord, may the dream concern those who hate you, and its interpretation concern your enemies." (Dan. 4:19).

What loyalty! His devotion was not based on the character of his king. It was based on the character of the One who assigned him the position of service. Some would have had an "I told you so" response to their boss if God judged them in the same way. The world has seen our "holier than thou" attitude, and they're not impressed. Responses like Daniel's become noticed. They display the kingdom in its purity and power. They are revolutionary.

Chapter 4 records what is possibly the greatest conversion of all time: that of Nebuchadnezzar. He was the darkest ruler ever to live. His final recorded words are: "Now I, Nebuchadnezzar, praise and extol and honor the King of Heaven, all of whose works are truth, and His ways justice. And those who walk in pride, He is able to put down" (Dan. 4:37). He was saved from hell because of the leavening power of the kingdom of God.

For massive worldwide revival to reach it's dominating potential, it must be taken out of the four walls of the Church and launched into the marketplace. (See Mark 6:56.) Quietly, powerfully, decisively invade through service; and when you run into a person with an impossibility, let him know the reality of Heaven is within arm's reach! And "let your peace come upon it" (Matt. 10:13).

For massive worldwide revival to reach it's dominating potential, it must be taken out of the four walls of the Church and launched into the marketplace.

Genesis 39:22—*The warden paid no attention to anything under Joseph's care, because the Lord was with Joseph and gave him success in whatever he did.*

BOOK QUOTE: *When Heaven Invades Earth* [Chapter 16]

GOD had spoken to Joseph about his purpose in life through dreams. God prospered him wherever he went because he was a man of promise. As a great servant, he obtained favor in Potiphar's house. When Potiphar's wife tried to seduce him, he said no. She then lied and had him put in prison, where he again prospered. While circumstances had gone from bad to worse, God was establishing the qualities of leaven in His man.

Sometime later, Pharaoh had two troubling dreams. Joseph interpreted the dreams and then operated in the gift of wisdom by giving the king counsel as to what to do next. The king honored him by putting him second in command over the entire Egyptian Empire.

Joseph gives us an illustration of forgiveness. His brothers come to him (unknowingly) because of famine in their land. When he finally reveals who he is, and the obvious fulfillment of his dreams, he says, "But now, do not therefore be grieved or angry with yourselves because you sold me here; for God sent me before you to preserve life" (Gen. 45:5).

Infiltrating the system involves both purity and power. To be effective as leaven in the *Babylonian system*, we must rethink our understanding of these subjects. God's people must find a heart to see others succeed. The ability to express loyalty and forgiveness before someone is saved may be the key to touching that individual's heart.

Personal integrity is the backbone of all life and ministry, and our credibility is founded on this one thing. We can be gifted beyond measure. But if we can't be trusted, the world will turn a deaf ear to our message. Integrity is holiness, and holiness is the nature of God. Yieldedness to the Holy Spirit is at the heart of the integrity issue.

Infiltrating the system involves both purity and power.

Mark 6:56—Wherever He entered, into villages, cities, or the country, they laid the sick in the marketplaces, and begged Him that they might just touch the hem of His garment. And as many as touched Him were made well. NKJV

BOOK QUOTE: *When Heaven Invades Earth* [Chapter 16]

ANY gospel that doesn't work in the marketplace, doesn't work. Jesus invaded every realm of society. He went where people gathered. They became His focus, and He became theirs.

We see businessmen use the gifts of the Spirit to identify the needs of their co-workers and customers. A young teammate laid hands on the star running back of his high school football team after he had been knocked out of the game with a serious leg injury. After the running back was healed, he returned to the game acknowledging God had healed him!

Teams of people bring hot meals to our local hotels to touch the needy. A hotel owner gave us a room for a season just so we would have a place to pray for the many sick patrons.

Some invade the bars looking for people who need ministry. The gifts of the Spirit flow powerfully in these environments.

Yards in the poorest communities are mowed and cleaned, while others clean the insides of the homes. Some go house to house looking to pray for the sick. Miracles are the norm.

Not only does Jesus care for the down and outer, but He also loves the up and outer. (The wealthy are some of the most broken of our cities.) Parents become Little League coaches. Some lead after-school programs in our public schools. Others volunteer at a local hospital, or become trained as chaplains for the police department or local high schools. People visit their sick neighbors seeing God do the impossible.

Where does life take you? Go there in the anointing and watch the impossibilities bow to the name Jesus.

Any gospel that doesn't work in the marketplace, doesn't work. Jesus invaded every realm of society.

John 12:36—*Put your trust in the light while you have it, so that you may become sons of light.*

BOOK QUOTE: *When Heaven Invades Earth* [Chapter 16]

BUCK fully embraced taking the gifts into the marketplace. He was selected for jury duty and the Lord spoke to him: "Justice must prevail." When the trial phase was finally over and the jury began to deliberate, Buck was able to share his testimony.

When it was time to cast their verdict, they were evenly divided. Their point of contention was the definition of a *criminal*. The man being tried fit six of the seven qualifications needed for him to be considered guilty. The seventh was questionable. So Buck brought a rose in a vase the next day and asked, "What are the parts of a rose?" They listed the petals, stem, leaves, thorns, etc. So he asked them, "Do you see all those parts of this rose?" They responded, "Yes, everything but the thorns." He asked, "Is it still a rose without those thorns?"

They said, "Yes!"

Buck stated, "And this man is a criminal!"

Now all but two agreed he was guilty. Buck proceeded to expose a secret sin in both jurors' lives. Both jurors changed their vote.

Buck first brought the gift of wisdom into the deliberations. It helped to bring clarification that benefited even unbelievers. He brought a word of knowledge, something that he could not have known in the natural, to expose the sin in two people who had rejected God's dealings. In the end the will of God prevailed in the situation—justice!

Being involved in the supernatural through spiritual gifts is what makes the invasion effective. The Kingdom of God is a Kingdom of power! We must be in pursuit of a fuller demonstration of the Spirit of God. Pray much and take risks.

The ultimate example of this invasion is Jesus. In Him, the supernatural invaded the natural.

Pray much and take risks.

Amos 3:7 (NASB)—*The Lord God does nothing unless He reveals His secret counsel to His servants the prophets.*

BOOK QUOTE: *When Heaven Invades Earth* [Chapter 17]

It's important to understand God's promise and purpose for the Church so that we might become dissatisfied—so that we will become desperate.

Revival is not for the faint of heart. It brings fear to the complacent because of the risks it requires. The fearful often work against the move of God—sometimes to their death—all the while thinking they are working for Him. Deception says that the changes brought about by revival contradict the faith of their fathers. As a result, the God-given ability to create withers into the laborious task of preserving. The fearful become curators of museums, instead of builders of the Kingdom.

Others are ready to risk all. The faith of their fathers is considered a worthy foundation to build upon. Change is not a threat, but an adventure. Revelation increases, ideas multiply, and the stretch begins.

God's activities on earth begin with a revelation to mankind. The prophet hears and declares. Those with ears to hear respond and are equipped for change.

In order to understand who we are and what we are to become, we must see Jesus *as He is*. We are about to see the difference between the Jesus who walked the streets healing the sick and raising the dead, and the Jesus who today reigns over all. As glorious as His life was on earth, it was the *before* side of the Cross. Christianity is life on the resurrection side of the Cross.

Revelation creates an appetite for Him. He doesn't come in a "no frills" model. There's no economy class Holy Spirit. He only comes fully equipped. He is loaded, full of power and glory. And He wants to be seen as He is, in us.

Change is not a threat, but an adventure.

Ephesians 3:4-5—In reading this, then, you will be able to understand my insight into the mystery of Christ, which was not made known to men in other generations as it has now been revealed by the Spirit to God's holy apostles and prophets.

BOOK QUOTE: *When Heaven Invades Earth* [Chapter 17]

THE power of one word from His mouth can create a galaxy. His promises for the Church are beyond all comprehension. Our predisposition toward a weak Church has blinded our eyes to the truths of God's Word about us. This problem is rooted in our unbelief.

We lack understanding of who we are because we have little revelation of who He is. We know a lot about His life on earth. Yet that is not the example of what the Church is to become. What He is today, glorified, seated at the right hand of the Father, is the model for what we are becoming!

What God has planned for the Church in this hour is greater than our ability to imagine and pray. Such statements cause some to fear the Church will not be balanced. Fear of disappointment has justified our unbelief. What is the worst that could happen if I pursued what is reserved for eternity? God could say no. We make a big mistake to think we can figure out what has been reserved for Heaven, from this side of Heaven.

Because many fear excess, mediocrity is embraced as balance. Such fear makes complacency a virtue. And it's the fear of excess that has made those that are resistant to change appear noble-minded. Excess has never brought an end to revival.

This generation is a generation of risk takers. And not all the risks taken will be seen as real faith. Some will come to light as steps of foolishness and presumption. But they must be taken just the same. How else can we learn? Make room for risk takers in your life that don't "bat a thousand." They will inspire you to the greatness available in serving a Great God.

We make a big mistake to think we can figure out what has been reserved for Heaven, from this side of Heaven.

Ephesians 3:10,11—*That now the manifold wisdom of God might be made known by the church to the principalities and powers in the heavenly places, according to His eternal purpose…. NKJV*

BOOK QUOTE: *When Heaven Invades Earth* [Chapter 17]

THERE are many things mentioned in Scripture about the Church that have yet to be fulfilled. Jesus intends for us to become mature before He returns. One of the signs of maturity is wisdom.

Wisdom is to be displayed by us *now*. It is clear that God intends to teach the spirit realm about His wisdom through those made in His image—us.

Solomon was the wisest man ever to live, apart from Jesus who is wisdom personified. (See 1 Corinthians 1:30.) The depth of Solomon's wisdom was actually identified by these three attributes: *excellence, creativity, and integrity.*

The wisdom of God will again be seen in His people. The Church, which is presently despised, or at best ignored, will again be reverenced and admired. The Church will again be a praise in the earth. (See Jeremiah 33:9.)

Let's examine the three elements belonging to Solomon's wisdom:

Excellence is the high standard for what we do because of who we are. Excellence comes from viewing things from His perspective.

In pursuing this virtue, we do all to the glory of God, with all our might. A heart of excellence has no place for the poverty spirit that affects so much of what we do.

Creativity is not only seen in a full restoration of the arts, but is the nature of His people in finding new and better ways to do things.

This anointing will also bring about new inventions, breakthroughs in medicine and science, and novel ideas for business and education. The list is endless. The sky is the limit. Arise and create!

Integrity is the expression of God's character seen in us. And that character is His holiness. Holiness is the essence of His nature.

It is clear that God intends to teach the spirit realm about His wisdom through those made in His image—us.

Ephesians 5:27—That He might present her to Himself a glorious church, not having spot or wrinkle or any such thing, but that she should be holy and without blame. NKJV

BOOK QUOTE: *When Heaven Invades Earth* [Chapter 17]

GOD's original intent for mankind is seen in the passage, "For all have sinned and fallen short of the glory of God" (Rom. 3:23). We were to live in the glory of God. That was the target when God created mankind. Our sin caused the arrow of His purpose to fall short.

The glory of God is the manifested presence of Jesus. Imagine this: a people that are continually conscious of the presence of God, not in theory, but the actual presence of God upon them!

We will be a Church in which Jesus is seen in His glory! It is the Holy Spirit's presence and anointing that will dominate the Christian's life. The Church will be radiant. "The latter glory of this house will be greater than the former" (Hag. 2:9 NASB).

Imagine a beautiful young woman prepared for a wedding. She has taken care of herself by eating right and getting all the exercise she needs. Her mind is sharp and she is emotionally secure and free. By looking at her, you'd never know she had ever done anything wrong. Guilt and shame do not blemish her countenance. She understands and exudes grace. According to Revelation 19:7, she made herself ready. Romance will do that to you. The tools are in place for such an event. The Church must now use them.

The former is a biblical description of the Bride of Christ. When we see how great God is, we'll not question His ability to pull this one off. Paul makes a statement to the church at Corinth that he didn't want to return to them until their obedience was complete. That is the heart of God for the Church. And so, Jesus, *the perfect One*, will return for *the spotless one* when He views our obedience as complete.

It is the Holy Spirit's presence and anointing that will dominate the Christian's life.

Ephesians 4:13—Till we all come to the unity of the faith and of the knowledge of the Son of God, to a perfect man.... NKJV

BOOK QUOTE: *When Heaven Invades Earth* [Chapter 17]

THE *unity of faith* is the *faith that works through love* is mentioned in Galatians 5:6. Love and faith are the two essentials of the Christian life.

Faith comes from the Word, specifically, "*a Word freshly spoken.*" Faith is what pleases God. It is active trust in Him as Abba Father. He alone is the source of such faith. It comes as the result of Him speaking to His people. Unity of faith means we will hear His voice together, and demonstrate great exploits. It is a lifestyle—as in having *unity in our ideas about faith*. The exploits of the present and coming revival will surpass all the accomplishments of the Church in all history combined.

The Church will receive a fresh revelation of Jesus, especially through the book of Revelation. That revelation will launch the Church into a transformation unlike any experienced in a previous age. *As we see Him, we become like Him!* The coming increase in revelation of Jesus will be measurable through new dimensions of worship—corporate throne room experiences.

Olympic athletes never get to the games by gifting alone. It's the powerful combination of a gift brought to its full potential through discipline. That is the picture of the Church becoming a mature man. It is singular, meaning we all function together as one. All its members will work in perfect coordination and harmony, complementing each other's function and gift, according to the directions given by the head. This was not a promise to be fulfilled in eternity. While I don't believe that this is speaking of human perfection, I do believe there is a maturity of function, without jealousy, that will develop as His presence becomes more manifest. We need to embrace this as possible because He said it is.

Love and faith are the two essentials of the Christian life.

Ephesians 3:19—To know the love of Christ which passes knowledge; that you may be filled with all the fullness of God. NKJV

BOOK QUOTE: *When Heaven Invades Earth* [Chapter 17]

THE Church will know the love of God by experience. This will go beyond our ability to comprehend.

The experiential love of God, and the corresponding fullness of the Spirit is what is necessary to bring us to the full stature of Christ—Jesus will be accurately seen in the Church, just as the Father was accurately seen in Jesus.

*And it shall come to pass in the last days, says God, That I will pour out of My Spirit on **all flesh**; Your sons and your **daughters** shall prophesy, Your **young** men shall see visions, Your **old** men shall dream dreams. And on My **menservants** and on My **maidservants** I will pour out My Spirit in those days; And **they** shall prophesy (Acts 2:17-18 NKJV).*

This passage quoted from Joel 2 has never been completely fulfilled. It had initial fulfillment in Acts 2, but its reach was far greater than that generation could fulfill. First of all, *All flesh* was never touched by that revival. But it will happen.

First Corinthians 12-14 is a wonderful teaching on the operation of the gifts of the Spirit. But it is so much more. It is a revelation of a body of believers who live in the realm of the Spirit that is essential for last days' ministry. These manifestations of the Holy Spirit will be taken to the streets where they belong. It is there that they reach their full potential.

This generation will fulfill the cry of Moses for all of God's people to be prophets. We will carry the Elijah anointing in preparing for the return of the Lord in the same way that John the Baptist carried the Elijah anointing and prepared the people for the coming of the Lord.

*The experiential love of God, and the corresponding fullness of the Spirit is what is necessary to bring us to the full **stature of Christ**...*

John 14:12 (NKJV)—*He who believes in Me, the works that I do he will do also; and greater works than these he will do, because I go to My Father.*

BOOK QUOTE: *When Heaven Invades Earth* [Chapter 17]

JESUS' prophesy of us doing greater works than He did has stirred the Church to look for some abstract meaning to this very simple statement. *Greater* means "greater." And the *works* He referred to are "signs and wonders." He showed us what one person could do who has the Spirit without measure. What could millions do? That was His point, and it became His prophecy.

This verse does not refer to *quantity* of works, but *quality*. Millions of people should be able to surpass the shear numbers of works that Jesus did simply because we are so many. But that waters down the intent of His statement. The word greater is *mizon* in the Greek. It is found 45 times in the New Testament. It is always used to describe "quality," not quantity.

God is not the kind of Father who gives us a command to ask for something without fully intending to answer our request. He directs us to pray this prayer because it is in His heart to fulfill it. The safest prayers in existence are the ones He tells us to pray. His answer will be *beyond all we could ask or think*. And it is "*according to the power that works in us*" (Eph.3:20).

The present reality of the Kingdom will become manifest and realized in the everyday life of the believer. That world will break into this one at every point where the Christian prays in faith. The lordship of Jesus will be seen, and the bounty of His rule will be experienced. While the full expression of His Kingdom may be reserved for eternity, it has never entered our minds what God would like to do before then. It's time to explore that possibility.

The lordship of Jesus will be seen, and the bounty of His rule will be experienced.

Acts 20:32— *Now I commit you to God and to the word of His grace, which can build you up and give you an inheritance among all those who are sanctified.*

BOOK QUOTE: *When Heaven Invades Earth* [Chapter 17]

WOULDN'T it be wonderful to have churches so explosive in the supernatural that we would have to find ways to calm them down? That's what Paul had to do with the Corinthian church. The instructions about the gifts of the Spirit were given to a people who had so much they needed to organize it. "Let everything be done decently and in order" (1 Cor. 14:40). You can't organize what you don't have. *Everything* has to be done before you can add a structure to make it more effective. Order is a poor substitute for power. But if you have much power, you'll need good order. *Only in that case* will order add a new dimension to the role of power in the Church.

Each move of God has been followed by another, just to restore what was forfeited and forgotten. And we still haven't arrived to the standard that they attained, let alone surpassed it. Yet, not even the early Church fulfilled God's full intention for His people. That privilege was reserved for those in the last leg of the race. It is our destiny.

As wonderful as our spiritual roots are, they are insufficient. What was good for *yesterday* is deficient for *today*. It's not that *everything* must change for us to flow with what God is saying and doing. It's just that we make too many assumptions about the *rightness* of what presently exists. Those assumptions blind us to the revelations still contained in Scripture. In reality, what we think of as the *normal Christian life* cannot hold the weight of what God is about to do. Our wineskins must change. There is very little of what we now know as Church life that will remain untouched in the next ten years.

What was good for **yesterday** *is deficient for* **today**.

Isaiah 64:4— *Since ancient times no one has heard, no ear had perceived, no eye has seen any God besides you, who acts on behalf of those who wait for Him.*

BOOK QUOTE: *When Heaven Invades Earth* [Chapter 17]

IT has never entered the mind what God has prepared for us while on this earth. His intent is grand. Instead of limiting ourselves by our imagination and experience, let's press onto a renewed hunger for things yet to be seen. As we pursue the Extravagant One with reckless abandon, we will discover that our greatest problem is the resistance that comes from between our ears. But faith is superior. It's time for us to make Him unconcerned about whether or not He'll find faith on the earth.

The Kingdom is in the now! Pray for it, seek it first, and receive it as a child. It is within reach.

In a recent meeting we had a remarkable level of breakthrough in the miraculous. Deafness, blindness, arthritis, and many other afflictions were healed through God's saving grace. There were between 40 and 50 healings in this meeting of about 200 people.

One notable miracle happened to a three-year-old boy named Chris, who had clubfeet. He had sores on the tops of his feet where they would rub on the carpet in his effort to walk. God began to touch him. They put him down and for the first time in his life his feet were flat on the ground! He stared in amazement at his feet, reaching down he touched the sores.

We returned home and watched the video of that evening. We were so thrilled with the miracle that it took us awhile to notice that Chris was intently trying to tell us something. My wife, who was holding the camera, had asked him, "What happened to you?"

Looking into the camera, he answered saying, "Jesus big! Jesus big!"

The only thing we can figure is that he had an encounter with Jesus who came and healed him.

Instead of limiting ourselves by our imagination and experience, let's press onto a renewed hunger for things yet to be seen.

1 Peter 1:13—*Therefore, prepare your minds for action; be self-controlled; set your hope fully on the grace to be given you when Jesus Christ is revealed.*

BOOK QUOTE: *The Supernatural Power* [Chapter 1]

*I*T is unnatural for a Christian to not have an appetite for the impossible.

It had been an awesome Sunday night in the presence of God. When it was all finished—the prayer and praise, the teaching and the time of asking God for miracles—one of my staff members walked from the sanctuary into the hallway and saw a man jumping up and down saying, "Oh my gosh, oh my gosh!" His pants seemed too big for him—he was holding them up so they wouldn't slump around his ankles. He was puzzled, but knew God must have done something. When we asked around we learned that the man had been healed that night after receiving prayer. The tumors he'd come in with had instantly disappeared. He'd come all the way from a neighboring state because doctors had given him only two weeks to live. In his mind, we were his last stop on the way to heaven or on the way to a miracle. He came into the sanctuary where he continued to jump up and down with great joy, very much healed and very much in need of a new wardrobe.

How did it happen? The Kingdom of God had come crashing into his infirmity and overwhelmed it. It was another great night and another great victory over the enemy.

That same weekend a woman drove to our church from two states away because she was having difficulty breathing. The doctors had found what they believed was lung cancer. Her family had to help her into the building. After receiving prayer, she left pain-free, able to breathe without any restriction.

Again, Kingdom reality vanquished earthly affliction.

... we were his last stop on the way to Heaven or on the way to a miracle.

Psalm 77:14—*You are the God who performs miracles; you display your power among the peoples.*

BOOK QUOTE: *The Supernatural Power* [Chapter 1]

Is that normal? Absolutely! But is it common in today's church? Not yet. But God is changing the way Christians think about the so-called impossible. He is teaching us to work hand-in-hand with the Kingdom so the reality of Heaven comes crashing into earthly problems and overwhelms them. The results are astonishing miracles, great victories over the enemy, healing, deliverance, revelation, and more. It's not hype; it's not baseless hope or theory. It's fact. The two stories I shared above are actual situations in which affliction was completely vanquished by Kingdom reality, and there are many more I will share throughout this book. Many churches see the miraculous happen on a weekly, even a daily, basis. As you can imagine, it's a revolutionary approach to Christian living—a return to the authentic.

I wish I could say I have always lived in the everyday miraculous, but I haven't. I've been a pastor for decades, but I didn't see miracles for most of that time. I believed in healing and deliverance, but neither I nor the people I pastored prayed for them with any success. We had correct doctrine, but not correct practice. However, a number of years ago God began to take us on a journey, giving us fresh Kingdom eyes to see what normal Christian living ought to be. Having missed much of the main activity of the Kingdom for so long, we were eager to get back to the original plan of God on this earth. It has been a wonderful learning experience!

> *. . .God is changing the way Christians think about the so-called impossible.*

Acts 2:43—*Everyone was filled with awe, and many wonders and miraculous signs were done by the apostles.*

BOOK QUOTE: *The Supernatural Power* [Chapter 1]

I have come to see that the normal Christian life means miracles, spiritual intervention, and revelation. It means peace, joy, love, a sense of well-being and purpose—all these traits that elude so many Christians. Written into the spiritual DNA of every believer is an appetite for the impossible that cannot be ignored or wished away. The Holy Spirit, the very Spirit that raised Jesus from the dead, lives in us, making it impossible for us to be content with what we can only see, hear, touch, taste, and smell. Our hearts know there is much more to life than what we perceive with our senses; we are spiritually agitated by the lack of connection with the realm of the supernatural. In the end, nothing satisfies the heart of the Christian like seeing so-called impossibilities bow their knees to the name of Jesus. Anything less than this is abnormal and unfulfilling.

To be effective believers, we must go well beyond the Christian life we have known. We must redefine "normal" Christianity so it lines up with God's idea of normal, not the definition we have accepted and grown accustomed to based on our experiences (or lack thereof). The normal Christian life begins with the realization that we were put here to do the will of God on earth as it is in Heaven—and what a joy it is to participate in that. Many of us have treated the will of God as if it's unknown or unknowable. Sincere believers might pray for days and weeks, looking more somber and beat-up all the time, and they'll tell you they're trying to find the will of God on a matter. I have done this, too! But the will of God is simpler and plainer than we have thought.

To be effective believers, we must go well beyond the Christian life we have known.

Philippians 2:13—*for it is God who works in you to will and to act according to his good purpose.*

BOOK QUOTE: *The Supernatural Power* [Chapter 1]

IN what is known as the Lord's Prayer, Jesus said clearly and concisely:

> *"Our Father in Heaven, hallowed be Your name. Your kingdom come. Your will be done on earth as it is in Heaven."* (Matthew 6:9-10).

The will of God is simply this: "On earth as it is in Heaven." Isn't it refreshing? When we pray, "Thy kingdom come, Thy will be done," we're praying for the King's dominion and will to be realized right here, right now. That is a life-transforming, paradigm-shattering way to "do" normal Christianity. What is free to operate in Heaven—joy, peace, wisdom, health, wholeness, and all the other good promises we read about in the Bible—should be free to operate here on this planet, in your home, your church, your business, and your school. What is not free to operate there—sickness, disease, spiritual bondage, and sin—should not be free to operate here, period. We are out to destroy the works of the devil (1 John 3:8). It's an awesome way to live!

When we make this our primary understanding of God's will, the other areas that trouble us so much will seem to sort themselves out (Matt. 6:33).

When we make this our mission, lives are set free, bodies are restored, darkness lifts from people's minds, the rule of the enemy is pushed back in every way imaginable. Businesses grow healthy, relationships flower again, people re-connect with their calling and purpose in life, churches grow, and cities feel the effects of having the Kingdom flourishing within them. Energy is freed up for Kingdom works in ways I have never seen before. Things happen regularly that are so extraordinary it's like stepping into the pages of a good novel. But it's not a made-up lifestyle; it's the lifestyle for which we were made.

We are out to destroy the works of the devil.

Acts 15:21—*Rather, as it is written: 'Those who were not told about Him will see, ad those who have not heard will understand.'*

BOOK QUOTE: *The Supernatural Power* [Chapter 1]

A young man named Brandon, who is a graduate of Bethel School of Supernatural Ministry, was visiting friends. They were at a restaurant and the waitress came to take their order. Brandon began to perceive things in his heart about the woman's relationship with her mother, and he shared them with her. The waitress was amazed, and she became so emotional that she had to take a break.

While the waitress was away, Brandon noticed an Asian couple staring at him from across the room. The woman had wrist braces on because she suffered from carpal tunnel syndrome, and one of her hands was completely frozen in a fist. Brandon asked if he could pray for her. She said that they were Buddhist, but were willing to receive prayer. He prayed and she was healed on the spot. The whole family was instantly overjoyed and began praising Jesus, right at their table. They said they had been praying to their ancestors for a long time for her hands to be healed, but the prayers hadn't worked. Brandon explained who Jesus is, and they received the gospel with wonder and thankfulness. He went back to his table and for the rest of the evening, the healed woman sat there opening and closing her hand in amazement.

About that time, the waitress came back and asked if she could talk with Brandon outside. She wanted to know more about God. Brandon shared further insight that the Holy Spirit gave him about her life and told her about Jesus' love. She gave her heart to the Lord and was filled with the Holy Spirit right there.

That sounds like something out of the Bible, but it is another very recent display of God's love from a normal Christian like you and me.

...they received the gospel with wonder and thankfulness.

Hebrews 13:20-21—*May the God of peace...equip you with everything good for doing His will, and may He work in us what is pleasing to Him, through Jesus Christ, to whom be glory for ever and ever. Amen.*

BOOK QUOTE: *The Supernatural Power* [Chapter 1]

ONE of the major functions of miracles and supernatural living is to offer immediate, irrefutable proof of what God wants to happen on earth. It demonstrates who God is by showing what His reality looks like.

Has it ever occurred to you that one of your jobs on earth is to prove the will of God? To show other people what He is like? To allow Him to overwhelm the enemy's works through you? Most people don't know how God behaves, or what's inside His heart for each one of us. Your calling and my calling as believers may be too massive to fully understand, but the Bible's command is clear: Our job is to demonstrate that the reality that exists in Heaven can be manifested right here, right now. We are not just to be people who believe the right things about God, but people who *put the will of God on display*, expressing it and causing others to realize, "Oh, so *that's* what God is like." Healing and deliverance and restoration do much more than solve the immediate problem; they give people a concrete demonstration of who God is.

One young man from our church was summoned for jury duty. While he was serving, a gang member got saved and three people were healed, one of them in front of a mocking crowd. This young man had so boasted in the Lord that many of the other jurors were publicly making fun of him. So he turned to an afflicted person, prayed, and the person was healed. The crowd went silent. Another man in a wheelchair stood before the people in the courthouse, moving his hands and displaying the healing power and love of Jesus Christ.

Has it ever occurred to you that one of your jobs on earth is to prove the will of God?

Psalm 145:12—*So that all men may know of Your mighty acts and the glorious splendor of Your kingdom.*

BOOK QUOTE: *The Supernatural Power* [Chapter 1]

OUR staff and students from our ministry school, have gone a number of times to a nearby university that is a major center of New Age spiritualism. The most popular religion on campus is witchcraft. My senior associate was invited to speak in a class on Christianity and the supernatural. A young lady who was tormented by demons began to manifest under their influence. My associate commanded them to leave, and she was delivered in front of many wide-eyed students! She was filled with so much joy that they had to carry her out of the classroom so the next class could begin. My associate began to call people out, pointing at them and speaking strong prophetic words into their lives that touched the secret things of their hearts. Some dropped to the floor instantly as if they'd lost their strength. Others sat there with their mouths gaping. And on it went until those witches and warlocks who had devoted their lives to the powers of hell knew there was a mighty God in Israel, and in the Church!

During worship one morning at our church, a woman who had esophageal cancer felt the fire of God come upon her. She turned to her husband and said, "God healed me."

They went to the doctor and the doctor said, "This kind doesn't go away." But he examined her anyway and told her in complete astonishment, "Not only is it gone, you have a brand new esophagus."

During another service we were reading the Bible, and a man in the congregation suddenly couldn't see the words clearly. Everything went blurry. He didn't figure out why until he got home and took off his glasses and could see fine without them. God healed his vision without anyone praying for him.

. . . those. . . who had devoted their lives to the powers of hell knew there was a mighty God in Israel, and in the Church!

Matthew 5:13—*You are the salt of the earth....*

BOOK QUOTE: *The Supernatural Power* [Chapter 1]

HE said those words to Adam and Eve so they would extend the boundaries of His garden—representing His government, His will—to the ends of the earth. His idea was to have a planet engulfed in His glorious rule, with mankind flawlessly "proving the will of God" on earth as it is in Heaven. It is a beautiful, breathtaking picture, and it remains God's goal for you and me, for the Church and for all of mankind. God has never wavered in what He wants for this planet and from you and me.

Of course, we know that the original plan got derailed, and that Adam forfeited the rulership God gave him over the earth, putting humanity into slavery to the enemy. Paul wrote,

"You are that one's slaves whom you obey..." (Romans 6:16).

But God had a plan of redemption in place: Jesus would come to reclaim all that was lost. God told the evil one,

"And I will put enmity between you and the woman, and between your seed and her Seed; He shall bruise your head, and you shall bruise His heel" (Genesis 3:15).

When that prophecy was fulfilled in the death and resurrection of Jesus Christ, God took back the authority man had given away and reclaimed our purpose on this earth. He gave us a clear field to run toward the original goal—and run with all our might. We, the Church, are called to extend His rule in this earthly sphere, just as Adam was called to do.

He gave us a clear field to run toward the original goal—
and run with all our might.

Matthew 28:19—Therefore go and make disciples of all nations, baptizing them in the name of the Father and of the Son and of the Holy Spirit...

BOOK QUOTE: *The Supernatural Power* [Chapter 1]

IN essence Jesus said, "Go heal the sick, preach the good news, demonstrate who I am and what I am like. Extend My Kingdom!"

But too few of us today follow those precise instructions. We get caught up in side arguments, intellectual skirmishes, theories, and emotional head-trips. We become enamored of our own talents and spiritual giftings, thinking we can direct our own course simply by putting our gifts and talents to use as we see fit. Though well-intentioned, we become self-appointed in our commissions, honestly believing we are submitting to God. In reality, it isn't possible to prove the will of God on earth as it is in Heaven unless we are completely plugged into the primary mission God gave us. We put it this way: *There is no co-missioning without* **sub**-*mission to the primary mission.*

So what is the primary mission?

"For this purpose the Son of God was manifested, that He might destroy the works of the devil." (1 John 3:8).

That was Jesus' assignment; it was Adam and Eve's assignment; it was the disciples' assignment. Believers, *that is your assignment as well.* God's purpose in saving you was not simply to rescue you and let you keep busy until He shipped you off to Heaven. His purpose was much bigger, much more stunning: He commissioned you to demonstrate the will of God, "on earth as it is in Heaven," transforming this planet into a place radiant and saturated with His power and presence. This is the very backbone of the Great Commission, and it should define your life and mine.

He commissioned you to demonstrate the will of God, "on earth as it is in Heaven,"...

Matthew 25:35—*For I was hungry and you gave Me something to eat, I was thirsty and you gave Me something to drink, I was a stranger and you invited Me in.*

BOOK QUOTE: *The Supernatural Power* [Chapter 1]

WHEN we do the will of God, we bring Kingdom reality crashing into the works of the devil. We initiate conflict between earthly reality and heavenly reality, becoming the bridge and connection point that makes it possible through prayer and radical obedience to assert the rulership of God. Not long ago, a woman with a broken arm came to our church with her wrist in such pain that we couldn't even touch her skin to pray for it. We held our hands away and prayed, and within moments God healed it completely. She had no pain and was twisting the wrist all around. The arm was totally different than it had been seconds earlier. Kingdom reality had overwhelmed one of the devil's works. *That's* the normal Christian life I'm talking about.

We have an annual holiday feast, in which families from the church adopt a table in our gym and decorate it with Christmas decorations. The tables are set with our finest china, crystal, and silverware. We then bus the needy to this event held in their honor. This past year we served prime rib. We started with 34 roasts to feed two seatings of about 500 people each. After serving 19 roasts in the first seating we realized that the 15 we had left were not enough for the 200 workers plus the second group of 500. The decision was made to not feed the workers. But when they went back into the kitchen there were 22. Seven more had mysteriously appeared. The workers were then fed, as was the second group of needy people. That should have exhausted our mysterious 22 roasts, but there were 12 more left after everyone had eaten! Multiplying bread is great, but I really like seeing prime rib multiply!

Kingdom reality had overwhelmed one of the devil's works.

Acts 5:12—*The apostles performed many miraculous signs and wonders among the people....*

BOOK QUOTE: *The Supernatural Power* [Chapter 1]

AREN'T you tired of talking about a gospel of power, but never seeing it in action? Aren't you tired of trying to carry out the Great Commission without offering proof that the Kingdom works? We tell people how great the product is, but seldom demonstrate or prove it.

We have improperly defined how the Kingdom of God operates, missing the bulk of what Jesus taught. Some teach that the Kingdom of God is for the distant future or the past, not here and now. Some consign all the promises of God in the Bible to the millennium or to eternity because the accepted wisdom is that we're going to barely make Heaven. But Jesus taught and demonstrated that the Kingdom of God is a present-tense reality—it exists now in the invisible realm and is superior to everything in the visible realm. In the same way that Jesus is fully God and fully man, so the Kingdom is fully now and fully then. He spent His ministry showing us how to bring Kingdom power to bear on the works of the devil. *Our ministry should do the same.* We can't be self-commissioned, relying on our ministry gifts to carry out the Great Commission. We can't afford to work apart from the supernatural intervention of Kingdom reality. Our assignment has never been about what we can do for God, but what can God do through us. That is the essence of the gospel: to do exactly what Jesus did and destroy the works of the devil.

That is normal Christianity. Miracles are normal. Salvation and deliverance are normal. Revelation, prophetic insight, and words of knowledge are normal. But to return to that original mission, we must radically change the way we think. We must *repent* and *renew our minds.*

Revelation, prophetic insight, and words of knowledge
are normal.

Jeremiah 6:19—Hear, O earth! Behold, I will certainly bring calamity on this people—The fruit of their thoughts, because they have not heeded My words nor My law, but rejected it. NKJV

BOOK QUOTE: *The Supernatural Power* [Chapter 1]

THE only way to consistently do Kingdom works is to view reality from God's perspective. That's what the Bible means when it talks about renewing our minds. The battle is in the mind. The mind is the essential tool in bringing Kingdom reality to the problems people face. God has made it to be the gatekeeper of the supernatural.

To be of use to the Kingdom, our minds must be transformed. We find a clue to what that word means in the transfiguration of Jesus when He talked with Moses and Elijah. The reality of Heaven radiated through Jesus, and He shone with incredible brilliance. His body revealed the reality of another world. The word *transformed* in that passage is the same word we find in Romans 12:2. The renewed mind, then, reflects the reality of another world in the same way Jesus shone with Heaven's brilliance. It's not just that our thoughts are different, but that our way of thinking is transformed because we think from a different reality—from heaven toward earth! That is the transformed perspective. The renewed mind enables His co-laborers to prove the will of God. We prove the will of God when put on display the reality of Heaven. The un-renewed mind, on the other hand, brings about a completely different manifestation.

At times in church history the intellectual aspect of the mind has been so exalted that it has wiped out a real lifestyle of faith. Theology has been exalted at the expense of belief. Academic assessment has replaced firsthand, supernatural experience. There is good reason not to let the mind dictate how we will believe. But Christians often react to error and create another error in the process. Pentecostals have often downplayed the mind's importance, implying that it has no value at all.

The mind is the essential tool in bringing Kingdom reality to the problems people face.

Luke 24:45—*Then He opened their minds so they could understand the Scriptures.*

BOOK QUOTE: *The Supernatural Power* [Chapter 1]

MANY Christians instinctively distrust the mind, thinking it is irredeemably corrupt and humanistic. However, the mind is actually a powerful instrument of the Spirit of God. He made it to be the gatekeeper of Kingdom activity on earth. When a mind goes astray God's freedom to establish His will on earth is limited. The mind is not to be tossed out; it is to be used for its original purpose. If the mind weren't vitally important to our walk with Christ, Paul wouldn't have urged us to "be transformed by the renewing of our minds." In fact, only a renewed mind can consistently bring Kingdom reality to earth.

Yet many of us live with un-renewed minds, which are of little use to God. People who are out of sync with the mind of Christ seldom get used, because their thoughts conflict with the mind of Christ. They are self-appointed in their mission and are not in submission to the primary mission. As a result, they are working entirely outside God's intended commission.

When we come into agreement with the primary mission, our minds become powerful tools in God's hands. This explains why there is such an intense war being waged for your mind. Every thought and action in your life speaks of allegiance to God or to satan. Both are empowered by your agreement. Renewing your mind means learning to recognize what comes from hell, and what comes from Heaven, and agreeing with Heaven. That is the only way you will complete your divine assignment. God designed your mind to be one of the most supernaturally powerful tools in the universe, but it needs to be sanctified and yielded to the Holy Spirit so you can carry out His designs, creative ideas, and plans in your everyday life.

Every thought and action in your life speaks of allegiance to God or to satan.

Matthew 3:8—*Produce fruit in keeping with repentance.*

BOOK QUOTE: *The Supernatural Power* [Chapter 1]

RENEWING the mind begins with repentance. That is the gateway to return to our original assignment on earth. Jesus said, "Repent, for the kingdom of Heaven is at hand" (Matt. 4:17). To many Christians, *repent* refers to having an altar call where people come forward and weep at the altar and get right with God. That is a legitimate expression of repentance, but it's not what the word repentance means.

Re means to "go back." *Pent* is like the penthouse, the top floor of a building. Repent, then, means to go back to God's perspective on reality. Without repentance we remain locked into carnal ways of thinking. When the Bible speaks of carnality, it doesn't necessarily mean obvious, disgusting sin. Most Christians have no appetite for sin; they don't want to get drunk or sleep around, but because they live without the demonstrated power of the gospel, many have lost their sense of purpose and gone back to sin. Having a renewed mind is often not an issue of whether or not someone is going to Heaven, but of how much of Heaven he or she wants in his or her life right now.

Jesus said that "unless one is born again, he cannot see the kingdom of God" (John 3:3). Jesus was speaking practically. He was saying that when our minds are renewed, we will see the Kingdom displayed and proven as He did in His earthly ministry. That's what it means to "see" the Kingdom of Heaven. Our souls long to see such things. We have inside of us an unrelenting hunger to watch the Kingdom break into this realm—and not just to watch but to participate, to become the connecting point and gateway for God's power.

Without repentance we remain locked into
carnal ways of thinking.

Romans 2:4—Or do you show contempt for the riches of His kindness, tolerance and patience, not realizing that God's kindness leads you toward repentance?

BOOK QUOTE: *The Supernatural Power* [Chapter 1]

I walked into church one recent Sunday morning, greeting people before the meeting, and in the back I met a homeless gentleman who'd come as a guest of someone else. He had a cast on his arm and was treating it with great care. So I said, "Hey, what happened to your arm?"

He said, "I fell off a 20-foot bridge and shattered my wrist."

"How about if we pray for that?" I asked.

"Okay," he replied.

We prayed and I told him, "Now move it around."

He moved it and his jaw dropped. He looked in complete astonishment at the lady who brought him because he had been completely healed in a moment of time. His wrist was fine. When the invitation came for people to give their lives to Christ later in the service, he was the first to come forward. Once again we see that "His kindness leads us to repentance" (Rom. 2:4).

That is a simple, everyday example of proving that the Kingdom works on earth. It is not mind-over-matter, or something spooky and weird. It is going back to God's perspective of reality and living as if we really believe it. His purpose—His reality—is to raise up a delegated group of people who work with Him to destroy the works of the devil, who demonstrate and prove the will of God here on earth as it is in Heaven. That is the core of the Great Commission, and it is your privilege and mine to co-labor with Him in it.

His purpose—His reality—is to raise up a delegated group of people who work with Him...

Acts 26:20—*I preached that they should repent and turn to God and prove their repentance by their deeds.*

BOOK QUOTE: *The Supernatural Power* [Chapter 1]

MOST Christians have repented enough to be forgiven, but not enough to see the Kingdom. They go part of the way, then stop. Life is so much fun when we experience the miraculous and partner with the supernatural! It's an honor and privilege and responsibility that too many of us have feared and ignored.

Without power, the gospel is not good news. Paul was so concerned about properly presenting the gospel that he changed his way of doing ministry between one assignment and the next. You recall he was in Athens, preaching the gospel at Mars Hill where philosophers gathered to talk. They loved to exchange ideas and debate intellectual ideas of the day, but their talks were mostly meaningless and void of power or truth. Paul came into their midst and gave a brilliant message that is honored to this day by Bible schools around the world for its conciseness. (See Acts 17.) Then he gave an opportunity for people to come and to meet Jesus—and only a small handful of people got saved.

What a disappointment! This was, after all, the apostle Paul, who stirred up entire cities with the message and power of God, who was tossed in jail for disturbing the peace. Later, in Ephesus, the city was absolutely turned upside-down by his teaching and the demonstration of God's power. All the occult practitioners brought their piles of books and burned them spontaneously. There was massive repentance. Paul had also been to the third heaven, the realm of God, had seen things unutterable and impossible to describe. But when he went before this group of intellectuals and presented the gospel in a superbly intellectual way, there were very few converts. In fact, Acts 18:1 says, "After these things Paul departed from Athens and went to Corinth."

Most Christians have repented enough to be forgiven, but not enough to see the Kingdom.

Matthew 10:7-8—He told His disciples, "And as you go, preach, saying, 'The kingdom of Heaven is at hand.' Heal the sick, cleanse the lepers, raise the dead, cast out demons." NKJV

BOOK QUOTE: *The Supernatural Power* [Chapter 1]

I F Paul was like any other preacher, he had his share of *blue* Mondays where he re-evaluated the Sunday service a thousand times over, trying to figure out what he could have done better. As Paul was coming to Corinth, I believe he was evaluating his message, which was brilliant but had produced few converts. Looking ahead, he knew he would be preaching the gospel in Corinth. At this point, he described what he was thinking:

> *And I, brethren, when I came to you, did not come with excellence of speech or of wisdom declaring to you the testimony of God. For I determined not to know anything among you except Jesus Christ and Him crucified. I was with you in weakness, in fear, and in much trembling. And my speech and my preaching were not with persuasive words of human wisdom, but in demonstration of the Spirit and of power, that your faith should not be in the wisdom of men but in the power of God* (1 Corinthians 2:1-5).

Paul didn't write, "I wanted your faith to be in the name of the Lord Jesus Christ." He used the phrase, "That your faith...[would be] in the power of God." Today there is a difference between preaching in Jesus' name and preaching with power. In Paul's day there was seldom a difference. Power was part and parcel of the gospel, as it should be for us in our everyday lives.

The gospel was presented in its wholeness, of course, in the life of Jesus who taught with power. Whenever He taught on the Kingdom, He would heal people. It wasn't one or the other; it was both. He showed us that proving the will of God means not only declaring the Kingdom is at hand, but demonstrating its effects.

Power was part and parcel of the gospel, as it should be for us in our everyday lives.

John 5:19—*Jesus gave them this answer: "I tell you the truth, the Son can do nothing by Himself; He can do only what He sees His Father doing, because whatever the Father does the Son also does.*

BOOK QUOTE: *The Supernatural Power* [Chapter 1]

MANY believers think miracles and power are for extra-special anointed people of God. Many get hung up on the idea that Jesus did miracles as God, not man. In reality, Jesus had no ability to heal the sick. He couldn't cast out devils, and He had no ability to raise the dead. He had set aside His divinity. He did miracles as man in right relationship with God because He was setting forth a model for us, something for us to follow. If He did miracles as God, we would all be extremely impressed, but we would have no compulsion to emulate Him. But when we see that God has commissioned us to do what Jesus did—and more—then we realize that He put self-imposed restrictions on Himself to show us we could do it, too. Jesus so emptied Himself that He was incapable of doing what was required of Him by the Father—without the Father's help. That is the nature of our call—it requires more than we are capable of. When we stick to doing only the stuff we can do, we are not involved in the call.

Jesus lived in constant confrontation and conflict with the world around Him, because Kingdom logic goes against carnal logic. A renewed mind destroys the works of the devil so that earthly reality matches heavenly reality. It proves the will of God not just in word but in deed. It heals the sick, frees those enslaved to sin, brings joy where there was sadness, strength where there was weakness, explosive creativity and world-changing ideas and inventions where there was lack of invention. It causes the Kingdom of God to be expressed "on earth as it is in Heaven."

That's normal Christian living.

> *. . . the nature of our call—*
> *it requires more than we are capable of.*

Matthew 3:2—*"Repent, for the kingdom of Heaven is near."*

BOOK QUOTE: *The Supernatural Power* [Chapter 2]

WE were born to live under an "open Heaven." Without that blessing we will fail to resource earth with Heaven's resources.

My wife and I were at a service in Fortuna, California, with several others from our school and staff. Many local pastors were also in attendance. They, having embraced the message of the Kingdom, encouraged their congregations to participate. Healing was extremely easy that night. (Healing is always easy in the sense that "we don't do it—God does!" But sometimes it just seems to flow better than others. This was one of those nights.) Out of about 200 people there were approximately 40 to 50 who acknowledged that God had healed their bodies that night.

There was a woman with a destroyed optical nerve; the doctors had said that she would never see out of that eye again, but she was healed and can now see. A deaf person was also instantly healed that night, as was a woman bound to a wheelchair because of crippling arthritis. She danced and shouted, expressing the joy of her deliverance. Another wonderful miracle took place as our students prayed for a child with club feet. He also was healed. Because the leaders stood together in unity and love, the *miracle realm* was very easy to enter into.

We have hungered for more, prayed for more, and now we are receiving unprecedented insight into our privileges and responsibilities in the Kingdom of God. These insights aren't just being pondered; people are acting on them, and more and more, God's will is being done on earth as it is in Heaven. "Your kingdom come, your will be done on earth as it is in Heaven" (Matthew 6:10).

. . . God's will is being done on earth as it is in Heaven.

Galatians 1:12—*I did not receive it from any man, nor was I taught it; rather, I received it by revelation from Jesus Christ.*

BOOK QUOTE: *The Supernatural Power* [Chapter 2]

I am incredibly excited about the revolution I see taking place in the Church.

Let's start by going back to the first mention of the House of God in the Bible. It's found in Genesis 28, which says:

Now Jacob went out from Beersheba…Then he dreamed, and behold, a ladder was set up on the earth, and its top reached to heaven; and there the angels of God were ascending and descending on it. And behold, the Lord stood above it and said: "I am the Lord God of Abraham your father and the God of Isaac; the land on which you lie I will give to you and your descendants…. Then Jacob awoke from his sleep and said, "Surely the Lord is in this place, and I did not know it." And he was afraid and said, "How awesome is this place! This is none other than the house of God, and this is the gate of Heaven!"…And he called the name of that place Bethel… (Genesis 28:10,13,16-17,19 NKJV).

Because this is the first mention in the Bible of the House of God, this passage defines the nature of this subject for the rest of Scripture. There are several aspects of this house that we should pay attention to. First, Jacob said, "God is here and I didn't even know it." This tells us that it is possible to be in the presence of the "House of God" (which we'll begin to define in a moment) and never know it's there. In other words, without a revelation—in Jacob's case, a dream—we can be oblivious to the presence and work of God in our lives or around us.

… without a revelation…we can be oblivious to the presence and work of God in our lives or around us.

Isaiah 53:11—*After the suffering of his soul, he will see the light of life and be satisfied...*

BOOK QUOTE: *The Supernatural Power* [Chapter 2]

I have been in church services and meetings and have watched time and again as God transforms one person's life dramatically and utterly, but the person sitting next to him or her is clueless that God is even in the house. They're thinking of what they'll eat when they get home, while other people are having total spiritual reconstruction just a few feet away. I don't know how or why that works, but it happens all the time.

One of my former elders, Cal Pierce, founder of the Spokane Healing Rooms and author of *Preparing the Way*, was a self-confessed "bored" board member when I came on as pastor. I had called for a special leadership meeting because of what God was starting to do in the church shortly after our arrival. It was obvious that I needed to introduce this new move of God to our leaders so they could actually "lead the charge." Cal did not like what was happening in the church and was attending the meeting out of duty. But God came upon him in one of the most sovereign acts I have ever witnessed. The Holy Spirit came upon him powerfully and apprehended him for a new work. If the Holy Spirit has claws, this man experienced them! God drafted him in a moment of time for something new. He was already born again, headed to Heaven, but God had a purpose for his life that was much higher than he was experiencing. God shook off everything that had held him back. But as he was experiencing this spiritual transformation, there were many in that room who experienced and realized nothing. They were like Jacob before his dream. God was there, and they didn't know it.

God was there, and they didn't know it.

Genesis 28:22—*and this stone that I have set up as a pillar will be God's house...*

BOOK QUOTE: *The Supernatural Power* [Chapter 2]

An important thing about the House of God was that it functioned under an open Heaven, meaning the demonic realm was broken off and there was clarity between the realm of God's dominion and what was happening on earth. It was pictured in Jacob's dream as a ladder with angels ascending and descending (see Genesis 28). Angels ascend when they've completed an assignment and descend when they're on their way to carry out a supernatural task.

(I'm convinced that many angels have been waiting around for decades for Christians to live the risk-filled lifestyle God expects of us. Their job is to bring the reality of God's rule into situations that afflict and torment humans. Hebrews 1:14 tells us, "Are they not all ministering spirits sent forth to minister for those who will inherit salvation?" Angels are necessary to complete the assignment of the Lord. Psalm 104:3 says that God "walks on the wings of the wind." The wind is described as an angelic presence. God is actually ushered into a situation by *riding* on angelic presence. A lifestyle without risks has little need for angelic assistance.)

Jacob awoke from his dream and declared that the place he was in was "none other than the house of God." He couldn't have meant a physical shelter because there were no buildings there. He couldn't have meant the house of God was an organization, tribe, or religious group, because there weren't other people around. He probably was as confused as anyone what the dream meant, and as far as we know he didn't get the answer to his puzzling prophetic dream. The answer arrived hundreds of years later in the person of Jesus, who was the initial fulfillment of this prophecy.

A lifestyle without risks has little need for angelic assistance.

John 1:14—*And the Word became flesh and dwelt among us, and we beheld His glory, the glory as of the only begotten of the Father, full of grace and truth.*

BOOK QUOTE: *The Supernatural Power* [Chapter 2]

DWELT in this verse means "to tabernacle." Jesus *tabernacled* among us—He was the House of God made flesh—the place where God lived. He was the initial fulfillment of the prophetic picture in Genesis 28. The House of God was not a building, location, or denomination, but a Person. We see this illustration expanded later in the Gospel of John where,

> *Nathanael answered and said to Him, "Rabbi, You are the Son of God! You are the King of Israel!" Jesus answered and said to him, "Because I said to you, 'I saw you under the fig tree,' do you believe? You will see greater things than these." And He said to him, "Most assuredly, I say to you, hereafter you shall see Heaven open, and the angels of God ascending and descending upon the Son of Man"* (John 1:49-51).

The fulfillment of the House of God began with Jesus. He was the House of God on earth. But this concept did not stop with Him—far from it. He was the initial fulfillment of the House of God, but not the ultimate fulfillment. There is a big difference. For example, your conversion was not God's ultimate intent for you. It was His initial intent that set you up for the ultimate fulfillment, which is that you be filled with His fullness, living the normal Christian lifestyle as defined by what takes place in Heaven. God's initial fulfillment of the House of God was Jesus, the tabernacle of God on planet Earth.

. . . your conversion was not God's ultimate intent for you.

1 Corinthians 3:16—*Do you not know that you are the temple of God and that the Spirit of God dwells in you? NKJV*

BOOK QUOTE: *The Supernatural Power* [Chapter 2]

I have been to many cities that are known for their darkness. Yet the practices of occult leaders cannot block the open Heaven over any believer who abides in Christ. Even the demoniac, as tormented as he was, couldn't be stopped from his "God encounter" as he fell at Jesus' feet in worship! I never notice the lack of an open Heaven, unless I become impressed with the devil's accomplishments in that city.

Jesus said to His disciples in John 14:16, speaking of the Holy Spirit, "And I will pray the Father, and He will give you another Helper, that He may abide with you forever."

And in Ephesians 2:19-22:

Now, therefore, you are no longer strangers and foreigners, but fellow citizens with the saints and members of the household of God, having been built on the foundation of the apostles and prophets, Jesus Christ Himself being the chief cornerstone, in whom the whole building, being fitted together, grows into a holy temple in the Lord, in whom you also are being built together for a dwelling place of God in the Spirit.

We, the Church, the redeemed, are the tabernacle of the Holy Spirit, the eternal dwelling place of God! We are living stones, according to First Peter 2:4-5, fitly framed together, building the eternal dwelling place of God. The House of God is us! Jacob's dream was not just about the Messiah but about you and me and every born-again believer throughout history. It is the heart of our very identity.

We, the Church, the redeemed, are the tabernacle of the Holy Spirit, the eternal dwelling place of God!

1 Peter 2:5—You also, like living stones, are being built into a spiritual house to be a holy priesthood, offering spiritual sacrifices acceptable to God through Jesus Christ.

BOOK QUOTE: *The Supernatural Power* [Chapter 2]

THE House of God is the picture of God's intention for your life and for everything you do. He wants a house where He will dwell, where angels ascend and descend on assignment and the heavens are open over a people who abide in Him, meaning they stay connected in their affection and love for Him. God wants so much to invade this world with the reality of what was purchased on Calvary. But He waits for a people who will live the normal Christian life, putting themselves at risk, constantly tapping into the invisible resources of Heaven that have been standing idle. That is how we function as the House of God.

If we understand and are confident in our identity as the House of God, we can do great exploits. No power of darkness in any realm of creation can stop our fellowship with the Father. There is an open Heaven over each one of us, from the newest Christian to the most mature. Being the House of God means we have the exact authority Jesus has at the right hand of the Father. We are entitled and empowered to be His "House," His embodiment on earth. As a Christian at this very moment, you have absolute liberty and access to Heaven.

But some of our ladders have not been used in quite a long time. There are no angels coming or going because we haven't stepped into the area of the supernatural. That's our problem. To be the House of God, we must bustle and brim with the life, joy, healing, and peace that is normal in Heaven. We must set our hearts on being a House filled with His glory wherever we go.

There is an open Heaven over each one of us, from the newest Christian to the most mature.

Psalm 24:7—Lift up your heads, O you gates; be lifted up, you ancient doors, that the King of glory may come in.

BOOK QUOTE: *The Supernatural Power* [Chapter 2]

BESIDES ladders and houses, gates are also mentioned in Genesis 28. Jacob said, "This is none other than the house of God, and this is the gate of Heaven!" (Gen. 28:17). In this context and elsewhere in the Bible, "gate" seems to mean a place of transition and access. In the natural you might walk through a gate to go from your front yard to the sidewalk, or from your backyard to your driveway. In the same way, when we talk about the Church being the gate of heaven, we are referring to the place where the reality of His dominion becomes available for all of mankind—His world invades ours!

The Church is the gate of Heaven (another way of saying the House of God). Now Jesus introduced the idea of the gate of hell. When I was younger, I read this wrong somehow and thought it meant that "the gates of Heaven will prevail against the assault of the enemy." That fit my theology better back then. I saw the Church as a group of people locked inside a compound, shoulders against the gate, trying to hold the fort as the devil and his powerful minions beat against it. I saw the Church in a posture of fear and weakness, trying to protect what we had until God hurried up and rescued us from the big, bad devil. But Jesus gave us an opposite picture. He said, "The gates of hell will not prevail." The principalities and powers that set up dominions or "gates" all over the earth will not prevail against us! We are advancing and winning, and Jesus promises that in the end, no gate of hell will stand.

> *The Church is the gate of Heaven*
> *(another way of saying the House of God).*

2 Corinthians 10:15—...*bringing every thought into captivity to the obedience of Christ.*

BOOK QUOTE: *The Supernatural Power* [Chapter 2]

From that time Jesus began to show to His disciples that He must go to Jerusalem, and suffer many things from the elders and chief priests and scribes, and be killed, and be raised the third day. Then Peter took Him aside and began to rebuke Him, saying, "Far be it from You, Lord; this shall not happen to You!" But He turned and said to Peter, "Get behind Me, Satan! You are an offense to Me, for you are not mindful of the things of God, but the things of men" (Matthew 16:21-23).

HE didn't say, "Peter, you devil worshiper!" He didn't say, "You are filled with all kinds of occult practices and deceits." He said, "Your mind is filled with the things of man." A most important thing to remember is that the devil is empowered by human agreement! That mental posture was a gate from which satan was released to bring his destruction. To say, "I'm only human," is to say, "I'm only satanic." Humanity without Christ at the center is satanic in nature. When you've been given the Spirit of God, you lose the privilege of claiming, "I'm only human." You are much more than that! In fact Paul rebukes the church at Corinth for *behaving like mere men* (1 Cor. 3:3). Second Corinthians 10:5 confirms the location of the gate of hell.

The gate of hell is in our minds any time we agree with the enemy. I empower him any time I agree with a man-centered perspective or natural wisdom that does not know God. I empower demonic forces and become a gate to release his power to kill, steal, and destroy in my life. It's chilling, but the Bible indicates it's a fact.

The gate of hell is in our minds any time we agree with the enemy.

John 3:12— *If I have told you earthly things and you do not believe, how will you believe if I tell you heavenly things?*

BOOK QUOTE: *The Supernatural Power* [Chapter 2]

OUR goal is to agree with Heaven all the time, to let our minds be the gate of Heaven where angels ascend and descend freely on assignment from God. It's not that they literally flow through our minds. It's just that they are released through our agreement. The original New American Standard Bible confirms this when it says, "Whatever you bind on earth shall have been bound in Heaven, and whatever you loose on earth shall have been loosed in Heaven" (Matthew 16:19, NASB).

This was the entire focus of Jesus' ministry, and it's a great word of authority to us. Whatever we bind has already been bound. Our task is to see what is bound up there, and then bind it down here. Whatever is free in the heavenly realm to function needs to be released here. We are to be a gateway people for the free flow of heavenly realities into this planet.

How do we know what is bound and loosed in Heaven? Who tells us what Heaven's reality looks like? The only way to know these things and to function as the House of God and gate of Heaven is to have revelation of what is happening in Heaven. Otherwise, we're working in the dark. God has always wanted to release truth to His people, backed by the Word, of things that are found in heaven but have no earthly parallel.

Jesus desires to reveal things to us about what's happening in the spiritual realm that have no corresponding earthly picture. But, first we must learn to hunger for and receive revelation as part of our everyday lives. That revelation will help us to carry out our earthly assignments with greater precision and wisdom.

Our goal is to agree with Heaven all the time, to let our minds be the gate of Heaven where angels ascend and descend freely on assignment from God.

Ephesians 1:17b— *...give to you the spirit of wisdom and revelation in the knowledge of Him.*

BOOK QUOTE: *The Supernatural Power* [Chapter 3]

THE nature of revelation is it that it opens up new realms of living, of possibility, of faith. It is absolutely impossible to live the normal Christian life without receiving regular revelation from God. The Bible does not say, "My people perish for a lack of miracles," or lack of money, or because of bad relationships or bad worship leaders or insufficient nursery staff, or anything else we could list. It says, "My people are destroyed for lack of knowledge" (Hos. 4:6). Proverbs 29:18 says similarly, "Where there is no revelation, the people cast off restraint." A more correct and complete translation is: "Without a prophetic revelation, the people go unrestrained, walking in circles, having no certain destiny."

The biblical word *vision* doesn't mean "goals." Goals are fine, but this *vision* is referring to the spirit of revelation coming upon you, giving you a vision of things that are unseen. Revelation is so essential in our lives that without it we perish. This is not a nice vitamin pill we can take or leave. This is what we live by. Without unfolding prophetic revelation that expands your capacity to see life from God's perspective, you will perish. Without seeing your present circumstances through God's eyes, you will spiritually die. It is so vital that Paul wrote to the Ephesians—those who seemed to have their act together in every area, who experienced perhaps the greatest revival recorded in the New Testament—and said he prayed that God would give them the spirit of wisdom and revelation (see Ephesians 1:17b above).

If the revival-steeped Ephesian church needed to be reminded of the importance of revelation, we need to hear it much more. Revelation is critical to the normal Christian life.

Revelation is so essential in our lives that without it we perish.

1 Corinthians 2:11—*For who among men knows the thoughts of a man except the man's spirit within him? In the same way no one knows the thoughts of God except the Spirit of God.*

BOOK QUOTE: *The Supernatural Power* [Chapter 3]

MANY Christians don't tune in to God's revelation. Paul put it well when he wrote,

Now we have received, not the spirit of the world, but the Spirit who is from God, that we might know the things that have been freely given to us by God. ...But the natural man does not receive the things of the Spirit of God, for they are foolishness to him; nor can he know them, because they are spiritually discerned (1 Corinthians 2:12,14).

Right now in the room where you're sitting, movies are playing all around you. If you had the right receiver or satellite dish, you could pick them up. Just because you can't see the waves passing through doesn't mean they aren't there. With the right receiver you could watch any number of television shows, ball games, talk shows, or listen to private conversations on cell phones and short wave radio. But without the proper receiver, you won't pick up anything.

Likewise, the Bible says the natural man does not *receive* the things of the Spirit of God. If God is speaking on FM radio and we are on AM, we can turn that dial all the way to the left, then go slowly over every station. We can quote verses with every turn of the dial. We can claim the promises of God. We can do anything we want to, but as long as we are on AM and He is on FM, we are not going to receive His message because the natural man is receiving.

*. . . the natural man does not **receive** the things of the Spirit of God.*

Jeremiah 29:11—For I know the plans I have for you," declares the Lord, "plans to prosper you and not to harm you, plans to give you hope and a future."

BOOK QUOTE: *The Supernatural Power* [Chapter 3]

THE key is to be spiritually discerning—to open our spirit man to direct revelation from God. The Bible says,

But as it is written: "Eye has not seen, nor ear heard, nor have entered into the heart of man the things which God has prepared for those who love Him." But God has revealed them to us through His Spirit. For the Spirit searches all things, yes, the deep things of God (1 Corinthians 2:9-10).

The Holy Spirit searches for things that have never been heard by human ears or seen by human eyes. He is the greatest search engine in the whole universe. Talk about quick and accurate! He searches the greatest reservoir of information imaginable—the heart of the Father. Psalm 139:18 says that God's thoughts about each one of us outnumber the sands on every seashore on this planet: *"Were I to count them, they would outnumber the grains of sand. When I awake I am with you."*

According to Jeremiah 29:11, all those thoughts are for your welfare, benefit, and blessing. God has been around a long time, and He has had a long time to think about you. He's been living in the experience of knowing you long before you were ever born. He doesn't just have a few random thoughts about you here and there. For trillions of years, God has been thinking about you, and the Holy Spirit searches that whole archive and brings incredible treasures to you at precisely the right moment—if you're listening.

For trillions of years,
God has been thinking about you...

Proverbs 14:6—*The mocker seeks wisdom and finds none, but knowledge comes easily to the discerning.*

BOOK QUOTE: *The Supernatural Power* [Chapter 3]

MOST born-again people know what it's like to be in confusion or trouble and have someone speak a word that brings a supernatural invasion of peace into their soul. You might not even have all of the answers you thought you needed five minutes ago, but for some reason, you don't care. Their words were the spirit of revelation from God Himself. The same way that Jesus became flesh, the Holy Spirit becomes words, and when they are spoken, they bring life (John 6:63). We wrap our hearts around it, and eventually it will start making sense.

Some people get torrents of revelation, and others don't. This may depend on how we build our support structure. There are pillar truths in the gospel that form the most basic foundation of the structure. A man of understanding accepts God's additions and doesn't question them. He is not double-minded about them. That's how a person of understanding attracts greater understanding. You treasure something that God says, and that builds a foundation for greater revelation.

Another way to attract revelation is to obey what we know. One man came to Jesus and asked what to do to gain eternal life (Luke 10:25-28). Jesus said, "What does it say to do?" The man pressed Jesus for more, but Jesus wouldn't give him any new information. Until he walked in obedience, he wasn't going to get more.

Obedience is a signal to God that says, "God, I want to go the next step." That tender heart draws the spirit of revelation to a person and/or to a body of people. They begin seeing and hearing things they never heard or saw before. The Bible even says, "He will seal up that instruction in our heart in the night while we sleep" (Job 33:15-16).

The same way that Jesus became flesh, the Holy Spirit becomes words, and when they are spoken, they bring life.

Romans 16:25—*Now to him who is able to establish you by my gospel and the proclamation of Jesus Christ, according to the revelation of the mystery hidden for long ages past...*

BOOK QUOTE: *The Supernatural Power* [Chapter 3]

You'll know when God is speaking because it will have a freshness to it. It will always be better than anything you could have thought up yourself. And if He gives you new ideas, they will probably be impossible for you to accomplish in your own strength. His thoughts will so overwhelm you that you'll want to draw close to Him so they can be accomplished.

Revelation is for every single believer, not just for some "gifted" folks. The greater revelation that a person carries, the greater faith he or she is able to exercise. If I believe it's not God's desire to heal everybody then my revelation limits me every time a person comes to me who is sick. I have to settle it in my heart—is it really God's will to heal people? As long as I shun the revelation that God wants everybody to be healed and whole, I have cut myself off from releasing faith in that area. Revelation enlarges the arena that our faith can function in. Deception shrinks our area of faith.

If you believe that only the Benny Hinns of the world can pray for the sick and get consistent success, then your faith will operate within the limits of that misconception. But what if Jesus' words come alive to you, as in Matthew 10:1-42 where He sent them out and told them to heal the sick, raise the dead, cleanse the leper, and cast out devils? What if you realized that the lifestyle Jesus lived and taught is meant to be *your* lifestyle? Revelation would broaden the boundaries for your faith to operate in.

Revelation is for every single believer, not just for some "gifted" folks.

Matthew 13:10-11—*The disciples came to Him and asked, "Why do you speak to the people in parables?" He replied, "The knowledge of the secrets of the kingdom of heaven has been given to you, but not to them."*

BOOK QUOTE: *The Supernatural Power* [Chapter 3]

REVELATION is not something you can dig out of a theological book or study guide. It's not even something you can unravel in the Bible all by yourself. Revelation is locked up in a realm the Bible calls "mystery." A mystery cannot be hunted down and trapped like an animal. It can't be discovered by persistent searching. It must be revealed. We don't unlock mysteries; they are unlocked for us. And they are only unlocked and revealed to those who hunger for them. Jesus said He concealed truth in parables so it remained a mystery to some, but not for others. In the same way He put gold in the rocks and said, "If you want it, go find it and dig it out." The Bible says, "It is the glory of God to conceal a matter, but the glory of kings is to search out a matter" (Proverbs 25:2).

God doesn't take the pearls of revelation—those things that were gained through hardship and difficulty, conflict and irritation—and freely throw them out to anybody. If we want to receive revelation we need the assistance of God's Spirit. Paul confirms this when he tells the Corinthians that he did not speak using the wisdom of man but the wisdom that comes from the mystery of God. He tells them that this is "hidden wisdom" that comes from the Spirit of God. (See 1 Corinthians 2:6-8.)

Revelation is locked up in a realm the
Bible calls "mystery."

1 Corinthians 2:4—*My message and my preaching were not with wise and persuasive words, but with a demonstration of the Spirit's power, so that your faith might not rest on men's wisdom, but on God's power.*

BOOK QUOTE: *The Supernatural Power* [Chapter 3]

WE cannot enter into revelation without the assistance of the Spirit of God. First Corinthians 2:6-8 confirms this when it says:

However, we speak wisdom among those who are mature, yet not the wisdom of this age, nor of the rulers of this age, who are coming to nothing. But we speak the wisdom of God in a mystery, the hidden wisdom which God ordained before the ages for our glory, which none of the rulers of this age knew; for had they known, they would not have crucified the Lord of glory.

Unfortunately, mystery is not something that most people in the Western world appreciate. We have this idea that God knows our address and if He wants us to have an insight or experience, He will send it to us. We don't want to work for it or hunger after it. The spirit of self-pity has found tremendous home in this culture, but self-pity doesn't attract a visitation of God. Faith does. Faith moves the economy of Heaven. It is the very currency of Heaven.

Mystery should be a continual part of your life. You should always have more questions than answers. If your encounters with God don't leave you with more questions than when you started, then you have had an inferior encounter. A relationship with God that does not stir up that realm of mystery and wonder is an inferior relationship. It would help all of us a great deal if we had to walk out of a few more church services, scratching our heads, wondering what just took place. He is the God of wonder, the God of awe! But tenderness of heart enables us to come into the realm of revelation that unlocks the mysteries of God.

We cannot enter into revelation without the assistance of the Spirit of God.

Jeremiah 33:3—*Call to Me and I will answer you and tell you great and unsearchable things you do not know.*

BOOK QUOTE: *The Supernatural Power* [Chapter 3]

WE can't snap our fingers and cause ourselves to have revelation; we still must hunger for it and pursue it (See Jeremiah 33:3 above.)

The word *mighty* is an Old Testament word that is similar to the New Testament word *mystery*. It's a picture of something that is out of reach, unattainable, behind fortification. God has hidden mighty and mysterious things *for* us, not *from* us. He has already allotted to us this mysterious realm of the Kingdom, but it doesn't come to just anyone. It comes to those who are open and hungry for it. Jeremiah used the word *call*, which means "to cry out to the Lord in a very loud voice." Picture a person desperate enough to open his or her heart fully and issue a deep cry from the spirit. That deep part of man calls to the deep part of God (Ps. 42:7). That opening of the heart determines the level of revelation we receive. Few people I know receive substantial revelations or visitations of God without reckless pursuit. Most people I know who receive revelation cry out day and night for that fullness of the Holy Spirit. Casual prayer gets casual revelation. Deep cries cause God to "hear you" and "answer you" and "show you great and mighty things you do not know."

This is the Old Testament equivalent of the promise of Ephesians 3:20 when it says,

"Now to Him who is able to do exceedingly abundantly above all that we ask or think, according to the power that works in us."

First Corinthians 2:9 says, "Eye has not seen, nor ear heard, nor have entered into the heart of man the things which God has prepared for those who love Him."

Casual prayer gets casual revelation.

2 Peter 1:2—*Grace and peace be multiplied to you in the knowledge of God and of Jesus our Lord.*

BOOK QUOTE: *The Supernatural Power* [Chapter 3]

PRAYER—the desperate cry of the heart of man—initiates the beginning of revelation to your heart and mind.

The spirit of revelation opens up our knowledge of who God is, and from that comes the release of power from Heaven. That power gives us access to all things pertaining to life and godliness. That encounter with God will not only shape the world around you, it will shape the world *through* you.

The most revered people in the Old Testament were the prophets because of the spirit of revelation that came upon them. Kings feared them. They knew that they could do anything in secret and the prophets would know. The Bible even says, "Surely the Lord God does nothing, unless He reveals His secret to His servants the prophets" (Amos 3:7). And now that spirit of revelation is not limited to people with unique gifts. It is liberally given to anyone who will pursue and ask—including you.

Hosea 6 says that we press on to know the Lord, meaning we seek an encounter with God, a revelation that launches us into a new awareness of how life is to be lived.

"Let us know, let us pursue the knowledge of the Lord" (Hosea 6:3).

The cry of Hosea was, "Let's press on—no, let's hunt down and chase the encounter with God that changes our understanding of reality." That is the kind of relentless pursuit each believer should have about the things of God. We need revelation to renew our minds, to help us prove the will of God on earth as it is in Heaven.

The spirit of revelation opens up our knowledge of who God is, and from that comes the release of power from Heaven.

Hosea 6:3—*Let us know, let us pursue the knowledge of the Lord.*

BOOK QUOTE: *The Supernatural Power* [Chapter 3]

I can't live life knowing there are realms of mystery, and keys to those realms, that are available to me but which I have not yet discovered. I can't sit back and say, "If it's God's will, He can drop a revelation into my lap." I need more, constantly. My spirit is hungry for things I have not yet known. Sometimes I get around certain people whose gifts and personality are so different yet so complementary to mine that I get revelation so fast in conversation I wish I had a tape recorder with me at all times. I get knowledge that connects 15 other things I've been thinking about and ties them all together. Those are wonderful times.

And yet I know that as Christians, we will always live in tension between what we understand and what remains a mystery. Years ago a famous author made a comment on a series of books he had written saying, "I don't know what is wrong with them, but they are too perfect. They answer every question and remove the realm of mystery. So I know something is wrong."

We cannot afford to live only in what we understand because then we don't grow or progress anymore; we just travel the same familiar roads we have traveled all of our Christian life. It is important that we expose ourselves to impossibilities that force us to have questions that we cannot answer. It is a part of the Christian life, which is why the Christian life is called "the faith." The normal Christian life is perfectly poised between what we presently understand and the unfolding revelation that comes to us from the realm of mystery.

It is important that we expose ourselves to impossibilities that force us to have questions that we cannot answer.

Amos 9:13—*"The days are coming," declares the Lord, "when the reaper will be overtaken by the plowman and the planter by the one treading grapes. New wine will drip from the mountains and flow from all the hills."*

BOOK QUOTE: *The Supernatural Power* [Chapter 3]

THE realm of mystery and revelation goes far beyond what we normally think of as "ministry." There are vast resources of revelation in Heaven for the areas of education and business, the arts and music, and these resources have yet to be tapped anywhere near to their fullness. There are melodies that have never been played or considered. There is lyrical content that would minister deeply to the Church and stir the world to conversion. Our job is to tap the revelation of the Lord in our area of talent or gifting so that we can accurately and powerfully reflect the King and His Kingdom.

I'm convinced that the pace of revelation will increase very rapidly in these last hours of history. Amos 9:13 says, "the plowman [will] overtake the reaper," meaning the seasons won't be so distinct anymore. They will overlap so that planting and harvesting occur in the same motion. We will live in a supernatural season when understanding will come much more quickly and bear fruit much more dramatically. We already see acceleration in history in the development of technology, science, and medicine. The knowledge of man is increasing, but don't think for a moment that God will not do equally and more so for the Church in spiritual matters. He is looking for men and women of understanding. He is ready to add the plywood to the frame of understanding, but we've got to have the framing in place first. He is ready to put on the drywall and the decorations and release revelation to each of us in quantities we've not yet known.

... the pace of revelation will increase very rapidly in these last hours of history.

Jeremiah 31:34—*No longer will a man teach his neighbor, or a man his brother, saying, "Know the Lord," because they will all know me, from the least of them to the greatest.*

BOOK QUOTE: *The Supernatural Power* [Chapter 3]

I believe that the pace of revelation will increase very rapidly in these last days. That acceleration of revelation is beginning in our day. God is presently wooing people into intimacy so they know how He thinks and moves. People are coming alive to that wooing and, in the process, to their sense of destiny. It's not about the greatness or accomplishment of any particular person or church. It's about the purposes of God being unveiled on the planet. On-going revelation and encounters with the power of God launch us into understanding of things we've never understood before.

Presently, every denomination, church, and group seems to have revelation into certain Kingdom matters. Nobody has the whole picture; God refuses to give it all to one person or one group because He wants us to be interdependent members of one another. But in these last days God is going to release a Spirit of revelation over the Church where we repent over our areas of great difference because we see Him as He is, we hear His word as He declares it, and we are literally taught by the Spirit. We are coming into an hour where there will be a common revelation, (see Ephesians 4:13) a time when, as the Bible says, "all shall know Him" (Jer. 31:34). I believe it is talking about an hour when the people of God will simultaneously hear and see similar revelations, no matter the group or church.

Let's be people of on-going, life-changing revelation from God. But let's never allow revelation to stop there. It must lead to direct, hands-on experience to have any effect at all.

Let's be people of on-going, life-changing revelation from God.

Proverbs 20:5—*The purposes of a man's heart are deep waters, but a man of understanding draws them out.*

BOOK QUOTE: *The Supernatural Power* [Chapter 4]

FOLLOWING an extended time of ministry in Africa, a ministry team from our church went to Johannesburg, South Africa. They came across a homeless man named Peter who was in a wheelchair. Peter shared how he'd been paralyzed for 11 years after falling from a height of 4 stories. He couldn't feel anything from his waist down and could barely move his arms. The day before, local hoods had taken him to a field and left him to die. Peter had given up on life, but heard God say, "If you stay here, you're going to die." So he crawled all the way back to town using only his arms.

The team prayed for him and Peter's leg started shaking crazily. "What's happening to me?" he cried out. He began to weep and repent for being mad at God. They lifted him up and he began to walk. The man who had pushed Peter's wheelchair for many years was saved, too, and they all sang together, "Our God is an awesome God."

People stopped out of curiosity, and soon they were saved and filled with the Holy Spirit. Then a car drove up, and the driver was impatiently trying to get past the crowd. Team members approached the car and discovered that one of its occupants had been the one who robbed Peter and left him in the field to die. That man got out of the back seat and fled from the scene. The other two saw how Peter was healed, and they gave their lives to Christ. In all there were around a dozen new Christians, some filled with the Holy Spirit, and a cripple who wasn't crippled anymore. We must require an experience from what we believe.

In all there were around a dozen new Christians, some filled with the Holy Spirit, and a cripple who wasn't crippled anymore.

Luke 8:21—*He replied, "My mother and brothers are those who hear God's Word and put it into practice."*

BOOK QUOTE: *The Supernatural Power* [Chapter 4]

RECEIVING revelation is not enough; we need experience in putting revelation into practice. You see, renewing the mind is not merely reading words on a page and having a moment of revelation about a particular verse. That passes for renewal of the mind in many churches, but at best that's only half the equation. Renewal comes as revelation leads you *into a new experience with God*, as those people had that day in South Africa. You may have a moment of inspiration while reading the Bible or listening to someone preach from the Scriptures, but without taking the next step into experience, the process stalls and there is no renewal.

Jesus put it this way in John 5:39:

You search the Scriptures, for in them you think you have eternal life; and these are they which testify of Me.

This says clearly that revelation is meant to bring us into an encounter with God, and if it doesn't, it only makes us more religious. Revelation is never given to increase our head knowledge. That's a by-product, at best. We are probably all so "smart" in biblical things that we could drown in the flood of information! Some theologians read the Scriptures 12 hours a day and have no clue about the Kingdom of God. They can recite endless evidence of their knowledge, but there is nothing revelatory or transforming about their lives. That has happened to many Christians who have at times embraced a routine of reading Scripture without letting the reading lead to experience. To renew the mind we must not just *think* differently but *live* differently, in a new experience of the empowerment of the Holy Spirit.

Renewal comes as revelation leads you
into a new experience with God,...

Isaiah 52:7—How beautiful on the mountains are the feet of those who bring good news, who proclaim peace, who brings good tidings, who proclaim salvation, who say to Zion, "Your God reigns!"

BOOK QUOTE: *The Supernatural Power* [Chapter 4]

THREE young people from our church were at an ice cream shop one evening when they suddenly felt the presence and power of God come upon them, almost like a burst of fire. Realizing that God was up to something, they looked around for an opportunity to participate in the impossible and they saw a young man on crutches. They approached him and struck up conversation. He said he had fallen from 15 feet in the air into 2 feet of water, breaking his tailbone. He didn't reveal it then, but he was a star running back at one of the local high schools. They prayed for him and suddenly he dropped his crutches and started jumping up and down. Then he took off running back and forth as fast as an athlete in competition. People in the parking lot stared in amazement and befuddlement. He kept yelling, "Praise God! Praise God! I've always wanted God to do something like this to me!" He was completely healed.

Those young people put into practice their revelation of God's power to heal. Instead of having a simple evening at the ice cream shop, they sought out an opportunity for God to do a miracle. That's how to put revelation to work!

When God reveals things to us, we must put those things to work. If we don't, we will lose the power and opportunity that revelation offers us. Jesus warned, "When anyone hears the word of the kingdom, and does not understand it, then the wicked one comes and snatches away what was sown in his heart" (Matthew 13:19).

When God reveals things to us, we must put those things to work.

Matthew 13:23—*But the one who received the seed that fell o good soil is the man who hears the word and understands it. He produces a crop, yielding a hundred, sixty or thirty times what was sown.*

BOOK QUOTE: *The Supernatural Power* [Chapter 4]

THE revelation of the Kingdom is spoken of as a living seed of another world that carries with it new possibilities. But when a person hears the word but doesn't understand it, the enemy has open access to that seed and can snatch it away. In our culture, we define understanding as nothing more than cognitive reasoning, coming to conclusions, fully comprehending. In Eastern culture, which is the culture of Scripture, understanding is an *experience*. It means engaging in activities that involve our five senses. In fact, the Greek word for *understanding* in this verse means "learning which takes place through the five senses." It means *doing*, as in *practical human experience*. The biblical view of understanding means far more than to give mental assent; it means to practice in real life what one has come to know by revelation. That's why the Jewish leaders said the words above to Jesus.

To understand also means yielding to something before you can explain, define, or describe it. Biblical understanding far surpasses the intellect. Hebrews 11:3 says, "By faith we understand that the worlds were framed by the word of God, so that the things which are seen were not made of things which are visible." We don't have faith because we understand, but we understand because we have faith. In other words, it is imperative to accept and understand things without completely satisfying your intellect. Biblical learning takes place in the spirit first, and as we obey the Spirit of God, our spirit communicates it to our minds so we intellectually understand. But understanding is not required for obedience. A *normal Christian* is "one who obeys the revelations and promptings of the Holy Spirit without understanding." Understanding usually unfolds in the experience.

We don't have faith because we understand, but we understand because we have faith.

Hebrews 11:3—*By faith we understand that the worlds were framed by the word of God, so that the things which are seen was not made of things which are visible.*

BOOK QUOTE: *The Supernatural Power* [Chapter 4]

To understand, we must obey revelations and put them into practice. As an example, let's say I speak to my church about caring for the poor. People may be moved in their emotions. But if they don't do something practical within the next two to three weeks—perhaps finding a poor family to help out, or volunteering at a soup kitchen—then that word is open to be taken from the heart, where it has the place to transform their lives. Revelation takes us only halfway there; experience leads us all the way. The great tragedy is that if you don't move into experience, that revelation remains locked in your mind so you think it's active in your life. The next time you hear a message about helping the poor you might say, "Amen. The other people in this room need to hear that," even though you have done nothing to help the poor. Hearing without doing has locked you into a form without power.

There are great audiences, great crowds of people, great denominations and movements that would fight to the death to defend divine healing, or prophecy, or many other practices, but they never see those things happen. They think, "I understand the concept. I agree that it happens. If it's God's will, He knows my address and He can give me that grace." They have the revelation, but can't point to any proof of its validity in their personal experience. They can't show anyone how to do it. Their mental concept insulates them from the conviction that anything more needs to happen. They develop anesthesia that deadens their sensitivity to personal transformation. They are robbed of experience and can only recite back principles. It is pure religion, form without power.

Revelation takes us only halfway there;
experience leads us all the way.

2 Corinthians 5:20—*We are therefore Christ's ambassadors, as though God were making His appeal through us.*

BOOK QUOTE: *The Supernatural Power* [Chapter 4]

JESUS said in John 3:13, "No one has ascended to heaven but He who came down from heaven, that is, the Son of man who is in Heaven." Strange verse, isn't it? We tend to only think of Heaven as a place that is out in space somewhere instead of a place that coexists with us. We have a difficult time comprehending and wrapping our hearts around this statement, and so we let it become a nice, encouraging statement with no practical application to our lives. What does it mean, the Son of Man who is in Heaven? What does it say about our job here on earth? Doesn't it mean that, like Jesus, we should live in a posture of dwelling in heavenly realms and living toward the afflictions, infirmities, and difficulties of the world around us? Shouldn't we function as ambassadors of another world, living in the realm of faith, which is the realm of the Spirit, which is called "the kingdom"?

But most of us have not realized that we can demand that the truth become an experience. Revelation should change our hearts before we could ever explain what we learned. The Bible says we are, as a matter of fact, seated at the right hand of the Father in Christ Jesus in heavenly places. This was written for us to experience, not so we have good theology, or so that our doctrinal statements are accurate and concise. Statements like this are launching pads into encounters where we experience the very things that are on the page. Jesus here is showing us what is possible to any person that has been cleansed of sin by the blood of Jesus.

Revelation should change our hearts before we could ever explain what we learned.

Luke 22:29—And I confer on you a kingdom, just as my Father conferred one on Me.

BOOK QUOTE: *The Supernatural Power* [Chapter 4]

WHILE the experience of salvation by faith has always been a part of the true Church, this revelation was put on the back burner for most. But a few hundred years ago, it was moved to the forefront, and the Church began to proclaim again that salvation is only by faith. Many died not knowing the assurance of their salvation. But because the Church embraced this revelation wholeheartedly, teaching it, practicing it, building up people's faith in it, today we consider it the simplest thing in the world. We pray for a sinner to receive Jesus, and we have absolutely no doubt that he or she will be instantly converted. Many of us don't realize that it's only "easy" now because previous generations labored in planting and watering this revelation by putting it into practice. For two centuries the Church in this nation has not lost sight of the power of conversion. It has taught it, preached it, gone into the streets with it, written books about it. Today we are riding the wave of a heritage of faith that has increased for many generations.

A similar thing happened with worship. Over the last hundred years or so, worship has changed significantly. It used to be staid and somber, never personal in its expression to God. Then certain churches and movements began to worship with exuberance, loud voices and raised hands—expressions that most mainstream Christians of the day rejected and ridiculed. Those "extreme worshipers" paid a price. But today you can go into almost any brand of church and see people exalting the name of Jesus with hands and voices raised. Our understanding of this revelation has come through experience and practice, and the church's "mind" has been renewed.

Today we are riding the wave of a heritage of faith that has increased for many generations.

James 5:16—*Therefore confess your sins to each other so that you may be healed. The prayer of a righteous man is powerful and effective.*

BOOK QUOTE: *The Supernatural Power* [Chapter 4]

CHRISTIANS are absolutely responsible for bringing divine healing to people, "proving the will of God," bringing earthly reality into line with what's true in Heaven. Healing is part of the normal Christian life. God put it in His book; He illustrated it in the Jesus' life. He told us to emulate what Jesus did. So why is it so easy for us to be fully convinced when we pray for someone to be saved that our prayer will work, and yet when we pray for healing we find it difficult to believe they will be healed? Because salvation, as it pertains to a born-again experience, has been embraced and taught continuously by the Church for centuries, while the revelation of healing has not been widely embraced, and has even been fought. Today in many churches, if you pray for people to be healed you are considered to be working under the influence of the devil, while disease is considered a gift from God to make people better Christians! Think about how badly the Church has backslidden, to believe such lies! We have tolerated the deception that accuses God of doing evil, which is why today healing remains so controversial, little-practiced and little-understood.

What would have happened if centuries ago Christians had embraced the power of the gospel to bring healing to the physical body, to the emotions, and to the mind? What if the Church had plowed through that tough soil for generation after generation? Instead of a few "heroes of healing" marking the trail of history, the entire Body of Christ would recognize healing as an essential part of the Great Commission. Normal Christians would see deformities and say, "No problem." Cancer, "No problem." Missing limbs, "No problem." We would pray in power without one iota of doubt.

Christians are absolutely responsible for bringing divine healing to people...

John 9:1-2—*As He went along, He saw a man blind from birth. His disciples asked Him, "Rabbi, who sinned, this man or his parents, that he was born blind?"*

BOOK QUOTE: *The Supernatural Power* [Chapter 4]

Can you imagine Jesus telling blind Bartimaeus, "This blindness is a gift from My Father to make you a better person"? And yet that's the approach most Christians take. They don't understand healing because they have no experience with it. They have not put the revelation into practice. I've grown so tired of people praying for blind people and asking God to open the eyes of their heart. The problem is with their natural eyes! The Church doesn't know what to do with blind people, or anyone with a real affliction.

When you put a revelation into practice, you won't get it 100 percent right. You might not even get it 50 percent right. But you will learn, and you will grow into a level of maturity you wouldn't otherwise have. At our church, the only way we know to learn is to experiment. We fail a lot and occasionally we get it right. But we are light years ahead of where we would have been had we not tried at all. I know people today who get excited when they come across somebody who is physically ill or dying. They see crutches, canes, wheelchairs, and casts, and they rejoice. One young man I know walks into a store and sees somebody with a broken leg and thinks, "God loves me so much that He put a man with a broken leg right in front of me." Then he ministers to them and people get healed! His perspective is absolutely reversed. He does not avoid the impossible; he is drawn to it. He is convinced that God is showing him favor by putting somebody in front of him who needs a supernatural intervention.

When you put a revelation into practice, you won't get it 100 percent right.

Romans 1:17—*For in the gospel a righteousness from God is revealed, a righteousness that is by faith from first to last, just as it is written: "The righteous will live by faith."*

BOOK QUOTE: *The Supernatural Power* [Chapter 4]

ONE pastor and his wife in my area have a passion for healing. They were in a Target parking lot and saw a man with metal crutches, his body twisted up. He was in obvious pain. The pastor's wife asked if she could pray for him and so they took him aside. The man was miserable, and had been praying for 18 years to die. He allowed them to pray and his body untwisted and became straight. He sprinted around the parking lot, came back, picked up his metal crutches, and threw them across the parking lot. He was absolutely set free and healed.

That's what happens when we unpack our revelation and put it to work in people's lives!

One of the most bizarre healings I've seen involved a man who so injured his leg that doctors severed the tendons in his ankles, turned his foot outward for balance and put pins in to lock his ankle. He had no movement, no flex, but he could walk in a limited way. I had a word of knowledge about God healing somebody's left ankle, and this man responded and received prayer. I don't know exactly what God did, but the man gained full use of his ankle, in spite of the complex mechanisms meant to keep it stationary.

Jesus had one concern about His return and it wasn't that He would find people who were excessive. He wants to find faith (see above).

When you put your revelation into practice, what used to be impossible will begin to look logical. Your area of faith will expand. That revelation will bring you into an experience and empower you to do the works of the Kingdom.

When you put your revelation into practice, what used to be impossible will begin to look logical.

Acts 19:11-12—*God did extraordinary miracles through Paul, so that even handkerchiefs and aprons that had touched him were taken to the sick, and their illnesses were cured and the evil spirits left them.*

BOOK QUOTE: *The Supernatural Power* [Chapter 5]

ONE Sunday night a young man in our church fell in the back of the sanctuary and broke his arm. The healing of broken bones, even the ones from decades ago that healed incorrectly, had become commonplace. I found him laid out on the ground, his arm clearly broken. I got down on the ground with him, put my hand on his arm, looked at the break—and suddenly fear stole into my mind. I forgot every miracle I had ever seen, and I said, "Let's call the doctor." Now, I wouldn't fault anyone for calling the doctor in that circumstance. For most it would be the proper thing to do. But for me the moment was personally revealing. I switched from supernatural mode to natural mode. My experience with miracles hadn't fully shaped me. I repented and apologized to the mother a week or so later, not because I felt guilty or ashamed, but because I realized I had a long way to go in having my mind renewed.

We must become students of miracles. That means the miracles we experience must shape how we think. Miracles can be dazzling and dramatic, but they are not primarily designed to dazzle us. God gives us miracles to train us how to see differently. A miracle is a school. We may flunk every test. You can see this happen all the time in churches. When God does a miracle, some people say go home and their life continues on in the very same pattern as before, only now they have one more fun thing they got to see God do.

We must learn to "see" by observing the effect of the unseen world on all that is visible. Miracles provide that opportunity more than any other Christian activity.

We must become students of miracles.

Mark 8:17-18—Do you still not see or understand? Are your hearts hardened? Do you have eyes but fail to see, and ears but fail to hear?

BOOK QUOTE: *The Supernatural Power* [Chapter 5]

JESUS' disciples participated in a mind-boggling miracle of a great multiplication of food (see Mark 6). The multiplication actually took place in *their* hands, not in Jesus' hands, and that's a key point to remember. But—and here's where they flunked the test—later that day, Jesus told them to cross over to the other side in their boat, and He went to a mountainside to pray. There, He saw in His spirit the disciples straining at rowing, almost ready to lose their lives, so He came walking on the sea close enough to check on them. They saw Him and screamed for fear, and He ended up coming into the boat. The winds and the waves stopped. The disciples were completely amazed "For they had not understood about the loaves, because their heart was hardened" (Mark 6:52).

The disciples did everything Jesus said to do, and yet when they got to the next problem, it came to light that they didn't learn the lesson from the previous one.

They should have seen their role in the miracle. Because they didn't see their role in the previous miracle, the next time they encountered a problem and Jesus wasn't in the boat, they had no solution. Jesus had said, "*You* give them something to eat." He didn't say, "I'll do it for you." It was at their touch, their obedience, that the food multiplied. And yet they missed the whole point.

Jesus' goal wasn't to send them into a storm so He could show up and be the hero. He planned to pass by, but they weren't understanding the lesson. They did not extract the nutrients from the last miracle. That hardness of heart prevented them from becoming deliverers, and so Jesus had to deliver them once again.

It was at their touch, their obedience, that the food multiplied. And yet they missed the whole point.

Matthew 13:33—*Another parable He spoke to them: "The kingdom of Heaven is like leaven, which a woman took and hid in three measures of meal till it was all leavened."*

BOOK QUOTE: *The Supernatural Power* [Chapter 5]

JESUS spoke of leaven in Mark 8:13-21:

And He left them, and getting into the boat again, departed to the other side. Now the disciples had forgotten to take bread, and they did not have more than one loaf with them in the boat. Then He charged them, saying, "Take heed, beware of the leaven of the Pharisees and the leaven of Herod." And they reasoned among themselves, saying, "It is because we have no bread." But Jesus, being aware of it, said to them, "Why do you reason because you have no bread? Do you not yet perceive nor understand? Is your heart still hardened? Having eyes, do you not see? And having ears, do you not hear? And do you not remember? When I broke the five loaves for the five thousand, how many baskets full of fragments did you take up?" They said to Him, "Twelve." "Also, when I broke the seven for the four thousand, how many large baskets full of fragments did you take up?" And they said, "Seven." So He said to them, "How is it you do not understand?"

He was warning them about influences on the mind that can rob us of the nutrients of revelation and renewal. Three kinds of leavens are mentioned: the leaven of Herod, the Pharisees, and the Kingdom. These leavens are alive and active today and they greatly affect how you think, how you live, and everything about your life.

Leaven is a picture of influence on our minds. Leaven in the natural realm causes dough to rise. The fire of difficulty causes the leaven in your life to be exposed and brought to the surface. If your mind is permeated by Kingdom leaven, then the Kingdom reality of faith will come to the surface.

The fire of difficulty causes the leaven in your life to be exposed and brought to the surface.

2 Corinthians 4:4—*The god of this age has blinded the minds of unbelievers, so that they cannot see the light of the gospel of the glory of Christ, who is the image of God.*

BOOK QUOTE: *The Supernatural Power* [Chapter 5]

THE leaven of Herod is an atheistic influence based on the strength of man and man-based systems, like politics, popular will, and persuasion. Herod's leaven excludes God entirely. Its statement of faith is a cynical, "God helps those who help themselves." If you found yourself in the boat without bread, the person under this influence would advise, "Next time write a list and remember to bring bread. You are the answer to your own problem. Take responsibility for yourself. Be a self-made person."

Herod's leaven represents one of the big problems in the Church: practical atheism. Large numbers of Christians are practical atheists who disbelieve in an active God. No church's written doctrine would declare there is no God. But believers face situations daily without bringing God into the picture. Like Herod, they say there is no divine intervention in practical living. They are professing Christians but live exactly like their atheist neighbors whenever they face a problem. They don't think to get God's counsel through His Word, or invite God to intervene.

American culture is permeated with the leaven of Herod. We're a country of self-made people, pioneers who think that through determination, discipline, and administrative excellence we can accomplish whatever we want. Sometimes the Church falls into the deception of thinking that whatever we can accomplish in our own strength has been directed or honored by God. But many things the Church has done in the last hundred years, God had nothing to do with. We have money, we have unity of heart and mind, and we have some administrative skills to accomplish our goals. But it doesn't mean they were born in the heart of God. They may have been born of our desire to accomplish something great, whether or not God was involved in our efforts.

. . . believers face situations daily without bringing God into the picture.

Psalm 25:14—*The secret of the Lord is with those who fear Him, and He will show them His covenant.*

BOOK QUOTE: *The Supernatural Power* [Chapter 5]

PHARISEE leaven represents the religious system. It embraces God in theory, but not in practice or experience. The concept of God is essential to the Pharisaical mind, but the experience of God is completely removed. The Pharisees have God in form but without power. Pharisees provides explanations, not solutions.

People under the influence of Pharisee leaven can know Jesus the wrong way, like the people of Nazareth did. They knew Jesus in form, but not in relationship or demonstration (see Mark 6). Today, countless millions in the Church have been satisfied with Pharisee leaven. They are content with some documentation that they belong to a certain brand of church, but they are entirely unplugged from an active, invasive, here-and-now God.

Under the influence of this leaven, many Christians find explanations for physical illnesses that do not bring the power of God into the picture. They say, "That person is tormented by that particular affliction, but with the lifestyle he leads, it's no wonder." They feel cocky at explaining the problem, and yet they are powerless to provide a solution, and they vilify anyone who tries.

Jesus exposed the core characteristic of the influences of Herod and the Pharisees: both are based on the fear of man. Both are primarily motivated by what people think. But when we are influenced by Kingdom leaven, we don't fear what people think about us. God is raising up a people who are considerate, compassionate, and caring, but who are also not motivated one bit by a fear of man. Instead they live out of the fear of God.

Proverbs 29:25 says, "The fear of man brings a snare, but whoever trusts in the Lord shall be safe."

The fear of God makes our sight clear. The fear of man makes us endlessly confused.

... when we are influenced by Kingdom leaven, we don't fear what people think about us.

Matthew 15:9—*They worship Me in vain; their teachings are but rules taught by men.*

BOOK QUOTE: *The Supernatural Power* [Chapter 5]

JESUS warned against Herod's and the Pharisees' leavens because they work against the renewal of our minds. In the immediate context when Jesus spoke these words, the great failure of the disciples was that they were afraid because they didn't pack a lunch, and Jesus had multiplied food for them twice. Their thought life began with what they lacked, and so they contradicted the revelation God had just given them about supernatural provision. They built their thought life on the improper foundation. In the previous chapter of Mark, Jesus said to another set of people, "Thus you have made the commandment of God of no effect by your tradition" (Matt. 15:6). That's what happened to the disciples. The plug gets pulled on God's power whenever we resort to tradition rather than the continual, fresh hearing of the Word of God. Tradition isn't necessarily an evil thing; it's just usually yesterday's word. The Bible says faith comes from hearing—not from having heard.

The disciples had that fresh word, but they didn't get it. "Why do you reason because you have no bread?" Jesus said. "Do you not yet perceive nor understand? Is your heart still hardened?" (Mark 8:17). He did not talk to them this way before they fed the multitudes, because they had no reference point. They did not know by experience what God could do. But God led them into the experience expecting them to make that miracle the new standard for their lives.

When God does a miracle for you, and you get to see it and be a part of it, He is teaching you how to see into the invisible realm. A miracle is a tutor, a gift from God to show us what exists on the other side.

*The Bible says faith comes from hearing—
not from having heard.*

Malachi 3:2—*But who can endure the day of His coming? Who can stand when He appears? For He will be like a refiner's fire or a launderer's soap.*

BOOK QUOTE: *The Supernatural Power* [Chapter 5]

Y OU and I can be the most Kingdom-minded people on the planet when things are going well. We can see dozens healed, dozens saved, have great times of worship. But then I might go home and the car breaks down and suddenly I'm out $3,000. Then the computer shuts off and the phone system goes out, and the neighbor's mad at me. The fire of circumstance expands whatever leaven is influencing my mind. Malachi 4:1 says, "For behold, the day is coming, burning like an oven."

He is talking about a series of events that will draw certain influences to the surface where we can plainly see them—whether we like them or not.

I wish my first response to adversity was always to have faith. Sometimes it takes me a day or two, sometimes only a few minutes to get my heart and mind right. There are times when I get so troubled, so provoked and anxious, and I know biblically there is no reason for it. I always wonder, how can I be so worried and bogged down by pressures when He bought me with a price, gave me His Son, and will freely give me all things? Only because the leaven of Herod or the Pharisees has worked its way into my soul, and the pressure caused the leaven to rise.

Kingdom thinking knows that anything is possible at any time. It's activated when you and I with tender hearts surrender to the thought patterns of God, when we receive His imaginations and say "yes." We want our minds to be full of Kingdom leaven, Kingdom influence. We want miracles, and we want those miracles to have their full effect on us, changing the way we see and behave.

The Bible says faith comes from hearing—
not from having heard.

Mark 4:39-41— *Then He arose and rebuked the wind, and said to the sea, "Peace, be still!" And the wind ceased and there was a great calm. But He said to them, "Why are you so fearful? How is it that you have no faith?" And they feared exceedingly, and said to one another, "Who can this be, that even the wind and the sea obey Him!"*

BOOK QUOTE: *The Supernatural Power* [Chapter 5]

THE storms of life, like miracles, can present terrific challenges and opportunities for us to grow. But it makes a great deal of difference which kind of storm you're in. Some storms, though sent by the devil, can provoke us and invite us to use the revelation we already have. They are miracles waiting to happen. Mark 4:35-38:

> *On the same day, when evening had come, He said to them, "Let us cross over to the other side." Now when they had left the multitude, they took Him along in the boat as He was. And other little boats were also with Him. And a great windstorm arose, and the waves beat into the boat, so that it was already filling. But He was in the stern, asleep on a pillow. And they awoke Him and said to Him, "Teacher, do You not care that we are perishing?"*

The disciples' storm was sent by the devil to keep them from the will of God. So many of us see the storm and pray what the disciples prayed when they saw Jesus sleeping in the boat: "Don't You care that we're perishing?" Jesus got up and answered their prayer. Most of us feel good when God answers our prayers. But Jesus turned to them and said, "How come you don't have any faith?"

"Wait a minute," they might have thought. "I had enough faith to come and to talk to You! And You did what I asked!" No, it is our responsibility to command that obstacle to disappear. Most people's ministry involves trying to get God to fix problems on earth when we should be commanding the storms to be calm. We should see situations from Heaven's perspective and declare the word of the Lord—and watch Heaven invade.

Some storms, though sent by the devil, can provoke us and invite us to use the revelation we already have.

Jonah 1:8—*So they asked him, "Tell us for who is responsible for making all this trouble for us?"*

BOOK QUOTE: *The Supernatural Power* [Chapter 5]

THERE are storms that God sends to show us we're going in the wrong direction:

But the Lord sent out a great wind on the sea, and there was a mighty tempest on the sea, so that the ship was about to be broken up…. So the captain came to him, and said to him, "What do you mean, sleeper? Arise, call on your God; perhaps your God will consider us, so that we may not perish"
(Jonah 1:4-6).

Jonah's storm was sent by God to turn him back to the will of God. Some people face storms because they took a left when God took a right. God brings a storm in His mercy to drive them back. Others face storms *because they are in the middle of God's will.* He doesn't like the storm, but He wants to train you to use tools He's given you to calm the storm.

Most of us find ourselves in a storm and instantly conclude our job is to cry out to God to intervene and change our circumstance. But that's not the purpose of the storm. God never allows a storm without first providing the tools to calm the storm. He wants us to use those tools to bring about a miraculous result. Think of the greatest conflict or crisis in your life in the last year. I assure you, with some examination, you can identify the tools God put in your life to take care of that problem. He allows problems into our lives so we can defeat them—not only so we can cry out to Him every time. The tools will be in the boat with us, but the enemy will fan the winds of fear to get us to forget where the tools are.

God never allows a storm without first providing the tools to calm the storm.

Jonah 2:7—*When my life was ebbing away, I remembered you, Lord, and my prayer rose to you, to your holy temple.*

BOOK QUOTE: *The Supernatural Power* [Chapter 5]

I love and respect the ministry of intercession. But many intercessors moan, weep and are depressed all of the time and call that intercession. They never come into a place of faith when they pray. There have been seasons when I prayed great lengths of time, very diligently, very disciplined, very impressive if I were to have counted the hours. God never penalized me because He knew the sincerity of my heart. But in reality, of the time I spent praying, very little of it was in faith. Most of it was in depression, discouragement or "burden."

The tragedy is that many believers can't yet distinguish the difference between the burden of the Lord and the weight of their own unbelief.

The worse some people feel when they're through praying, the more they feel gratified to be an anointed intercessor. It's okay to start there, but do whatever is necessary to arrive at a place of faith.

That kind of wayward intercession is the opposite of what Jesus expects of us when we face storms. If Jesus is sleeping in your boat, it's not because He's waiting for you to wake Him up with your wailing or earnest prayers. It's because you have divine purpose. He's wanting you to use the tools He has given you to bring about the "heavenly" result. Some teachers teach that God likes to wait until the last minute to intervene and show His sovereignty. They think that's His way of showing He was in control the whole time. You hear people say, "God's never early or late, but He's always right on time." But God doesn't always work that way. If He always intervenes at the last minute, it's often because we didn't use the tools we'd been given in the first place!

. . . many believers can't yet distinguish the difference
between the burden of the Lord and the weight
of their own unbelief.

Psalm 144:1—*Praise be to the Lord my Rock, who trains my hands for war, my fingers for battle.*

BOOK QUOTE: *The Supernatural Power* [Chapter 5]

IF you are facing a spiritual battle, it is usually because you have been trained for that moment. It means you have experienced things in your life that should have taught you how to respond to the present storm. When problems come, you should already know the right thing to do. You shouldn't have to seek God in hours of discouraged prayer. You should be ready to step in and say, "I believe God for a miracle in this situation. That backslidden child will return home. That disease in your body is broken in the name of Jesus. That financial crisis is over." The time to pray is beforehand, like Jesus did, crying out to God in private times when nothing was going wrong. That's how to store up power and create an inner atmosphere of peace and faith that you take with you into the troubling situation.

Let's not waste our miracles. Let's not watch God do something awesome, then give a little golf clap, a little "amen" and walk away unchanged. Let's recognize that we are equipped for each storm. We have been trained by past miracles to see present solutions. Let's allow the leaven of the Kingdom to fill our minds, replacing the leaven of Herod and of the Pharisees. Let's allow our revelation and experience of God to forever change the way we approach this life.

We need to look at the most common hindrances that get in the way of our minds being renewed, and keep us from fully living the normal Christian life. And we need to know how to overcome them!

If you are facing a spiritual battle, it is usually because you have been trained for that moment.

2 Corinthians 9:8—*And God is able to make all grace abound to you, so that in all things at all times, having all that you need, you will abound in every good work.*

BOOK QUOTE: *The Supernatural Power* [Chapter 6]

THERE are common obstacles people come up against as they seek to live in the supernatural and renew their minds. I heard a story of a European family who wanted to move to the United States, so they worked hard and saved enough money to take a ship across the Atlantic. They also saved as much as they could to buy cheese and crackers, provisions they could eat as a family in the small ship's cabin they would occupy. The family huddled in their cabin eating their meager provisions, listening to the laughter of people in the hallway on their way to eat in the banquet room. On the last night the captain announced they would make landfall in the United States the next day. The father decided to celebrate by taking the family to the banquet room where everyone else on the ship had been eating for three weeks. He approached the captain and asked how much the meal cost. The captain looked at him in surprise and said, "You mean you haven't been eating there? Those meals were included in the price of the fare."

I strongly believe that many Christians eat cheese and crackers, in spiritual terms, when our "fare" bought us a full banquet. I'm not talking about financial wealth, although God destroyed the power of poverty at the Cross. I'm talking about salvation and the forgiveness of sin. Too often Christians live under the influence of yesterday's failures, blemishes, and mistakes. When we do, we depart from the normal Christian lifestyle and live under the influence of a lie. Needless to say, this lie halts the renewing of our minds and keeps us from living in the "everyday miraculous" that should be normal for every born-again believer.

I strongly believe that many Christians eat cheese and crackers, in spiritual terms, when our "fare" bought us a full banquet.

Revelation 12:10—*For the accuser of our brothers, who accuses them before our brothers, who accuses them before our God day and night, has been hurled down.*

BOOK QUOTE: *The Supernatural Power* [Chapter 6]

WHY do people receive God's forgiveness but constantly live under the shadow of their failures? I used to willingly live under the guilt and shame of bad decisions from yesterday because I thought it helped me walk in humility.

Others similarly resist forgiveness because they don't want to be prideful. Remembering how rotten they are makes them feel good, but it's actually a subtle form of pride.

When we succumb to guilt and shame, we give in to the oldest temptation in the Bible: the temptation to question our identity and God's identity. The first temptation was not to partake of forbidden fruit, but to question what God had said. The serpent said, "Has God indeed said, 'You shall not eat of every tree of the garden'?" (Gen. 3:1b). Once he got them to doubt God's integrity and identity, it was easy to lure them into foolish actions. And this is the devil's strategy with you and me.

Probably 95 percent or more of all counseling that churches undertake is simply to help people stop questioning what God has said and to stop questioning who we are in Christ. We are the people God loves, the people God forgives. We are the House of God, the gate of Heaven on earth. Moses asked God, "Who am I that I should go to Pharaoh, and that I should bring the children of Israel out of Egypt?" (Gen. 3:11).

God appeared to ignore the question by answering, "I will certainly be with you" (Gen. 3:12). But that was the answer!

Moses said, "Who am I?"

God said, in effect, "You are the man God goes with." Who are you, brother or sister? You are the person that God hangs around with. You are clean and forgiven. That is your identity!

You are the person that God hangs around with.

1 Corinthians 6:19-20—*You are not your own; you were bought at a price.*

BOOK QUOTE: *The Supernatural Power* [Chapter 6]

GOD is never honored when we deny what Jesus did for us. He suffered so we would be free. What parent delights in seeing his or her child suffer? Neither does God delight in seeing us suffer with the effects of guilt and shame. Yet we often ascribe that evil motive to the Father.

This may come as a shock to you, but when Jesus bought you, He bought your problem! Isaiah 61:1 says the prison would be opened for those who were bound. In truth, prisoners are usually in prison because they did something wrong. How does biblical justice set a prisoner free when there is a price to pay? It depends on your definition of "justice." Once you come to Jesus in repentance, He aims for true justice, which addresses not you but the power that influenced you. Maybe you cheated on your taxes, or wrongly criticized a friend, or did something more horrible than that. When you truly repent and are forgiven, you become a partner with the Lord in addressing it. You do everything possible to make restitution, but there is no longer any guilt and shame. Now His justice is aimed at the powers of hell that deceived you into acting on greed, or anger, or whatever it was. You now are in a place to inspire people to walk uprightly in that area.

The word likewise in Romans 6:11 above means "evaluate, take an account of, do the math and come to a conclusion." We either believe that His provision was adequate or we don't. Unfortunately, many believers constantly battle a phantom self-image from the past with no assurance of their present identity in Christ. Forgiveness seems like a theory or an impractical truth. Yet it is the most practical truth there is.

... when Jesus bought you, He bought your problem!

Romans 6:2-4—*How shall we who died to sin live any longer in it? Or do you not know that as many of us as were baptized into Christ Jesus were baptized into His death? Therefore we were buried with Him through baptism into death, that just as Christ was raised from the dead by the glory of the Father, even so we also should walk in newness of life. NKJV*

BOOK QUOTE: *The Supernatural Power* [Chapter 6]

ARE you washed in the blood of Jesus? Then you need to think of yourself as dead to sin. It's not a mind-over-matter thing, but has everything to do with the power of supernatural thinking. It's waking up to what's been true since the moment you met Jesus.

For if we have been united together in the likeness of His death, certainly we also shall be in the likeness of His resurrection, knowing this, that our old man was crucified with Him, that the body of sin might be done away with, that we should no longer be slaves of sin. For he who has died has been freed from sin. Now if we died with Christ, we believe that we shall also live with Him, knowing that Christ, having been raised from the dead, dies no more. Death no longer has dominion over Him. For the death that He died, He died to sin once for all; but the life that He lives, He lives to God (Romans 6:5-10).

The blood of Jesus wiped out the power and record of sin in your life. Your old nature is dead. It hasn't been put on a shelf, or in a closed room, or imprisoned—it has been crucified. Period.

We went from rotten sinners to born-again saints in a single moment when we accepted salvation. Once the blood of Jesus has wiped out sin, you can't get any cleaner. That doesn't mean we can avoid the hurdles and issues that come with changing your life and renewing your mind. Maturity is a process. My associate Kris says, "You are not a sinner; you are a saint. It doesn't mean that you can't sin; it just means that you are no longer a professional." That's the story of your life.

We went from rotten sinners to born-again saints in a single moment when we accepted salvation.

Romans 8:38-39— *For I am persuaded that neither death nor life, nor angels nor principalities nor powers, nor things present nor things to come, nor height nor depth, nor any other created thing, shall be able to separate us from the love of God which is in Christ Jesus our Lord.*

BOOK QUOTE: *The Supernatural Power* [Chapter 6]

IT's difficult if not impossible to demonstrate the will of God "on earth as in Heaven" if we don't think of ourselves as truly forgiven, and if we hang onto a false view of our identity. It effectively cancels out most of our potential. We were designed to triumphantly demonstrate the reality of the Kingdom, but many of us strip our goal down to survival: "If I can get through the day without being discouraged, I will have succeeded."

Our first thought of each day should be the reality of the Kingdom: "His mercies are new for me every morning!" (Lam. 3:23). Friend, you are forgiven! There's nothing anybody can do to change that. When the enemy brings up a sin from your past, he is talking about something non-existent. It's completely legal for you to say, "I didn't do that. The person who did that is dead. This person has never done that." Either the blood of Jesus is completely effective, or it's not effective at all. And it does not just wipe away the punishment so that when you die you don't go to hell; rather, the blood of Jesus has the power to completely transform us into a new creation in Christ.

There is no power, no circumstance, no person, no strategy of the devil, nothing in existence right now in heaven or on earth that can separate you from the love of God. In Romans 8:38-39, Paul mentions the present and the future but doesn't mention the past, because the past can separate you from your awareness of the love of God, if you let it become your present identity. Remember, Jesus bought your sin, not to bring it up again but to destroy it so you don't have to think about it anymore.

We were designed to triumphantly demonstrate the reality of the Kingdom, but many of us strip our goal down to survival...

Lamentations 3:22-23—*Because of the Lord's great love we are not consumed, for His compassions never fail. They are new every morning; great is your faithfulness.*

BOOK QUOTE: *The Supernatural Power* [Chapter 6]

I finally figured out that the secret to always being encouraged is to live in denial. The enemy puts a request across my desk and I stamp "request denied" on it. He tells me I'm one thing; I deny that assertion and rest in my true identity in Christ. The Bible says that if I walk in the light as He is in the light, I have fellowship with Him, and the outcome is that the blood of Jesus continuously washes me clean (see 1 John 1:7). If I am open and honest and stay right in my relationships with God and with people, the blood of Jesus keeps me clean 24 hours a day.

Thinking of ourselves as rotten sinners, always recalling the bad thing we did in our past, robs us of a renewed mind and keeps us from stepping into the supernatural, normal life. God is never honored when we recall and live under the influence of our sins and blunders of yesterday. Many people grow older and live with so much regret. I could go back to that way of thinking really quickly, but I know better now. I know the right way is to embrace your forgiven-ness. Insist on your identity in Him. Let your heart be light with the realization that His mercies are new *for you* each morning. You'll not only be happier, you'll be much more effective for the Kingdom.

You might dwell on this for a while and let it saturate your understanding. Live in this truth and let it multiply in your life over the next few days. You'll see a major difference when you start living free and forgiven, with no baggage to haul around. In the next chapter we discuss remembering as a way of renewing our minds.

*Let your heart be light with the realization that His mercies are new **for you** each morning.*

Ephesians 4:23—...to be made new in the attitude of your minds.

BOOK QUOTE: *The Supernatural Power* [Chapter 7]

AN associate of mine, Mike, and I were in the airport in Vancouver, Canada, waiting in line at Starbucks (one of my favorite places). As I stood there enjoying the aromas, the sights and sounds of the coffee shop, and the anticipation of my next cup of coffee, I noticed Mike was taking a long time with the cashier. It didn't occur to me that anything important was happening. I was simply there getting coffee as we waited for our next flight. Then I saw him take the cashier's hand, and they closed their eyes and bowed their heads in prayer. When they had finished, Mike joined me and told me that as he was ordering, he had seen a spirit of suicide on her, and he began to minister to her and broke that power. She told him, "God sent you in here today." I was caught off guard because all I was thinking about was coffee! My mind had momentarily forgotten the more important things in life.

It's easy for our minds to stray into natural thinking only, for our faith to erode so subtly that we don't notice it happening. Little by little we can begin to think "practically," leaning on natural wisdom instead of Kingdom reality. One of the great tools for keeping a Kingdom mindset is to meditate on and remember God's Word, devising ways of reminding ourselves of His promises to us, and then passing those promises and remembrances on to the next generation of believers. Without taking practical steps to remember and meditate on the truth, we will easily forget what God has promised. By degrees, we will become earthly minded, and that's what we must avoid if we're to successfully live the normal Christian life.

One of the great tools for keeping a Kingdom mindset is to meditate on and remember God's Word...

Isaiah 26:3—*Thou will keep him in perfect peace, whose mind is stayed on Thee.*

BOOK QUOTE: *The Supernatural Power* [Chapter 7]

IN Eastern occult religions, meditation means emptying the mind. But biblical meditation is the opposite—it's filling the mind with God's truth. Every person, saint and sinner alike, meditates every day. The question is, what are you meditating on? A person with a renewed mind derives joy even in even negative circumstances because joy comes not by what is seen but by what God says. God is not a liar and He will keep His Word. But worry reasons with you, saying, "Years ago you disobeyed the Lord, and now you will reap what you sowed." This "good argument" might cause you to shift your meditation from God's Word to worry. Soon that little voice has grown so big it's like a megaphone in your ear. You forget that God said He would keep us in perfect peace, which means divine health, prosperity, wellness of being, soundness of mind. *Stayed* or *fixed* means "braced, lodged in an immovable position." But when we listen to worry, we become "unfixed." Why does worry shout so loudly for our attention? Because if we look at it long enough, it will gain our trust. Pretty soon we begin praying out of fear, and eventually we quit praying and start looking for sympathy. We have trusted that other voice, and it won the affections of our heart.

We must get our minds set on spiritual things because as long as we fill our minds with what's happening in the natural, we restrict our effectiveness. We may rise up now and then and score a victory with the gift of faith, but we won't have the continual influence of Kingdom transformation flowing through us.

What's the solution? To meditate on the Word and give ourselves every opportunity to remember what is true.

. . . as long as we fill our minds with what's happening in the natural, we restrict our effectiveness.

Habakkuk 2:2—*Write the vision and make it plain on tablets, that he may run who reads it.*

BOOK QUOTE: *The Supernatural Power* [Chapter 7]

Gᴏᴅ has given us the tools to be able to focus our minds on Him. He tells us meditate on the Word and give ourselves every opportunity to remember what is true. The Bible tells us clearly about how to do this in Habakkuk 2 (see above).

People need motivation to run. That's the main reason I travel and speak and write as much as I can. I want to give other people the fuel they need to get up and go. I want them to have whatever revelation I have, just as I feed on the revelation given to me by others. To participate in the active, awesome work of the Kingdom we can't casually row, row, row our boat gently down the stream. We've got to run!

That's why I do as Habakkuk advised and write down God's ideas about my life whenever they are revealed to me. I mark up and underline my Bible every which way. I write down prophecies I've received on note cards and in my computer, and I carry those with me wherever I go. I post Post-It notes on the dashboard of my car. I put them all over the church sometimes so that when I walk around and pray I see cards everywhere, reminding me of what God is saying. I keep a journal for my children and my grandchildren that they might see what God did in my lifetime. We even have a staff member at our church whose entire job description is to record the miracles that happen in and through our church and with our ministry teams. I want people to know the great and mighty works of the Lord long after we're gone, so they can run with the vision even further.

To participate in the active, awesome work of the Kingdom we can't casually row, row, row our boat gently down the stream.

Psalm 119:97-98—Oh, how I love your Law! I meditate on it all day long. Your commands make me wiser than all my enemies, for they are ever with me.

BOOK QUOTE: *The Supernatural Power* [Chapter 7]

A written record is only useful when you review it. Take apart the word "review." Re means "to go back," and view means "to see." *Go back* over God's promises until *you can see!* Sometimes I need to re-visit those prophetic words that were spoken over me. They are the facts of my life, because God spoke them. It's not simply positive thinking or using my imagination to trick myself into believing some alternate reality. It's meditating on what God has said until I can see it and run with it.

At times I will ask people, "Remind me what happened in such-and-such city when we ministered there. Tell me the story again." The person will say, "Oh, man, that guy with no hip joint got up and walked. And the deaf lady heard for the first time. That broken bone was healed. Remember?" Those conversations remind me of things I have forgotten and reestablish the cornerstones of my thought life. I force my imaginations to become Kingdom imaginations. The testimony of what the Lord has done helps us to remember who God is, what His covenant is like and who He intends to be in our lives. Every testimony of His work in someone's life is a prophecy for those with ears to hear. It is a promise that He'll do the same for us because "*God is no respecter of persons*" (see Acts 10:34). And "*He is the same yesterday, today and forever*" (see Heb. 13:8). But the testimony must be heard, spoken, written down, and reviewed. Israel fell into great backsliding when they forgot the testimony (the spoken or written record of what God has done). But when they recalled the testimony of what God did before, anticipation increased, and so did the miracles.

The testimony of what the Lord has done helps us to remember who God is, what His covenant is like and who He intends to be in our lives.

Malachi 3:16—*Then those who feared the Lord spoke to one another, and the Lord listened and heard them; so a book of remembrance was written before Him for those who fear the Lord and who meditate on His name. NKJV*

BOOK QUOTE: *The Supernatural Power* [Chapter 7]

SOMETIMES God reviews what is written in His book of remembrance, and He shapes the future because of what was done in the past. It happened with Cornelius in the Book of Acts:

> *He and all his family were devout and God-fearing; he gave generously to those in need and prayed to God regularly. One day at about three in the afternoon he had a vision. He distinctly saw an angel of God, who came to him and said, "Cornelius!" Cornelius stared at him in fear. "What is it, Lord?" he asked. The angel answered, "Your prayers and gifts to the poor have come up as a memorial offering before God"* (Acts 10:2-5).

That's a wonderful promise that our gifts and work for the Lord are never forgotten or overlooked. But at other times, God instructs us to actively remind Him of what we've done. He invites us to engage Him in this way and to review the circumstances of our lives before Him so that through this interaction we are transformed. When Israel crossed the River Jordan, the leaders of the tribes each took a stone and made a pile on the Promised Land side of the river (see Josh. 4). The stones were to trigger their memories about what God had done. But they also served to remind God of their condition, their need, and their obedience. Memorial stones that we put before God—in the form of prayer and generosity—remind Him of our condition, our need, and our obedience. Is it possible that God has chosen not to know certain things so that He could discover them in His relationship with us? He gives us a stunning privilege of putting before Him stones of remembrance to remind Him of our past faithfulness.

God instructs us to actively remind Him of what we've done.

Hebrews 11:11—*By faith Sarah herself also received strength to conceive seed, and she bore a child when she was past the age, because she judged Him faithful who had promised. NKJV*

BOOK QUOTE: *The Supernatural Power* [Chapter 7]

THE record of Scripture gives us a good idea of what is written in the book of remembrance. Take the example of Sarah in Genesis 18,

> *Laughed within herself, saying, "After I have grown old, shall I have pleasure, my Lord being old also?" And the Lord said to Abraham, "Why did Sarah laugh, saying, 'Shall I surely bear a child, since I am old?' Is anything too hard for the Lord? At the appointed time I will return to you, according to the time of life, and Sarah shall have a son." But Sarah denied it, saying, "I did not laugh," for she was afraid. And He said, "No, but you did laugh!"*
> (Genesis 18:12-15)

She didn't just give an embarrassed giggle. The Hebrew word for laugh tells us she was *mocking* what God had said. Not only that, she lied about it when God confronted her.

In Hebrews (see above), the record sounds different than the reality! This tells us something precious: the book of remembrance doesn't have a record of our mistakes. Genesis 18 was recorded for human benefit, so you and I could identify with those who followed God in the past. But Hebrews 11 is how it's recorded in the book of remembrance. Once the blood has been applied, there is no record of sin anymore. God brags all over Heaven about Sarah, and He does the same about you and me.

Renewing the mind becomes possible when we remember, record, review, and remind ourselves and God of what He has done in the past, and of our obedience. It is a sure way to solidify your identity in Him, and to mold your mind so it conforms to the mind of Christ.

Once the blood has been applied, there is no record of sin anymore.

1 Thessalonians 1:3—*We continually remember before our God and Father your work produced by faith, your labor prompted by love, and your endurance inspired by hope in our Lord Jesus Christ.*

BOOK QUOTE: *The Supernatural Power* [Chapter 8]

ONE of the toughest lessons a Christian can learn is how to trust and praise God in the uncertain time between a promise and its fulfillment. It is a powerful act of spiritual warfare to stand in the middle of death and disease, conflict and unresolved issues, and to cause your spirit to rise and give thanks to God.

One of our missionaries, Tracey, was driving from South Africa when the bus ahead of her went out of control and crashed at about 60 miles per hour. Passengers were thrown from the vehicle. She and other motorists discovered a gruesome scene as they went victim to victim. Many had life-threatening injuries, traumatic head injuries, and were laying unconscious. One woman was clearly dead. She had no vital signs, her head was facing her back, and she had one eye lying on her cheek. Our missionary, a Physician's Assistant, placed the bystanders by each of the injured persons. She then instructed, "*Speak life in Jesus' name.*"

Minutes later, the woman assigned to the dead passenger screamed. The "dead" woman had groaned, turned her head around, and begun to breathe again. To their amazement the woman's vital signs were strong, and her misplaced eye was back in its socket. That caused the others to pray all the more earnestly for their patients. Within a short period of time the unconscious victims had regained consciousness and those with serious wounds stopped bleeding.

When I heard that story, my mind kept coming back to the people who stood by and prayed even when the situation seemed hopeless. That's the kind of attitude we must have during times of uncertainty. We must declare the goodness and faithfulness of God even in the midst of our trial, before we have an answer.

It is a powerful act of spiritual warfare to stand in the middle of death and disease, conflict and unresolved issues....

Psalm 100:4—*Enter His gates with thanksgiving and His courts with praise; give thanks to Him and praise His name.*

BOOK QUOTE: *The Supernatural Power* [Chapter 8]

WHY do we have to endure uncertainty? That is a mystery, but the Bible hints at an answer when it gives a spiritual picture of a city called the community of the redeemed, or Zion (see Isa. 62). Isaiah 60:18 says, "But you shall call your walls Salvation, and your gates Praise." In Revelation we see this gate called praise again and discover that is made out of one solid pearl (see Rev. 21:21). Think for a moment. How is a pearl formed? Through irritation and conflict. A granule of sand gets inside an oyster shell, and a pearl forms around the granule to keep it from doing harm. The Bible's pairing of praise with irritation is not coincidental. When we are stuck in conflict and uncertainty, and yet we praise Him without manipulation, it is a sacrifice. It means we are reacting in a way that produces something beautiful. In that moment a gate is formed, a place of entrance where the King of glory can invade our situation.

Many people have no gate because they won't praise Him in the middle of apparent paradox. They get stuck wondering, "How can God promise to heal all of my diseases but I've got this problem in my body?" "How can God promise to provide, and yet I've been without a job for three months?" And yet Psalm 87:2 says, "The Lord loves the gates of Zion more than all the dwellings of Jacob." That gate—that place of praise in the midst of conflict—is where His presence rests, where the King Himself dwells. The gate is formed when we move above human explanation and into a place of trust.

When we are stuck in conflict and uncertainty,
and yet we praise Him without manipulation,
it is a sacrifice.

Psalm 103:3—...who forgives all your sins and heals all your diseases....

BOOK QUOTE: *The Supernatural Power* [Chapter 8]

WHEN some Christians find themselves in a place of uncertainty with no answer for their problem, they change their view of God and ascribe to Him character traits that are totally anti-biblical. They might convince themselves that He won't help them out of a financial hole because He isn't intervening in their affairs, though the Bible says, "And my God shall supply all your need according to His riches in glory by Christ Jesus" (Phil. 4:19). They may claim He won't heal them, though the Bible says He heals all your diseases and forgives all your iniquities (see Ps. 103:3).

Uncertainty causes some people to misunderstand who God is. They begin to deny God's true nature and embrace sickness and disease, poverty and mental anguish as gifts from God. That is a devastating lie from hell. It's actually blasphemous to attribute to God the work of the devil. But many Christians want answers so badly during times of uncertainty that they invent theological answers to make themselves feel good about their present condition. In doing so, they sacrifice the truth about God on the altar of human reasoning. That's what causes people to say things like, "God gave my aunt leukemia to teach her perseverance." No way. That has never happened. If somebody's body is racked with pain or wasting away because of disease, it's the devourer. It's not the job description of the Messiah. Again, the Bible says, "He forgives all your iniquities; He heals all your diseases." It would never enter our minds that God would give someone a drug habit or a drinking problem to help them become better people. So why would He condemn people to disease? Or poverty? Or depression? Or any other miserable condition?

Uncertainty causes some people to misunderstand who God is.

Psalm 145:9—*The Lord is good to all; He has compassion on all He has made.*

BOOK QUOTE: *The Supernatural Power* [Chapter 8]

People tend to respond in one of two ways when the answer they seek doesn't come. Let's see why those approaches don't work. First, they may accuse God. They do this by claiming that He won't heal them, though the Bible says He heals all your diseases in Psalm 103:2,3: "Praise the Lord, O my soul, and forget not all His benefits—Who forgives all your sins and heals all your diseases."

Let's get this straight: God is good all of the time. The devil is bad all of the time. We do ourselves a tremendous service to remember the difference between the two. Healing, salvation, wholeness, provision, and joy have already been given to us. They can't be recalled or returned. They are facts of Kingdom living. They were paid for by Jesus on the Cross.

Another that people respond to God when they their answer doesn't seem to come is to fall into deception. Christians fall into the deception that when the Bible talks about sufferings, it means all of the above afflictions. Not at all! The suffering referred to in the Bible means living between two conflicting realities and trusting and praising God through it all. Anybody can declare the greatness of God after they've won the Reader's Digest sweepstakes. But when you live in the middle of a conflict—of having a promise that is not yet fulfilled, or having a problem that seems to never get resolved—you rise above circumstance and declare that He is good all the time, no matter what.

Healing, salvation, wholeness, provision, and joy
have already been given to us.
They can't be recalled or returned.

Mark 9:22-23—*"If You can do anything, take pity on us and help us." Jesus replied, "'If you can'? Everything is possible for him who believes."*

BOOK QUOTE: *The Supernatural Power* [Chapter 8]

WHY do disease and addiction and all the other tools of the devil continue to torment the human race? It's my conviction that if we knew more about spiritual warfare, we could thwart much of what we see. What's needed to cure the incurable and do the impossible is warfare at a level that we have never experienced. There are two situations in the New Testament that support this view. In one, Jesus laid hands on a blind man and asked him if he saw anything. The man said, "I see men like trees, walking" (Mark 8:24). To get the complete miracle, the man needed a second touch from Jesus. He needed persistence. In another situation, a tormented child had a demon that threw him into the water and the fire to kill him. (See Mark 8:22,23 above.)

Jesus has no limitations and He is absolutely good all of the time. There was no question what He wanted in that situation, or what He could do. The responsibility for the impossible was not on Jesus but on the father of that child, and on the disciples who had been unable to drive out the demon.

Jesus said something to explain why the disciples saw their prayers unanswered: "This kind can come out by nothing but prayer and fasting" (Mark 9:29). Jesus neither prayed nor fasted in that particular moment when He healed the demonized boy. But He had a prayer vault filled with time He'd spent with the Father so that heaven could erupt into the natural world at a moment's notice. He exercised faith out of intimacy with God, as we should do. My inability to bring deliverance or healing has driven me to the throne. I must have more!

> *... if we knew more about spiritual warfare,*
> *we could thwart much of what we see.*

Romans 8:18—*For I consider that the sufferings of this present time are not worthy to be compared with the glory which shall be revealed in us. NKJV*

BOOK QUOTE: *The Supernatural Power* [Chapter 8]

WHEN we find ourselves in uncertain seasons of life, we are like the disciples in when they failed to heal the demon-possessed boy in Mark 9. They were the most miracle-experienced people on earth at that time. No one had seen more and done more than they, and yet they came up against something for which they could get no solution. We may find ourselves facing problems and not knowing where the tools are to bring about the solution. But that doesn't mean the problem is insurmountable. There is power in resolving in your heart that God is good all of the time, and that His will for healing and wholeness does not change, despite what we see in the natural.

You can rest knowing that two things are guaranteed to you. First, in every situation in which you suffer loss by the devourer, all things will work together for good. Did God design the evil in your life? No. Did He assign it to you? No. But He is so big that He can win with any hand. He can use your past sin or the devil's attacks to accomplish what He wants.

Second, our God is a God of vengeance. The devil never has final say in anything. That beast will be silenced and there will be absolute, complete vindication for every moment of infirmity, affliction, difficulty, torment, and temptation that you've ever experienced. We have the promise from Romans 8 (see above). The difficulty you experience in your finances, in that assault on your body, in that attack on your family or your emotions, is not worthy of comparison to the glory that will be revealed in you. Like Bob Mumford said a long time ago, "I read the last chapter and we win."

There is power in resolving in your heart that God is good all of the time,. . .

Mark 6:5-6—*Now He could do no mighty work there, except that He laid His hands on a few sick people and healed them. And He marveled because of their unbelief. Then He went about the villages in a circuit, teaching.*

BOOK QUOTE: *The Supernatural Power* [Chapter 8]

WHEN some Christians face uncertainty, they often become intellectually offended with God. Mark 6:1-4 illustrates this:

Then He went out from there and came to His own country, and His disciples followed Him. And when the Sabbath had come, He began to teach in the synagogue. And many hearing Him were astonished, saying, "Where did this Man get these things? And what wisdom is this which is given to Him, that such mighty works are performed by His hands! Is this not the carpenter, the Son of Mary, and brother of James, Joses, Judas, and Simon? And are not His sisters here with us?" So they were offended at Him. But Jesus said to them, "A prophet is not without honor except in his own country, among his own relatives, and in his own house."

This passage shows how an unregenerate mind is a horrible weapon that can be used against us, causing us to reject the very answer we need. The folks in Nazareth were stunned by Jesus' teaching at first. It stirred them up and caught their attention. When He started teaching in the synagogue, they said to each other, "Wow! Where did He learn this stuff? This is amazing!" They were impressed, and that created an environment in which Jesus could do miracles to illustrate the power of what He was teaching. But then they took stock of what was happening and said, "Wait a minute. We know this guy. He grew up here. We knew His dad, His mom, His sisters. How is He doing all these miracles?" Their minds became offended at Jesus. This is not the kind of offense where somebody hurts you. This is intellectual offense, when you have unanswered questions that block your ability to trust in the unseen.

> . . . *an unregenerate mind is a horrible weapon that can be used against us, causing us to reject the very answer we need.*

Psalm 103:1-2—*Bless the Lord, O my soul; And all that is within me, bless His holy name! Bless the Lord, O my soul, And forget not all His benefits.*

BOOK QUOTE: *The Supernatural Power* [Chapter 8]

MANY times I hear people say things like, "I wish I could believe God heals people today, but my grandmother died two weeks ago and we prayed for her and she didn't get healed." Grief separates people from God because they have questions, but no answers.

Questions are allowed in the Kingdom, *but lack of answers must not interrupt our heart-communion with God.* If we demand answers from God, then we are walking in the spirit of offense. Hosea 6:3 says, "So, let's press on to know the Lord." Those words "press on" can be translated "hunt." We should passionately pursue the Lord, in spite of not fully understanding Him or His ways. We are to run after Him even in the time of potential offense. The answer is always on the other side of our offense. Acts 14:22 promises, "We must through many tribulations enter the kingdom of God." Getting through the difficulty—without becoming defiant or demanding with God—will take us into the very thing God promised.

David gave a good example when he commanded his emotions and his mind to come into line with the truth about God in Psalm 103 (see above). That's a terrific prayer for us to pray when we're in the uncertain place, ready to take offense with God. We can yank our minds and emotions back into line with reality.

When you find yourself in an uncertain time, you can create a gate of praise by lifting your heart and your voice to God. Persistently pursue fellowship with God even though your uncertainty feels endless, and no answers have materialized. The suffering will last but a moment in God's grand plan for your life. Be thankful for the opportunity to persevere. And be assured—better times are on the way!

Persistently pursue fellowship with God even though your uncertainty feels endless. . .

1 Kings 3:9—So give your servant a discerning heart to govern your people and to distinguish between right and wrong. For who is to govern this great people of yours?

BOOK QUOTE: *The Supernatural Power* [Chapter 9]

MY wife Beni and I were worshiping one Sunday morning at our church when a woman came forward and began to worship in front of us. It's busy up in the front of our sanctuary anyway, so I didn't think this was unusual. But this particular woman's movements didn't seem to flow from the Holy Spirit, and so I tried to discern what was happening in my spirit man—the location of the indicator that tells you something isn't right. Usually that gift works well for me, but this time it was as though the Lord reached into my heart and turned it off. I didn't feel anything, good or bad. I wasn't getting any spiritual signals about what was taking place before me.

But something unusual did happen: I noticed a shift in the temperature of the air around me. I walked over to another part of the sanctuary and it was warm. I walked back to my seat and it was cold. I had a strong hunch that the devil was at work. I went to our main dancer and quietly asked her to worship before the Lord because we needed to break something in the spiritual realm. She got up there and began to dance and the moment she moved across the stage, the lady in front of me collapsed, as if she were a puppet and her strings had been snipped. Beni leaned forward and prayed with her. We discerned real sincerity, a heart that was right, but she needed deliverance and salvation. It turned into a wonderful story, but I want to draw your attention to the fact that signals in the physical realm—in this case, colder-than-normal air—helped lead to a spiritual breakthrough. The situation contained physical indicators of spiritual realities.

. . . signals in the physical realm. . .helped lead to a spiritual breakthrough.

Romans 12:1-2—*I beseech you therefore, brethren, by the mercies of God, that you present your bodies a living sacrifice, holy, acceptable to God, which is your reasonable service. And do not be conformed to this world, but be transformed by the renewing of your mind, that you may prove what is that good and acceptable and perfect will of God.*

BOOK QUOTE: *The Supernatural Power* [Chapter 9]

THE mind is grossly undervalued in charismatic/Pentecostal circles. The same is true of the physical body. Many see the body as evil in itself, something to be ignored, pushed aside, tolerated but never really used for Kingdom purposes. But God designed the human body to be more than a tent that you dwell in. It is an instrument of God that recognizes His presence and discerns what is happening in the Kingdom realm.

Christians use Romans 12:1-2 mostly when sending off a new missionary to a post somewhere overseas, or when people do some other kind of ministry that involves self-denial. I'd like to suggest that this passage is also speaking about our physical bodies' role in recognizing and working with God.

David had 30 to 40 years in which he came freely before the actual, manifested presence of God that was upon the Ark of the Covenant. God's glory radiated visibly from it. David was immeasurably impacted by God's presence: "My flesh longs for You…." (Psalm 63:1).

Was he speaking purely metaphorically? I don't think so. He was declaring that he'd been so affected by the presence and the glory of God that his body itself ached and cried out for more. What's true for David is true for us. In the same way that you and I might hunger for food or thirst for water, our physical bodies—not just our emotions, intellects, and spirits—can ache for God. And if we can hunger for God physically, then we can be satisfied by God physically. There is no such thing as hunger without the potential of fulfillment. You don't have an appetite for things that are non-existent. Rather, God has put within our makeup the capacity to recognize Him and His activities with our physical bodies.

There is no such thing as hunger without the potential of fulfillment.

Hebrews 5:14—*But solid food is for the mature, who by constant use have trained themselves to distinguish good from evil.*

BOOK QUOTE: *The Supernatural Power* [Chapter 9]

Touch, smell, sight, hearing, and taste can be trained to help us in the discernment process. Not only can we recognize the presence of God with our bodies, but those physical signs should help us discern good and evil. On that Sunday morning during worship, my spirit was telling me nothing about the woman in front of me, but the air temperature got the message across. Unfortunately, most Christians don't pay any attention at all to what happens to them physically when God shows up. I've got news for you: God's first language is not English. He communicates with us in various ways, through impressions of the heart, mental pictures, feelings, emotions, and physical sensations. When we ignore our bodies, we are at least sometimes ignoring the voice of God.

This is important because when we neglect the physical signs of the Kingdom, we can miss what God is doing. Sometimes Jesus walks by our boat and does not intend to get in the boat, figuratively speaking. He puts Himself within reach, but doesn't make it automatic. If we don't perceive that He is there, we will miss the opportunity. We misunderstand what we see and perceive physically with our senses, and miss opportunities to be with Jesus?

I have seen many Christians open up to the ways God speaks. They are perceiving what He is doing, calling out for Him to come into the boat. They are stepping into the adventure that says, "I want every part of my being to be utilized by God, that I might be useful in every situation." One day it will be normal for all Christians to discern the Kingdom with their five senses. But to get there, we have to train our senses.

One day it will be normal for all Christians to discern the Kingdom with their five senses.

Psalm 25:4-5—*Show me your ways, O Lord, teach me Your paths; guide me in Your truth and teach me, for You are God my Savior, and my hope is in You all day long.*

BOOK QUOTE: *The Supernatural Power* [Chapter 9]

PILOTS, when they're learning to fly, test themselves in flight simulators with the cabin pressurized as though they were at 40,000 feet. The instructor starts depleting the oxygen gradually so the pilot-in-training can recognize and observe what happens to his body when the airplane is losing oxygen. Every body responds differently. For some people, the hair on their arms hurts. For some, their ears ring. For some, the muscles in their legs ache. The important thing is to be familiar with how their own body reacts so if the oxygen masks don't fall properly, they can recognize from the physical signs that they are losing oxygen.

How do you react when God comes into the room in a special way? How do you manifest the presence of God? How do you feel, sense, or perceive God when He is moving around you? You need to know the answer to those questions to fully live the normal Christian life. Without understanding that God moves and communicates with us in the physical realm, our minds cannot fully come into line with Heaven's reality.

For me, it's been a process of discovery. I learned that the tangible anointing, the presence of the Holy Spirit for giftedness, is physically discernable. I can physically feel it, as though someone took a silk scarf and laid it over my hands. Why is that important? Not so we can wow each other with what we feel. The point isn't competition. The point is fine-tuning our perceptive abilities so we know when God has come into the room, and what He intends to do.

How do you react when God comes into the room in a special way?

2 Corinthians 6:12—*You are not restricted by us, but you are restricted by your own affections. NKJV*

BOOK QUOTE: *The Supernatural Power* [Chapter 9]

I'VE spoken with people who get a tingling on the back of their heads, or a fire in their hands when God begins to move. The Bible teaches that the power of God is concealed and hidden in the hands (see Hab. 3:4). When somebody talks about revival or healing, they ignite the area of the affection of my heart and the anointing is released through those affections.

One of our young men was walking through Safeway one time and he felt the anointing of God come on his hands. A man was coming into the store. He asked him, "Do you need a miracle in your body?" The man said, "As a matter of fact I do. I'm in excruciating pain, and have had several back surgeries." He prayed for him and the man was instantly healed, then listened to the gospel and was born again. The young man began to shout in the parking lot that God had healed this man, and somebody else was saved. It all started with having senses trained to discern good and evil, and recognizing a "God moment" even in that unusual setting.

I'm not saying that we can physically feel every time God is at work. I am saying we should pay attention to the physical signs. You'll learn how your body reacts. It may take you years, like it has for me. Sometimes I'll pray for somebody and I don't sense anything, but they get healed. Physical senses are not always a sure indicator, but they are an indicator that God does use. Let's not stall on the adventure of learning to recognize God's presence. God will use every part of who we are. Tune into your body and begin to perceive the anointing and presence of God.

Physical senses are not always a sure indicator, but they are an indicator that God does use.

2 Corinthians 6:1—*As God's fellow workers we urge you not to receive God's grace in vain.*

BOOK QUOTE: *The Supernatural Power* [Chapter 10]

THE normal Christian life is a partnership between God and each one of us, played out in everyday living as we become the gate of heaven, releasing the manifestation of God's reality for those around us. Paul called us co-laborers with Christ, partners in the work of heaven in this earthly sphere. But many Christians have a one-dimensional perspective of this idea of co-laboring. They think it's a robotic interplay between themselves and God in which their will is dialed down to zero and His will completely overtakes their desires and thoughts. But that is exactly the opposite of what the Bible says. Our ideas and desires and dreams have a monumental influence on how God carries out His plan. We are co-laborers, meaning that apart from Christ our work is not complete, and at the same time, amazingly, *His work on earth is not complete without us.* God sees us as contributors to what He is doing. He actually is interested in your desires and dreams and has opened up His plan on this planet to your influence.

This sounds almost blasphemous to modern Christians. Many of us, myself included, have prayed prayers in the past that say, "Oh God, take over my will!" That is easily one of the stupidest prayers anyone can pray. It totally devalues our will, which is one of the greatest things God ever created. Your will is so valuable that He wouldn't violate it even at the cost of His own Son. You and I are the pearl of great price. Without an independent will, we become animated playthings, dolls, programmed toys. But with a free will, we become lovers of God and willing co-laborers with Him. And when we co-labor with Him, our ideas can literally change the course of history.

Our ideas and desires and dreams have a monumental influence on how God carries out His plan.

James 2:23—*And the scripture was fulfilled that says, "Abraham believed God, and it was credited to him as righteousness," and he was called God's friend.*

BOOK QUOTE: *The Supernatural Power* [Chapter 10]

THE Bible shows us how co-laboring works. At the creation, God let Adam name all of the animals (see Gen. 2:19). Moses had one of the most intimate relationships with God in all of Scripture. He experienced God face-to-face, even mouth-to-mouth, some say. How did that relationship work? One time God said to Moses:

Go, get down! For your people whom you brought out of the land of Egypt have corrupted themselves.... They have made themselves a molded calf, and worshiped it and sacrificed to it, and said, "This is your god, O Israel, that brought you out of the land of Egypt!"...I have seen this people, and indeed it is a stiff-necked people! Now therefore, let Me alone, that My wrath may burn hot against them and I may consume them. And I will make of you a great nation (Exodus 32:7-10).

Moses responded,

Lord, why does Your wrath burn hot against Your people whom You have brought out of the land of Egypt with great power and with a mighty hand? ... Turn from Your fierce wrath, and relent from this harm to Your people. Remember Abraham, Isaac, and Israel, Your servants, to whom You swore by Your own self, and said to them, "I will multiply your descendants as the stars of heaven; and all this land that I have spoken of I give to your descendants, and they shall inherit it forever" (Exodus 32:11-13).

God's response?

So the Lord relented from the harm which He said He would do to His people (Exodus 32:14).

That's a breathtaking interaction. God wasn't playing some psychological game. He wasn't using reverse psychology to steer Moses to the right conclusion. He was interacting with Moses as a friend. This was a conversation between intimates, not servant and master.

Moses had one of the most intimate relationships with God in all of Scripture.

John 15:15—*No longer do I call you servants, for a servant does not know what his master is doing; but I have called you friends, for all things that I heard from My Father I have made known to you.*

BOOK QUOTE: *The Supernatural Power* [Chapter 10]

JESUS affirmed that we have friendship with God. Servants aren't co-laborers; friends are. There are major differences between the mentality of each. A servant is task-oriented, wanting to know exactly what is required so he or she can do it. But a servant doesn't know the master's business from the inside. We don't have servants today, so it's hard for us to understand, but imagine that you did have people living in your household who served you and carried out your will. A servant would know certain things about you, like your hobbies, whether you liked going to baseball games or out fishing, what you liked for dinner, what time you wanted coffee in the morning. But a servant would not share personal times with you. He wouldn't comfort you in your down times; you wouldn't invite the servants in to discuss family problems or major business decisions, or even minor ones. But God has elevated us from servants to friends. He invites us into a relationship that goes beyond employer-employee interactions. He is willing for us to engage Him…to change His mind, to direct His ideas, to share in His unfolding creative work. He doesn't lack for ideas. He just enjoys our participation.

When you become a friend of God, you don't lose the humility and obedience of a servant, but your relational perspective shifts. There is a point in our relationship with God where obedience is no longer the primary issue. That may also sound blasphemous, but it's a deep truth God wants to reveal more widely in the Church. There are levels of relationship with God that many of us have not conceived or experienced, and until we do, our co-laboring with Him will be more limited than it needs to be.

… God has elevated us from servants to friends.

Acts 13:22—After removing Saul, he made David their king. He testified concerning him: "I have found David son of Jesse a man after my own heart; he will do everything I want him to do."

BOOK QUOTE: *The Supernatural Power* [Chapter 10]

ONE of the most extraordinary examples of co-laboring was King David's idea for a temple. First Kings 8 recounts the building of the temple of Solomon, one of the most significant events in the Bible. At the temple's dedication, Solomon said,

> *Blessed be the Lord God of Israel, who spoke with His mouth to my father David, and with His hand has fulfilled it, saying, "Since the day that I brought My people Israel out of Egypt, I have chosen no city from any tribe of Israel in which to build a house, that My name might be there; but I chose David to be over My people Israel." Now it was in the heart of my father David to build a temple for the name of the Lord God of Israel (1 Kings 8:15-17).*

God said, "I didn't choose a city, I chose a man, and the temple was in the heart of the man." It's like He was saying, "The Temple wasn't my idea. David was my idea." Incredible! David's creativity and desires wrote history because God embraced them. This is absolutely foreign to most of our way of thinking. We wait for instructions and work hard to suppress our own ideas. We think anything we do for God must flow directly from the Throne and be carried out to the letter, as if from a heavenly instruction booklet. God's approach is different. He has made Himself vulnerable to the desires of His people. History unfolds according to what we do, what we pray, what we don't do and what we don't pray. He gave us Kingdom principles that set up our parameters. Then He said, "Dreamers! Come! Let's dream together and write the story of human history."

History unfolds according to what we do, what we pray, what we don't do and what we don't pray.

Psalm 103:5—...*who satisfies your desires with good things so that your youth is renewed like the eagle's.*

BOOK QUOTE: *The Supernatural Power* [Chapter 10]

SOMETIMES we think that if we really desire something, it must not be of God. It's as if we serve a barbaric God who wants to wipe out anything that springs from our own hearts. On the contrary, God is enamored of your desires. He wants to see what makes you tick. Jesus said, "If you ask anything in My name, I will do it (John 14:14). Yes, He made you and knows everything about you, but He can only commune with you as you open yourself up in relationship with Him. That's where pleasure is derived, when dreams and desires spark dialogue and interaction, and the co-laboring begins.

For many years I misunderstood the biblical concept of desire. Psalm 37:4 tells each of us:

"Delight yourself also in the Lord, and He shall give you the desires of your heart."

Like many pastors, I foolishly taught that if you delighted yourself in the Lord, He would change your desires by telling you what to desire. But that's not at all what this means. That verse literally means that God wants to be impacted by what you think and dream. God is after your desires. He's after intimacy with you. He has opened Himself to the desires of His people. He likes going back and forth with you, throwing out His idea and waiting for your response. Jesus even said, "Whoever you forgive, I forgive." Co-laboring is a huge aspect of ministry that many of us simply do not understand, because true friendship with God is so foreign to us.

. . . God wants to be impacted by what you think and dream.

Mark 11:24—*Whatever things you ask when you pray, believe that you receive them, and you will have them.*

BOOK QUOTE: *The Supernatural Power* [Chapter 10]

Some of our misunderstanding comes because we don't know which of our desires come from God, and which are carnal. The very word *desire* is made up of the prefix *de* meaning "of," and *sire* meaning "the Father." Desire is, by nature, of the Father. But before we come to Christ, our desires are corrupted because desire springs from what we commune with. For example, if we commune with anger over a past hurt, our desire will be for revenge.

When we commune with the Father, our desires are pure. What do you desire in that place of communion with the Lord? Once we come into the Kingdom, the straight and narrow road Jesus talked about becomes broad and big. The Kingdom is bigger on the inside than it appears on the outside. There is room for our desires, our creativity, our ideas. We don't think or dream independent of God, but because of Him. He essentially said, "I'm going to give you one huge idea, and I want it to shape every breath of your life, every bit of ministry, every prayer. The idea is, "On earth as it is in Heaven." Now, go! Run with it. Make it happen."

That mandate moves us out of robotic servanthood where we constantly ask, "Lord, do you want me to answer the phone when it rings? Should I talk to that person at the store, or pass by?" That's a form of dependence that doesn't always please God. Rather, God trusts the heart of a man who is lost in friendship with Him. As we come into intimacy with Him, more of what takes place is a result of our desires, not only of our receiving specific commands from Heaven. God begins to feed off your wishes and desires.

When we commune with the Father,
our desires are pure.

Ephesians 5:1—Be imitators of God, therefore, as dearly loved children....

BOOK QUOTE: *The Supernatural Power* [Chapter 10]

As a pastor, my first concern is always with God's agenda for us. When we consider other people for our board or leadership team, I am immune to their agendas until they lay them down and pick up my agenda, which God has given to me for our church. Then their agendas become important to me. Their desires and wishes come alive in my mind as they share them with me. I believe that's how the Father works. As He sees you and me surrender to His agenda, He's suddenly interested in hearing what we have to say. Our yieldedness and surrender make Him vulnerable to our dreams. It becomes a co-laboring effort.

As with any collaborative effort, the work we do with God bears our imprint and His. My wife gave birth to three of our children, and they bear my traits and hers. So when we co-labor with God, the result "looks" like Him and like us. For example, each of the four Gospels represents the same message, and yet each is unique and distinct, because each of the authors were unique and distinct. Even the present outpourings and revivals taking place across the world have completely different manifestations but the same Spirit because they flow through people with different giftings, personalities, relationships, and cultural settings.

Co-laboring isn't about having our way with God. He's not a cosmic bellhop to carry out whatever wish and desire we have. Neither does He rubber stamp every dream we come up with. But if He cancels one, it's only because He's got a better one in mind. And He would much rather listen to you dream than have you cower before Him asking for your next task.

Our yieldedness and surrender make Him
vulnerable to our dreams.

Proverbs 24:14—*Know also that wisdom is sweet to your soul; if you find it, there is a future hope for you, and your hope will not be cut off.*

BOOK QUOTE: *The Supernatural Power* [Chapter 10]

DREAMING with God unlocks deep reservoirs of creativity in each and every person, in different areas of gifting and talent. But in too many sectors of the Church, creativity is on lockdown because people fear their desires and dreams. Religion, cruel and boring, bottles up the creative impulse God has put inside of every person. Each of us has a right and responsibility to express ourselves creatively in whatever area of life interests us. Yet so many of us have the horrible habit of doing things the way they have always been done, for reasons of fear and safety. We're descendants of the Creator and yet we stick with old, tired methods. We ask God to do a new thing through us, but expect Him to do it in a familiar way.

Many Christians pray, and when their mind wanders they think it's the devil distracting them. That may sometimes be the case, but maybe our "devil" is too active our God too inactive. When your mind wanders, maybe God is leading you to creative solutions to problems. You may have been resisting ideas from heaven and keeping to a rigid, religious practice of prayer. Some business people get "off track" when they're praying, thinking about a deal or an opportunity, and at the end of the prayer time they think, "I just blew my whole prayer time thinking about something else." Guilt and condemnation come on them when God was actually swerving them over to a subject that was on His mind. He wanted them to think creatively and to interact with Him so He could release ideas they'd never had before.

In this relationship with the Lord, there's an exchange in His presence, and it shapes passions and dreams in us.

We ask God to do a new thing through us, but expect Him to do it in a familiar way.

Joel 2:28—And afterward, I will pour My Spirit on all people. Your sons and daughters will prophesy, your old men will dream dreams, your young men will see visions.

BOOK QUOTE: *The Supernatural Power* [Chapter 10]

RECENTLY while sharing a meal with some friends in a restaurant, I found myself thinking about the healing power of God sweeping through that place. It was a "grown up" daydream. The next day a prophet prophesied over me and called out certain things God had put in my heart. He said, "You find yourself daydreaming…" and he described the things I was daydreaming about. Then he said in the voice of the Lord, "You thought all this time this was you, but it's Me! It's Me! I was doing that; I was in the middle of that dream; I was the one stirring that up in you."

Daydreams can involve all kinds of new, creative ideas. God deposits novel thoughts and ways of expression that we've never had before. What is it like to have the God whose thoughts are as high as the heavens speaking into your thoughts? Has it ever happened in your life? I read once that every four-year-old is an artist. Then they go to school and are taught certain standards for art, so not every child remains an artist. I wouldn't say the system is always bad, but there is a drive to create in every person that is sometimes squelched.

When my oldest son was about ten years old, he was complaining about English class. "Dad, where am I ever going to use this?" he said. I listened to him go on and on about how boring English was, and I finally said, "Maybe you ought to pay extra special attention in English class. You might be one of those guys God uses to write books and you're going to need to learn this stuff." He got a faraway look and suddenly English class took on a whole new importance to him.

God deposits novel thoughts and ways of expression that we've never had before.

Hebrews 1:2—...*but in these last days He has spoken to us by His Son, whom He appointed heir of all things, and through whom He made the universe.*

BOOK QUOTE: *The Supernatural Power* [Chapter 10]

A man was walking down the road before there was AC electricity. They had to have a transformer every few feet. This man let his mind wander over the problem and God downloaded into his brain the entire concept of AC electricity. That one idea lit up entire cities from coast to coast. His daydreams revolutionized the world.

That's what Philippians 4:19 means when it says "according to His riches in glory by Christ Jesus." A Jewish rabbi was asked about that phrase and he said, "It means God, out of His realm of glory and dominion, will release to His people ideas, concepts, creative things, and witty inventions that will cause tremendous provision to come to them."

Pay attention to Kingdom imaginations. I don't mean the thundering voice, but the fresh ideas that gallop through your head throughout the day. It's entirely possible that they are sent to you by God. Some business people walk by a vacant lot and "see" a building sitting there, but they don't realize God is talking to them, drawing them to think creatively. Some musicians get an original tune stuck in their head, but they don't develop it. If we pay attention, we will pick up God's ideas. You see, the Church won't transform cities through continuous revival meetings but by allowing Kingdom creativity and power to flow into communities.

What would it be like to have ideas that transform a poverty-stricken area into a thriving business center? Or eradicate a particular disease? Or totally transform people's minds through a movie, book, or music CD? Why do you think there has been such an assault on artists in the Church? Because the enemy wants to separate us from the creative force that thinks outside the box. Those ideas can change the world.

... God, out of His realm of glory and dominion, will release to His people ideas, concepts, creative things, and witty inventions...

Proverbs 13:12—*Hope deferred makes the heart sick, But **when** the desire comes, **it is a** tree of life. NKJV*

BOOK QUOTE: *The Supernatural Power* [Chapter 10]

Your desires, far from being evil, are intended to make you strong and healthy in all areas of life. The Bible calls the fulfillment of your desires a tree of life.

When your desires are fulfilled, they become a tree of life to you. The tree of life provides continuous emotional strength, financial strength, wisdom, a mind that's at ease. That is God's desire for you and for every believer. The tree of life is mentioned in three books of the Bible. First it's in Genesis, in the center of the Garden along with the tree of the knowledge of good and evil (see Gen. 2:9). When Adam and Eve partook of the tree of the forbidden fruit, an angel blocked the way to the tree of life. It wasn't punishment; the tree of life added an eternal aspect to whatever it touched. In other words, if sinful man had partaken of the tree of life, mankind would have been permanently locked into a sinful condition.

The tree of life is mentioned again in the Book of Revelation 22:2, with a great prophetic picture of believers partaking of its fruit. That moment lies in the future and so the tree of life in Revelation tells us what will be. But the tree of life is also found in Proverbs, as we just read. The tree of life in Proverbs tells us *what can happen right now*. We can partake of the fruit of this tree in our everyday lives at this present time. God has figuratively placed this tree within our reach, and every bite of its fruit releases in us strength and eternal courage, a sense of destiny and purpose.

When your desires are fulfilled, they become a tree of life to you.

Proverbs 13:19—*A desire accomplished is sweet to the soul, But it is an abomination to fools to depart from evil.*

BOOK QUOTE: *The Supernatural Power* [Chapter 10]

THE Bible says the fulfillment of your desires is a tree of life. Where does that tree spring from? From the fulfillment of our individual, unique, God-given desires. Desire is part of God's system, His economy. He draws us into intimate friendship with Him, then responds to our desires and prayers, and answers them. When He does, it releases the courage of eternity into us.

When our desires go unfulfilled, our bodies and spirits suffer together. One of the causes of sickness and disease is disappointment that is never dealt with redemptively. People go through a disappointing circumstance and never get before God to have Him heal the hurts they pour out from their soul. The physical body inevitably reflects what's going on. I once ministered to woman with Crohn's disease; her colon had been dissolving for seven years. I asked her if she struggled with shame. She said she did, and I said, "Your body is sending you a message. Your colon is eating itself. The harshness you have toward yourself is making you sick, and your body is manifesting what you are doing to yourself emotionally." She repented for that sin and was instantly healed.

When a tree of life grows sturdy in our spirits, it bears wonderful fruit in all areas of life. The Bible talks about the fruit of the Spirit—love, joy, peace, patience, and so on. These are produced when we abide in Christ, when our desires are fulfilled as we are connected to Him, the Vine.

That fruit should increase as revival and revelation are passed down through the generations.

When a tree of life grows sturdy in our spirits, it bears wonderful fruit in all areas of life.

Deuteronomy 29:29—*The secret things belong to the Lord our God, but those things which are revealed belong to us and to our children forever, that we may do all the words of this law.*

BOOK QUOTE: *The Supernatural Power* [Chapter 11]

It's the Lord's desire that the supernatural territory we occupy, the realms of life where we consistently demonstrate His authority, grow larger and more powerful as we pass it on to the next generation. Inheritance is a biblical concept. Proverbs18:22 says, "Houses and riches are an inheritance from fathers."

The purpose of a natural inheritance is to give children a leg up so they don't have to start where their parents started. It's simply not true that everyone has to start at the same point and go through the same hardships. It's a biblical concept that one generation would provide a boost for the next.

A spiritual inheritance works the same way. It enables the next generation to start where the previous generation left off. It's the intent of the Lord for us to wake up to this, one of the most significant yet overlooked principles in the Christian life. He wants generations to pass on their spiritual inheritances. You see, with an inheritance, we get for free what someone else paid for. Sometimes we inherit graces from the Lord where we don't have to go through some of the processes a previous generation went through. That doesn't fit the do-it-yourself motto of the age, but it's the way it works with God. It's like when a person lays hands on other people to impart a grace for a certain area of life and ministry. Those people get the grace for free. That's the way things work in the Kingdom. We see somebody that has a great anointing in healing and we ask them to pray for us, and from that point on, we begin to pray for people and we see things happen that we never saw happen before. That's an inheritance.

A spiritual inheritance enables the next generation to start where the previous generation left off.

1 Corinthians 2:12—Now we have received, not the spirit of the world, but the Spirit who is from God, that we might know the things that have been freely given to us by God. NKJV

BOOK QUOTE: *The Supernatural Power* [Chapter 11]

A spiritual inheritance is about making us more effective and efficient in our representation of the King and His Kingdom. It's delightful, it's enjoyable, it's pleasant, it's encouraging, but it's not simply for personal consumption. It is to open doors so that the King and His Kingdom have influence in more places than before.

A spiritual inheritance differs from a natural inheritance in one key way: A natural inheritance gives us something we did not have before. But a spiritual inheritance pulls back the curtain and reveals what we already have permission to possess. That's why it says, "but those things which are revealed belong to us and to our children forever" (Deut. 29:29). Receiving a spiritual inheritance is like learning that years ago somebody put ten million dollars in your bank account. You had the money all along, but now you are at liberty to spend it, because you have knowledge that the money is there and belongs to you. This is what Paul was trying to get across when he wrote, "Therefore let no one boast in men. For all things are yours: whether Paul or Apollos or Cephas, or the world or life or death, or things present or things to come—all are yours. And you are Christ's, and Christ is God's" (1 Corinthians 3:21-23).

But as it is written: "Eye has not seen, nor ear heard, nor have entered into the heart of man

The things which God has prepared for those who love Him" (1 Corinthians 2:9-10).

When we learn of our inheritance, suddenly we have "spending power" with God. We call on resources we didn't know about before. When a previous generation passes on a spiritual inheritance, they pass on all the knowledge and experience they gained in a certain spiritual area.

When we learn of our inheritance, suddenly we have "spending power" with God.

2 Corinthians 3:18—*And we, who with unveiled faces all reflect the Lord's glory, are being transformed into His likeness with ever increasing glory, which comes from the Lord, who is the Spirit.*

BOOK QUOTE: *The Supernatural Power* [Chapter 11]

No generation has raised up the next to carry the momentum of a great outpouring of the Spirit, and had them take it to the next level. Time and again the ball gets dropped. The spiritual territory that was once occupied becomes unoccupied, and the enemy comes to repossess familiar turf. After some time another generation rises up, having become discontent, and begin to re-dig the wells of revival. But they start at about the same place as before. The well got filled with earth, symbolizing humanity, which is made of earth. We suffer setback after setback from generation to generation and what should be a point of passing the baton becomes a place of starting over.

The last 2,000 years of history show us that a revival will come and last two to four years, then fade out. Because of this pattern, an entire branch of theology has developed that says revival is supposed to arrive periodically to give the Church a shot in the arm— new enthusiasm, new hunger, new energy. But by saying that revival is an exception, a pit stop for refueling, normal Christianity is defined way down. I say rather that revival is not the exception; revival is normal. Signs, wonders, and miracles are as normal to the gospel as it is normal for you to get up in the morning and breathe. Revival is the Christian life; you can't dissect the two. We were never intended to live a season of life outside of the outpouring of the Spirit of God. He always takes us "from glory to glory" (2 Cor. 3:18). He is progressive in every move He makes. The nature of His Kingdom is that "of the increase of His government and peace there will be no end" (Isa. 9:7).

Signs, wonders, and miracles are as normal to the gospel as it is normal for you to get up in the morning and breathe.

Luke 12:42—*The Lord answered, "Who then is the faithful and wise manager, whom the master puts in charge of his servants to give them their food allowance at the proper time?*

BOOK QUOTE: *The Supernatural Power* [Chapter 11]

THE quickest way to lose something is to take a defensive posture where we maintain what we have instead of working to increase it. In the parable of the talents, God condemned the man who did not put his money to use, but buried it in the ground. (See Matthew 25.) To choose not to expand and increase is to choose to lose the very thing we are trying to protect.

This principle is further illustrated in Luke 11:24-26 where Jesus said,

> When an unclean spirit goes out of a man, he goes through dry places, seeking rest; and finding none, he says, "I will return to my house from which I came." And when he comes, he finds it swept and put in order. Then he goes and takes with him seven other spirits more wicked than himself, and they enter and dwell there; and the last state of that man is worse than the first.

When a person gets set free, there is a moment when he is absolutely clean and purged from filthiness. From that moment on he has the responsibility of managing that liberty. One of our greatest problems is the failure to occupy the inheritance that we've been given. Throughout the years, certain individuals broke into new spiritual territory: Smith Wigglesworth, Aimee Semple McPherson, A.B. Simpson, and many other giants of the faith we could name. They didn't start out as giants but they were possessed by a passion to pursue new territories that had not been occupied before. They began to possess territory that had not been possessed by anyone continuously since the days of the apostles. They did it at great personal risk and sacrifice, and entered into things that were completely unknown to the Church at that time.

One of our greatest problems is the failure to occupy the inheritance that we've been given.

Luke 11:24-26—*When an unclean spirit goes out of a man, he goes through dry places, seeking rest; and finding none, he says, "I will return to my house from which I came." And when he comes, he finds it swept and put in order. Then he goes and takes with him seven other spirits more wicked than himself, and they enter and swell there; and the last state of that man is worse than the first.*

BOOK QUOTE: *The Supernatural Power* [Chapter 11]

THE tragedy of history is that revival comes and goes, and subsequent generations build monuments around the achievements of the previous generation, but do not completely receive and occupy their inherited spiritual territory. What was gained by past generations has not been occupied and advanced by those who followed. The house is swept and clean, but because it was not occupied, the enemy came back seven times worse. The word house in Scripture can refer to an individual, a family, a local church, a denomination, even to your ministry, gift, and calling. But our country is pockmarked by institutions that once were advancing into unoccupied spiritual territory, and then became re-occupied by the enemy. For example, one of these former hot spots from a few centuries ago was once a great revival center. For a season it became almost the focal point of the nation. If you wanted to see what God wanted to do on the planet, you could look there. That place was Yale University. Yale's goal back then was not to raise up nice Christian people, but to raise up Holy Ghost revivalists. They paid a price to move into uninhabited territory. But today the school isn't producing revivalists, but anti-Christian secularists.

How do you get from revival center to secular stronghold? Gradually, by one generation after another, yielding territory instead of embracing their inheritance. Compromise starts when we fail to maintain what we have been given, when we stop moving into new territory, from glory to glory. When they began to compromise in that vital area, they backed up. The territory they once occupied became inhabited by the enemy and the very thing that was once a strength now became their greatest weakness.

What was gained by past generations has not been occupied and advanced by those who followed.

Psalm 78:6—...*so the next generation would know them, even the children yet to be born, and they in turn would tell their children.*

BOOK QUOTE: *The Supernatural Power* [Chapter 11]

SHOW me a church or a family whose forefathers broke into significant signs and wonders in the realm of healing, and I can assure you that if the following generations did not work to maintain and expand that previous standard, they were heavily afflicted and diseased. When the victories of past generations go unoccupied, they become the platform from which the enemy mocks the victories of the past generation. Perhaps they don't want to pay the same price their forefathers paid, or perhaps they end up forming organizations around past movements to preserve and defend the idea but not the practice of revival. Worse yet, that unoccupied territory becomes the military encampment from which the enemy launches an assault against the people of God to erase from their memories their inherited victories. When we back off of the standard that God has set, we literally invite the devourer to destroy.

Instead of building on the work of the John Lakes, Smith Wigglesworths, and Aimee Semple McPhersons, we build memorials to their memories, and forget what we should have inherited. We applaud the buildings they were in, we tell the stories of their great accomplishments, and the place that they occupied is now inhabited by the enemy himself. And so a generation like ours becomes dissatisfied once again, discontent at seeing a biblical standard and a lifestyle that falls short. And we once again have to re-dig a well, remove the humanistic, rationalistic approach to life that denies the Creator Himself and His involvement, intimate, personal involvement, in the affairs of man. We get back to the springs of life and joy.

When we back off of the standard that God has set, we literally invite the devourer to destroy.

Hebrews 10:39—*But we are not of those who shrink back and are destroyed, but of those who believe and are saved.*

BOOK QUOTE: *The Supernatural Power* [Chapter 11]

A few hundred years ago John Wesley began to occupy new spiritual territory. He was a pastor, but as a result of the presence and power of God on the Moravians, he was truly born again. He went back to England and became the father of the Methodist movement, a group of revivalists and fire-breathing believers. Thousands would gather in fields to hear Wesley preach. God would sweep through those meetings. The Methodists had a slogan: "Organized to beat the devil." They were called "Method-ists" because they created structure, not for structure's sake, but to set the boundaries for God to do something significant in their midst. Their discipling process is legendary. They pastored 100,000 people through this process of raising up leaders who would raise up leaders who would raise up leaders. It's an amazing story.

And yet, within recent days, that very movement ordained a lesbian minister. Let's not misunderstand—Jesus loves lesbians, but He intends to get them out of that lifestyle. The point is, territory broken into by John and Charles Wesley, by those in leadership and the many forgotten revivalist preachers, has been lost. Through a lifestyle of risk, they broke into uncharted territory. Wesley put a stake down and passed that ground on to the following generation, and they built monuments to his accomplishments as they withdrew from territory he once occupied, trying to make the gospel more palatable, more understandable. After all, it's not necessary to suffer all that persecution, to have all those bad things said about you. They withdrew, perhaps out of good, reasonable intent, but they left vacated territory behind them, and the very things they were strongest in—great deliverance and freedom from bondage—have become their greatest weakness.

Wesley put a stake down and passed that ground on to the following generation, and they built monuments to his accomplishments as they withdrew from territory he once occupied...

Psalm 33:12—*Blessed is the nation whose God is the Lord, the people He chose for His inheritance.*

BOOK QUOTE: *The Supernatural Power* [Chapter 11]

JOHN and Charles Wesley occupied new territory for God on this earth, but the generations that followed did not continue the revival. There are many other examples through history, but the point is simple. Every generation of revivalists has been father-less as it pertains to the move of the Spirit. Every generation has had to learn from scratch how to recognize the Presence, how to move with Him, how to pay a price. The answer to this tragedy is inheritance, where you and I receive something for free. What we do with it determines what happens in the following generations. God is serious about returning for a glorious Church. He's serious that nations should serve Him—not just a token representation from every tribe and tongue—but entire nations, entire people groups apprehended by God Himself.

Can you imagine what would happen if entire nations stepped into the gifts they have from God? Where the song of praise, the declarations of God and His greatness and goodness became visibly manifest on a people? That's His heart. But if we're to get there, we must understand and embrace our spiritual inheritance. We were never intended to start over from scratch every two or three generations. God wants to put each generation at a higher level than the previous one. Every generation has a ceiling experience that becomes the next generation's floor. We dishonor our forefathers and the great price they paid to get their breakthrough by not maintaining and expanding what they accomplished. They attained by tremendous risk and persevering under ridicule and rejection. The things we take for granted today cost the previous generation tremendously.

Can you imagine what would happen if entire nations stepped into the gifts they have from God?

Ephesians 1:3—*Praise be to the God and Father of our Lord Jesus Christ, who has blessed us in the heavenly realms with every spiritual blessing in Christ.*

BOOK QUOTE: *The Supernatural Power* [Chapter 11]

INHERITANCE helps us to build truth on top of truth. Instead of starting over each generation, we inherit certain truths that allow us to move forward into new areas. For example, when we come to Christ, we become *servants* of the Most High God. Servanthood is a very strong reality of our relationship with the Lord. But there is a superior truth, and that is friendship. Friendship is greater than servanthood. Both are true, and we don't leave servanthood to become a friend, but we build friendship on top of the experience and revelation of servanthood.

That is how we are to move into new territory, by building on precept after precept. Truth is progressive and multi-dimensional. It constantly evolves as we grow, though it never evolves into something that contradicts its foundations. There are measures and levels of anointing that cause the reality of the Scripture to change for us. In fact, a generation is now forming, I pray and believe, that will walk in an anointing that has never been known by mankind before, including the disciples. This generation won't need natural illustrations to help them understand what their spiritual task is. They will move into spiritual territory that defies the natural order. I said earlier in the book that God wants to give us revelations and experiences of Heaven that have no earthly parallel. Jesus told Nicodemus, *"If I have told you earthly things and you do not believe, how will you believe if I tell you heavenly things?"* (John 3:12).

This generation. . .will move into spiritual territory that defies the natural order.

John 4:35—*Behold, I say to you, lift up your eyes and look at the fields, for they are already white for harvest! NKJV*

BOOK QUOTE: *The Supernatural Power* [Chapter 11]

JESUS used two natural illustrations to illustrate the Christian life. One was childbirth and the other was wind. Then He said He had more to say about spiritual realities that have no earthly parallel. This is important, because we are brokers of a heavenly realm. We are here as ambassadors assigned, given dominion over a planet, to represent His Name, to do what Jesus did. What good are we if we can't understand and operate in the spiritual realm that has no natural parallel? But as the generations embrace their inheritance, I believe we will move into the season Jesus spoke about that defies the natural order.

We understand spiritual things through natural pictures. We compare evangelism to a harvest, because we are familiar with the process of sowing and reaping. But Jesus wants us to understand spiritual realities that have no natural picture.

With a superior revelation not bounded by the natural order, every day is harvest day. There is no waiting for the right season. People who seem impossible to win to the Lord will be won instantly, without any sowing or preparation or tending, if our anointing is equal to the revelation Jesus has for us in John 4:35. The anointing on a coming generation will be great enough that the natural order of things will no longer apply. With a low-grade anointing and revelation, we have to live by natural principles and restrictions to get spiritual results. But Jesus brings this revelation, which is almost frightening. He says, "Lift up your eyes," meaning, "With the way you see things right now, you cannot operate on the revelation I want to give you. But there is something available for a coming generation where their anointing is so extreme that every person will be ready for harvest."

We are here as ambassadors assigned, given dominion over a planet, to represent His Name, to do what Jesus did.

Colossians 2:17—*These are a shadow of the things that were to come; the reality, however, is found in Christ.*

BOOK QUOTE: *The Supernatural Power* [Chapter 11]

Jesus walked in such an anointing, carrying the Spirit without measure, which instantly defied the natural principles that illustrated spiritual truths. The more you and I become empowered and directed by the Spirit of God, the more our lives should defy the natural principles that release spiritual realities. It's not that the principles of harvest are no longer true. They are as true as they ever were, but they are superseded by a superior truth. What used to take years or months now takes weeks or days to solve.

Think of the Gadarene demoniac in Mark 5. The Church today would treat a man like that much differently than Jesus did. It wasn't long ago that Christians wouldn't even pray for an insane or deranged person. We sent them to asylums and to doctors to have their problem fixed. Now we at least have the courage to pray for them, and we're seeing breakthroughs. Multiple personality disorders and people who have suffered satanic ritual abuse are made right with prayer, and what used to be beyond our realm of faith now can be broken with the anointing we have. I doubt if we would do what Jesus did: He sent the man into ministry right after being saved! We would probably insist that he go through a longer process of healing and deliverance before being entrusted the position of being the director of evangelism for that region. With the average anointing we carry as a people, we would have to take him through months of counseling sessions, and many training classes to make sure he is *debugged*. But as the anointing increases, it increasingly defies natural laws. You will know it is increasing because it will bump up against the very boundaries and limits of faith you used to live within.

. . . as the anointing increases, it increasingly defies natural laws.

Ephesians 1:18—I pray also that the eyes of your heart may be enlightened in order that you may know the hope to which He has called you, the riches of His glorious inheritance in the saints.

BOOK QUOTE: *The Supernatural Power* [Chapter 11]

As the anointing begins to increase, it will increasingly defy natural laws. An examples of this is when Jesus came up to a fig tree, which had no fruit on it. It was not the right season for fruit. But He cursed it anyway. Why? Because He has the right to expect impossible fruit. He requires from us fruit that is impossible to bear. I truly believe that it is not normal for a Christian to not have an appetite for the impossible. It's completely abnormal; it's a deformity that comes through disappointment and/or bad teaching.

Remember the promise out of Amos 9:13,

"Behold, the days are coming," says the Lord, "When the plowman shall overtake the reaper, and the treader of grapes him who sows seed; the mountains shall drip with sweet wine, and all the hills shall flow with it."

That illustrates this very principle. We must lift our eyes to see from His perspective. A greater vision/revelation makes a greater anointing available, if I'll *earnestly pursue spiritual gifts* (1 Cor. 14:1). How do we know you've lifted them high enough? Because we can see differently—everyone ready for harvest. How does the plowman overtake the reaper? The growth stages are no longer restricted by natural laws of planting and harvesting, but have become supernatural in nature. The field is growing at the same time it is being harvested and planted. The seasons are overlapping. Why? Because a generation embraced its spiritual inheritance and in that new territory the anointing is strong enough to defy natural boundaries the Church has lived within for centuries.

. . .it is not normal for a Christian to not have an appetite for the impossible.

Proverbs 13:22—*A good man leaves an inheritance for his children's children.*

BOOK QUOTE: *The Supernatural Power* [Chapter 11]

WE are in the beginning stages of the season called "accelerated growth." It is possible, if we are willing to pour ourselves out, to lay the groundwork for another generation to come and use our ceiling as their floor, to build upon it, to bring things of the Church into a place where it must come to.

Righteousness causes us to realize that our daily decisions affect several generations away. We must learn to sow into the welfare of a generation we may never live to see.

If you're a first-generation believer, or if your family has been in the church for generations, by revelation you have access to an inheritance that is beyond your wildest imagination. We owe it to the generations in the past to occupy that territory because they paid a great price for it. We owe it to our family ancestors. We owe it to our children and grandchildren. Before Jesus returns there will be the community of the redeemed walking under the influence of their inheritance, *a city whose builder and maker is God.* There will be a generation that steps into the cumulative revelation of the whole gospel. There will be a generation that lifts their eyes and sees that supernatural season in which every single person is harvestable now, and have the anointing necessary to carry it out.

My cry is to see these things in my lifetime, so I'm giving my life for it. But I have told my kids and the young people I pastor, "If we don't get there together, take it on. Do not be shaped by the opinions of man, but be shaped by your value for His presence. Any price you pay in claiming more territory for God is well worth the exchange."

Righteousness causes us to realize that our daily decisions affect several generations away.

1 Corinthians 3:9—*For we are God's fellow workers; you are God's field, God's building.*

BOOK QUOTE: *Dreaming With God* [Chapter 1]

HERE is an important statement: God has made Himself vulnerable to the desires of His people. This is because God has called us to become His friends.

The disciples lived in awe of the One who called them to leave everything and follow. It was an easy choice. When He spoke, something came alive in them that they never knew existed. There was something in His voice that was worth living for—worth giving one's life for.

Everyday with Jesus was filled with a constant barrage of things they could not understand; whether it was a demoniac falling at Jesus' feet in worship, or the overbearing, religious leaders becoming silent in His presence; it was all overwhelming. Their lives had taken on a meaning and purpose that made everything else disappointing at best. Oh, they had their personal issues, for sure, but they had been apprehended by God and now nothing else mattered.

The momentum of the lifestyle they experienced would be hard for us to comprehend. Every word, every action seemed to have eternal significance. It must have occurred to them that to serve in the courts of this King would be far better than living in their own palaces. They were experiencing firsthand what David felt when he lived with God's presence as his priority.

Perhaps only Esther of old could really understand what that exaltation felt like, as she, a servant girl who descended from captives, was promoted to queen. "And who knows but that you have come to royal position for such a time as this" (Esther 4:14).

*. . . but they had been apprehended by God
and now nothing else mattered.*

John 15:14—*You are my friends if you do whatever I command you.*

BOOK QUOTE: *Dreaming With God* [Chapter 1]

Toward the end of His earthly life, Jesus gave His disciples the ultimate promotion. He told the twelve that He no longer called them servants, but friends. To be in the same room with Him, or even to admire Him from a distance, was more than they could have asked for. But Jesus brought them into His life. They had proven themselves worthy of the greatest promotion ever experienced by humanity—from servants to intimates. "*No longer do I call you servants, for a servant does not know what his master is doing; but I have called you friends, for all things that I heard from My Father I have made known to you*" (John 15:15). With this promotion, the disciples' attention would now shift from the task at hand to the One within reach. They were given access to the secrets in the heart of God.

When Jesus gave His disciples this promotion, He did so by describing the difference between the two positions. Servants don't know what their master is doing. They don't have access to the personal, intimate realm of their master. They are task-oriented. Obedience is their primary focus—and rightly so, for their lives depend on success in that area. But friends have a different focus. It almost sounds blasphemous to say that obedience is not the top concern for the friend, but it is true. Obedience will always be important, but friends are less concerned about disobeying than they are about disappointing. The disciples' focus shifted from the commandments to the presence, from the assignment to the relationship, from "what I do for Him" to "how my choices affect Him." This bestowal of friendship made the revolution we continue to experience possible.

. . . friends are less concerned about disobeying than they are about disappointing.

Colossians 1:21-22—Once you were alienated from God and were enemies in your minds because of your evil behavior. But now He has reconciled you...

BOOK QUOTE: *Dreaming With God* [Chapter 1]

JESUS has promoted us from the role of servant to the role of friend. Several paradigm shifts take place in our hearts as we embrace this promotion. First, *what we know* changes, as we gain access to the heart of the Father. His heart is the greatest resource of information we need to function successfully in all of life. Jesus paid the price of our access to the Father, thereby granting us the *freedom* that comes from the truth we gain through that unlimited knowledge of His heart. Liberty is found in this phase of the promotion.

Second, our *experience* changes. Encounters with God as an intimate are quite different from those of a servant. His heartbeat becomes our heartbeat as we celebrate the shift in our own desires. The realm of His presence becomes our greatest inheritance, and divine encounters our greatest memories. Personal transformation is the only possible result from these supernatural experiences.

Third, our *function* in life radically changes. Instead of working *for* Him, we work *with* Him. We work not *for* His favor but *from* His favor. In this position He entrusts us with more of His power, and we are naturally changed into His likeness more and more.

Fourth, our *identity* is radically transformed. Our identity sets the tone for all we do and become. Christians who live out of who they really are cannot be crippled by the opinions of others. They don't work to fit into other people's expectations, but burn with the realization of who the Father says they are.

*Instead of working **for** Him, we work **with** Him.*

Luke 10:42—*but only one thing is needed. Mary has chosen what is better, and it will not be taken way from her.*

BOOK QUOTE: *Dreaming With God* [Chapter 1]

WITH previous entries, we have been looking at how we have been promoted through Christ from being a servant to a friend. The classic example of the difference between servants and friends is found in the story of Mary and Martha. Mary chose to sit at Jesus' feet while Martha chose to work in the kitchen (see Luke 10:38-42).

Mary sought to please Him by being with Him while Martha tried to please Him through service. When Martha became jealous, she asked Jesus to tell Mary to help in the kitchen. Most servants want to degrade the role of the friend to feel justified in their works-oriented approach to God. Jesus' response is important to remember: "*Mary has chosen the better part.*" Martha was making sandwiches that Jesus never ordered. Doing more for God is the method servants use to increase in favor. A friend has a different focus entirely. They enjoy the favor they have and use it to spend time with their friend.

To say we need both Marys and Marthas is to miss the point entirely. And it simply isn't true. I've heard it said that nothing would ever get done if we didn't have Marthas. That, too, is a lie. That teaching comes mostly from servants who are intimidated by the lifestyle of friends. Mary wasn't a non-worker; she just learned to serve from His presence, only making the sandwiches that Jesus ordered. Working *from* His presence is better than working *for* His presence. Pastor Mike Bickle put it best when he said that *there are lovers and there are workers. And lovers get more work done than do workers!* A passionate lover will always outperform a good servant in pleasing Him.

And lovers get more work done than do workers!

Psalm 40:8—*I desire to do Your will, O my God; Your law is within my heart.*

BOOK QUOTE: *Dreaming With God* [Chapter 1]

WE usually think of the will of God as something static—fixed and unchangeable. We primarily associate it with specific events at certain times. The element missing in our understanding of this subject is our role in the unfolding of His will.

When God was going to destroy Israel, He told Moses to get out of the way, because He was going to kill the people that Moses had led out of Egypt into the wilderness. Moses then reminded God that they weren't his people—they were God's, and not only that, he didn't lead them out of Egypt, God did! God responded by basically acknowledging he was right, and then promised not to kill them. The astonishing thing isn't so much that God changed His mind and spared Israel; rather, it was that He expected Moses to come into the counsel of His will, and Moses knew it. Abraham was another who understood this. These covenant friends throughout history all seemed to have a common awareness of God's expectation that they be involved in the demonstration of His will, influencing the outcome of a matter. They understood that the responsibility rested on their shoulders, and they must act before God to get what people needed. The priestly role of an intercessor was never more clearly illustrated. The primary focus of His will wasn't whether or not to destroy Israel; it was to bring Moses in on the process. His will is not always focused on events; it is focused on His friends drawing near into His presence, standing in their roles as delegated ones. The will of God is as much process as it is outcome—often fluid, not static.

The will of God is as much process as it is outcome—
often fluid, not static.

John 16:23-24—*And in that day you will ask Me nothing. Most assuredly, I say to you, whatever you ask the Father in My name He will give you. Until now you have asked nothing in My name. Ask, and you will receive, that your joy may be full.*

BOOK QUOTE: *Dreaming With God* [Chapter 1]

As kids, many of us dreamed about being granted one wish. Solomon got the "one wish." When God appeared to Solomon and gave him that opportunity, it forever raised the bar of our expectations in prayer. The disciples were given the same "wish," only better. Instead of one blank check, they were given an unlimited supply of blank checks. And this gift was specifically granted in the context of their friendship with God.

Surrounding their promotion to friendship, Jesus gave His disciples this amazing list of promises. Each promise was a blank check they were to live by and use throughout their lives for the expansion of the Kingdom:

- *"If you abide in Me, and My words abide in you, you will **ask what you desire,** and it shall be done for you"* (John 15:7).
- *"You did not choose Me, but I chose you and appointed you that you should go and bear fruit, and that your fruit should remain, that **whatever you ask** the Father in My name He may give you"* (John 15:16).
- ***If you ask anything** in My name, I will do it* (John 14:14).

For us to properly receive what Jesus has offered us in these verses, any robotic understanding of what it means to be a follower of God has to change. God never intended that the believer be a puppet on a string. God actually makes Himself vulnerable to the desires of His people. In fact, it can be said, "if it matters to you, it matters to Him."

While much of the Church is waiting for the next word from God, He is waiting to hear the dream of His people. He longs for us to take our role, not because He needs us, but because He loves us.

Each promise was a blank check they were to live by and use throughout their lives for the expansion of the Kingdom.

Matthew 7:11—*If you, then, though you are evil, know how to give good gifts to your children, how much more will your Father in heaven give good gifts to those who ask Him!*

BOOK QUOTE: *Dreaming With God* [Chapter 1]

My mother's side of the family had a family reunion in the early '90s. Around 160 people came from all over the world to the campground we rented in northern California. Astonishingly, they represented 48 different pastors and missionaries.

On one of the evenings, someone had scheduled a square dance as a recreational activity. Now, I don't dance, except in worship. It doesn't matter to me if it's square dancing, or if it's on some nightclub dance floor, I simply don't dance.

When Beni, my wife, asked what I was going to do, I told her emphatically: "I don't dance!" She already knew my thoughts and wisely chose to not attempt the impossible, which was to talk me out of such an idea so that I could join in the family fun.

We went to the hall where the party was in full swing, as entire families were attempting to dance together. Then the unexpected happened. My daughter, Leah, then about ten years old, asked me if I would dance with her.

I am known for being unmovable. Some family members call it stubborn; I call it commitment. Yet in that moment I felt like I had been ambushed. To my horror, I found myself without a will saying, "Yes." Where was my toughness? What about my resolve? I had been "brought to my knees" by a little girl. Moments later I was on the dance floor, attempting what I knew better than to attempt. But the look in my little girl's eyes told me all was well. Her pleasure more than made up for my embarrassment. And I understood again how fathers willingly make themselves vulnerable to the desires of their children—and how God joyfully makes Himself vulnerable to the desires of His people.

> *. . . God joyfully makes Himself vulnerable*
> *to the desires of His people.*

Daniel 7:27—*Then the sovereignty, power and greatness of the kingdoms under the whole heaven will be handed over to the saints, the people of the Most High. His kingdom will be an everlasting kingdom, and all rulers will worship and obey Him.*

BOOK QUOTE: *Dreaming With God* [Chapter 1]

THERE is no question that spending time with God changes our desires. We always become like the one we worship. But it's not because we've been programmed to wish for the things He wants us to wish for; it's because in friendship we discover the things that please Him—the secret things of His heart. It is the instinct of the true believer to search for and find, that which brings pleasure to the Father. Our nature actually changes at conversion. It is our new nature to seek to know God and to please Him with our thoughts, ambitions, and desires.

Those who have the greatest difficulty with this line of thinking are those who consider this to be an assault on the doctrine of the sovereignty of God. There is no question; God is sovereign. But His position of rulership is not denied by our assignment to co-labor with Christ. One of my favorite quotes on this subject comes from my dear friend Jack Taylor. He says, *"God is so secure in His sovereignty that He is not afraid to appear un-sovereign."*

Many believers discount their desires, automatically trying to get rid of everything they want in order to prove their surrender to God. Their selfless approach overshoots the will of God and actually denies the fact that God is the Father of the dreams and abilities within them. Most still don't see the difference between the entrance *to* the Kingdom, and life *in* the Kingdom. We enter on a straight and narrow road, saying, *"Not my will but Yours be done."* The only door is Christ Jesus. The only way to find life in Christ is to come in complete abandonment to Him.

. . . His position of rulership is not denied by our assignment to co-labor with Christ.

1 John 3:1—*How great is the love the Father has lavished on us, that we should be called children of God! And that is what we are! The reason the world does not know us is that it did not know Him.*

BOOK QUOTE: *Dreaming With God* [Chapter 1]

THE question should not be, "are my desires from God?" The question should be, "With what, or with whom have I been in communion?" (These quotes are from Lance Wallnau.)

I can commune with God or with the enemy. If I ponder an offense I experienced years ago, and I begin to wonder if God ever judged that person, the desires of vindication and retaliation will stir up in my heart. Why? Because I have been fellowshipping with the *father* of bitterness, and those desires are the *children* formed in my heart.

If fellowshipping with evil can produce evil desires in us, how much more should time with God form desires in us that have eternity in mind and ultimately bring Him glory? The thing to note is this: these desires are not there by command; they are in our hearts because of our fellowship with God. They are the off-spring of our relationship with Him.

Life in the Kingdom, which is past the narrow entrance of salvation, is bigger on the inside than it is on the outside. Here we find the Lord saying that we're no longer servants, but friends. It's in that context He says that the Father will give us whatever we want. The emphasis is on *what you want*. Granted, we can't forget the context, or we'll just create more selfish people who confess Christ. Just as the Cross precedes the resurrection, so our abandonment to *His will* precedes God attending to *ours*. But the opposite emphasis also has dangers—if we never become people of desire, we will never accurately and effectively represent Christ on the earth.

*Just as the Cross precedes the resurrection, so our abandonment to **His will** precedes God attending to **ours**.*

2 Chronicles 7:11—Solomon successfully accomplished all that came into his heart....

BOOK QUOTE: *Dreaming With God* [Chapter 1]

"*...desire fulfilled is a tree of life*" (Proverbs 13:12 NASB). Solomon gave us this amazing statement. If there was anyone qualified to discuss *fulfilled personal desires* it was Solomon. We can't allow his disobedience later in life to deter us from the profound lessons learned through his obedience early in life. He experienced the power of having his heartfelt desires accomplished.

Solomon's words revisit the subject of the tree of life found in Genesis. It connected Adam and Eve to eternity. (After eating the forbidden fruit, the angel of the Lord guarded the way to the tree of life so that Adam and Eve could not eat its fruit; it made eternal whatever it touched. It would make their sinful condition permanent—an eternal, unredeemable state.) Here we are told that a believer will experience the tree of life as their desires are fulfilled. Those who taste the wonder of fulfilled desires in Christ will be given eternal perspective and identity through that fulfillment. The process of surrender, personal transformation, and fulfilled desires is the training ground for reigning with Christ forever.

Answered prayers, especially those that require supernatural intervention, make us happy! And happy people are fun to be with. Perhaps that's why Jesus was called the friend of sinners (see Luke 7:34). His joy exceeded all those around Him. Moment by moment, He saw His prayers answered by His heavenly Father. His joy was what many would consider extreme. In Luke 10:21, it says, "*Jesus rejoiced in the Spirit.*" The word *rejoiced* suggests "shouting and leaping with joy." (Footnote from the Spirit-Filled Life Bible.) Even proximity to Jesus brought joy. John the Baptist leapt for joy in his mother's womb because Mary, pregnant with Jesus, entered the room. Jesus' joy is contagious, and must become the mark of true believers once again.

The process of surrender, personal transformation, and fulfilled desires is the training ground for reigning with Christ forever.

1 Kings 8:15-17—Blessed be the Lord God of Israel, who spoke with His mouth to my father David, and with His hand has fulfilled it, saying, 'Since the day that I brought My people Israel out of Egypt, I have chosen no city from any tribe of Israel in which to build a house, that My name might be there; but I chose David to be over My people Israel.' Now it was in the heart of my father David to build a temple for the name of the Lord God of Israel.

BOOK QUOTE: *Dreaming With God* [Chapter 1]

AN extraordinary example of fulfilled dreams is illustrated in Solomon's building of a temple that his father, David, had planned. The building and consecration of Solomon's temple is one of the most significant events in the Bible. Yet at the temple's dedication, Solomon gave credit to his father.

God said that He didn't choose a city, He chose a man, and the idea for a temple was in the heart of the man. God basically said: The temple wasn't my idea. David was my idea. Incredible! David's creativity and desires helped write history because God embraced them. David gave us many Kingdom principles, which set the direction in which we are to live. It is as if he said, "Dreamers! Come! Let's dream together and write the story of human history." You are God's idea, and He longs to see the treasure that is in your heart. As we learn to dream with God we become co-laborers with Him.

God assigned Adam the task of naming all the animals (see Gen. 2:19). Names had much richer meaning in those days because they represented the nature of something. I believe that Adam was actually assigning to each animal its nature, its realm of authority, and the dimension of glory it would enjoy. In reality, Adam's assignment was to help define the nature of the world he was to live in. This co-laboring role was a creative role, complimentary to God the Creator. God brings us into these situations, not because He can't do it Himself. He delights in seeing all that He made come into its identity in Him by embracing its divine purpose. To embrace the privilege of creative expression is consistent with being made in the image and likeness of our Creator.

This co-laboring role was a creative role, complimentary to God the Creator.

Psalm 37:4—*Delight yourself also in the Lord, and He shall give you the desires of your heart. NKJV*

BOOK QUOTE: *Dreaming With God* [Chapter 1]

THE King James Bible highlights the role of our desires in the way it translates Mark 11:24, *"Therefore I say unto you, what things soever ye desire, when ye pray, believe that ye receive them, and ye shall have them."* We are to pay attention to our desires while we're enjoying the presence of God in prayer. Something happens in our time of communion with Him that brings life to our capacity to dream and desire. Our minds become renewed through divine encounter, making it the perfect canvas for Him to paint on. We become co-laborers with Him in the master plan for planet earth. Our dreams are not independent from God, but instead exist *because of* God. He lays out the agenda—*On earth as it is in Heaven*—and then releases us to run with it and make it happen! As we grow in intimacy with Him, more of what happens in life is a result of our desires, not simply receiving and obeying specific commands from Heaven. God loves to build on our wishes and desires, as He embraced David's desire for the temple.

This truth is risky from our perspective because we see those who live independent of God and only want Him to validate their dreams. True grace always creates a place for those with evil in their heart to come to the surface through increased opportunity. But the richness of this truth is worth pursuing in spite of the perceived danger, because only this truth enables the Church to come fully into her destiny through co-laboring with the Lord.

This divine destiny was announced by the Psalmist long before the blood of Jesus made it a possible lifestyle.

*Our dreams are not independent from God, but instead exist **because** of God.*

2 Timothy 1:6—*For this reason I remind you to fan into flame the gift of God, which is in you through the laying on of my hands.*

BOOK QUOTE: *Dreaming With God* [Chapter 2]

ONE of the most natural parts of being created in the image of God is the ability to dream. Yet many believers, in their attempts to please God, kill the very capacity He gave them. They reason, "To really please God I must get rid of everything to do with self!" It sounds spiritual, but it's more Buddhist than Christian. If we pursue that line of thinking we end up with neutered believers. Self-mutilation need not be physical to be a perversion. Anytime we try to cut away at what God placed in us, we enter a form of spirituality that is not Scriptural and contribute to a spirit that works against a truly effective witness. It is not wise to crucify the resurrected man and call it discipleship. The Cross is not for the new man; it's for the old man (Romans 6:5-9).

Confusion over our value and identity is sometimes acute in revival, as the outpouring of the Spirit always brings an increased awareness of our sinfulness. Some of the greatest hymns of confession and contrition have been written during such seasons. But the revelation of our sin and unworthiness is only half of the equation. Most revivals don't get past this one point, and therefore cannot sustain a move of God until it becomes a lifestyle. It's difficult to build something substantial on a negative. The other half of the equation is how holy He is on our behalf and who we are as a result. When this is realized, our identity changes as we embrace the purpose of our salvation by faith. At some point we must go beyond being simply "sinners saved by grace." As we learn to live from our position in Christ, we will bring forth the greatest exploits of all time.

As we learn to live from our position in Christ, we will bring forth the greatest exploits of all time.

Colossians 3:10—...and have put on the new self, which is being renewed in knowledge in the image of its Creator.

BOOK QUOTE: *Dreaming With God* [Chapter 2]

Our heavenly Father is the Creator of all, and the Giver of all good gifts. His children should bear His likeness, which means they should be creative. When unbelievers lead the way in inventions and artistic expressions, it is because the church has embraced a false kind of spirituality. It is not living in a true Kingdom mentality, which is the renewed mind. The renewed mind understands that the King's dominion must be realized in all levels of society for an effective witness to take place. Someone with a Kingdom mindset looks to the overwhelming needs of the world and says, "God has a solution for this problem. And I have legal access to His realm of mystery. Therefore I will seek Him for the answer!" With a Kingdom perspective, we become the answer in much the same way Joseph and Daniel were to the kings of their day.

To be free to dream with God, one must learn to be a co-laborer. The desire of the true believer is never independence from God. The goal is not to find ways to shape God's thinking, as though He were in need of our input. Instead it is to represent Him well. Learning to display His heart instinctively and accurately is the passion of true lovers of God. His heart is to redeem all people, and the tools He uses to display His goodness are gloriously vast, reaching into the heartfelt needs of every individual. Only divine wisdom can meet that challenge.

Learning the dreams of God for this world is our beginning place. Dreaming can be expensive. We know that the Father's dream of redeeming humanity cost Him the life of His Son. However, partnering with Him in His dreams will release in us a new capacity to dream like Him.

To be free to dream with God, one must learn to be a co-laborer.

Proverbs 8:29-31—*When He marked out the foundations of the earth; Then I was beside Him, as a master workman; and I was daily His delight, rejoicing always before Him, rejoicing in the world, His earth, and having my delight in the sons of men. NASB*

BOOK QUOTE: *Dreaming With God* [Chapter 2]

WISDOM and creativity are related subjects in the Bible. In fact, creativity is a manifestation of wisdom in the context of excellence and integrity. Wisdom is personified in Proverbs 8, and is the companion of God at the creation of all things. Therefore wisdom and creativity must not be separated in the mind of the believer. They are the essential tools needed to complete our assignment of being an effective witness to the lost. It is wisdom that makes our role in this world desirable to them. While most Christians have a value for wisdom, most do not have an equal value for the role of creativity in their God-given responsibilities. Yet it is creativity that illustrates the presence of wisdom: "*Wisdom is vindicated by all her children*" (Luke 7:35 NASB).

The six days of creation saw the most wonderful display of wisdom and art imaginable. As God spoke, the worlds were made. Light and beauty, sound and color, all flowed together seamlessly as wisdom set the boundaries for creation itself. Solomon, the man known for supernatural wisdom, discusses the co-laboring effect that wisdom had on that day in Proverbs 8 (see above).

Wisdom is given an artisan title of "master workman." Note the even more powerful phrases; "*rejoicing always before Him,*" "*rejoicing in the world,*" and "*my delight in the sons of men.*" Wisdom is not stoic as it is so often pictured. It's even more than happy; it is celebratory in nature and finds pleasure in the act of creation. But its greatest delight is in us! It has found perfect companionship with humanity. We were born to partner with wisdom—to live in it and display it through creative expression.

. . . creativity that illustrates the presence of wisdom. . .

Exodus 31:3-5—I have filled him with the Spirit of God in wisdom, in understanding, in knowledge, and in all kinds of craftsmanship, to make artistic designs for work in gold, in silver, and in bronze, and in the cutting of stones for settings, and in the carving of wood, that he may work in all kinds of craftsmanship. NASB

BOOK QUOTE: *Dreaming With God* [Chapter 2]

THE first mention of a person filled with the Holy Spirit in Scripture was Bezalel. He was called upon to head up a building project for Moses. It was wisdom that qualified him to take on this assignment, and it was wisdom that enabled him to design and build what was in God's heart.

> *Then Moses said to the sons of Israel, "See, the Lord has called by name Bezalel the son of Uri, the son of Hur, of the tribe of Judah. And He has **filled him with the Spirit of God,** in **wisdom,** in understanding and in knowledge and in all **craftsmanship**; to **make designs** for working in gold and in silver and in bronze, and in the cutting of stones for settings and in the carving of wood, so as to perform in every **inventive work.** He also has put in his heart to teach, both he and Oholiab, the son of Ahisamach, of the tribe of Dan. He has filled them with **skill to perform every work** of an engraver and of a designer and of an embroiderer, in blue and in purple and in scarlet material, and in fine linen, and of a weaver, as **performers of every work and makers of designs** (Exodus 35:30-35 NASB).*

Artistic design, excellence, and *inventive work* are a few of the characteristics of wisdom in this passage. If we combine Old Testament revelation and New Testament power in the Spirit we end up with believers who walk in wisdom, making practical contributions to the needs of society, who also confront the impossibilities of life through the provisions of the Cross, bringing solutions through supernatural display of miracles, signs, and wonders. Perhaps it is these two things working in tandem that should be considered *the balanced Christian life.*

Artistic design, excellence, and inventive work are a few of the characteristics of wisdom. . .

Zechariah 1:18-21—Then I lifted up my eyes and looked, and behold, there were four horns. So I said to the angel who was speaking with me, "What are these?" And he answered me, "These are the horns which have scattered Judah, Israel and Jerusalem." Then the Lord showed me four craftsmen. I said, "What are these coming to do?" And he said, "These are the horns which have scattered Judah so that no man lifts up his head; but these craftsmen have come to terrify them, to throw down the horns of the nations who have lifted up their horns against the land of Judah in order to scatter it. NASB

BOOK QUOTE: *Dreaming With God* [Chapter 2]

ZECHARIAH 1:18-21 is one of the more alarming passages in the Bible because God's tools for victory are not common knowledge for most of us today.

In these verses the people of God are being terrorized and scattered by abusive authorities and powers (horns). Hopelessness is the theme of the day, and the confidence that God is with them is at an all time low. The God of wisdom illumines a truth that is to awaken the people of God to His end-time plans. He sends forth His army to tear down military strongholds. Who are His soldiers? Craftsmen! Not since God first sent a choir into war has there been such an outlandish strategy for battle. This is a plan that only Wisdom could design.

When creativity is the normal expression of God's people there is something that happens to all who oppose Him. They become disheartened. The devil himself has no creative abilities whatsoever. All he can do is distort and deform what God has made. God is made known through His works. When His works flow through His children their identity is revealed, and there is an inescapable revelation of the nature of God in the land. He is irresistible to those who have eyes to see.

Craftsmen are not simply woodworkers and painters. Everyone, doing their God-given task with *excellence, creativity,* and *integrity* is a craftsman in the biblical sense. The opposition that surrounds us cannot stand against the demonstration of God's people wielding this great weapon of war. Micah tells us that in the last days the nations will come to His holy nation asking us to teach them the Word (see Micah 4:1-2). It is possible that this is their response to seeing us filled with the Spirit until His wisdom is on display.

. . . God's tools for victory are not common knowledge for most of us today.

2 Chronicles 9:3-4—When the queen of Sheba had seen the wisdom of Solomon, the house which he had built, the food at his table, the seating of his servants, the attendance of his ministers and their attire, his cupbearers and their attire, and his stairway by which he went up to the house of the Lord, she was breathless. NASB

BOOK QUOTE: *Dreaming With God* [Chapter 2]

THE world's definition of wisdom is focused on the attainment and use of knowledge. It's not wrong; it's just misleading. The church has adopted their incomplete definition, pursuing a wisdom that has no soul. Biblical wisdom sees with divine perspective, and is the creative expression of God, bringing practical solutions to the issues of everyday life.

Besides Jesus, Solomon was the wisest man to ever live. He caught the attention of his entire generation. People were in awe of his gift. The royalty in other nations envied his servants who had the privilege of being exposed to his gift on a daily basis. *A servant in the presence of wisdom is better off than being a king without wisdom.* The queen of Sheba was stunned by how wisdom affected simple things like clothing, buildings, and the like.

The effects of his gifts brought Israel into the greatest time of peace and prosperity they had ever known. Wisdom, through one man, changed a nation. What could happen with millions embracing this God-given opportunity?

The wisdom of God will again be reflected in His people. The Church, which is presently despised, will again be reverenced and admired. The Church will again be a *praise in the earth* (see Jer. 33:9).

The manifestations of wisdom are varied. But as mentioned earlier, its nature can be seen in three words—integrity, creativity, and excellence. Divine wisdom springs from *integrity*, and becomes manifest through *creative* expression with *excellence* as its standard. Wherever we find ourselves operating in any of these three expressions we are being touched by divine wisdom.

*Divine wisdom springs from **integrity**, and becomes manifest through **creative** expression with **excellence** as its standard.*

Proverbs 8:11—*...for wisdom is more precious than rubies, and nothing you desire can compare with her.*

BOOK QUOTE: *Dreaming With God* [Chapter 2]

THE nature of wisdom can be seen in three words—integrity, creativity, and excellence. Divine wisdom springs from *integrity*, and becomes manifest through *creative* expression with *excellence* as its standard. We are going to examine the first two.

Integrity – a) Adherence to moral and ethical principles; soundness of moral character; honesty. b) The state of being whole, entire, or undiminished. c) A sound, unimpaired, or perfect condition. *Synonyms*: honesty, truth, truthfulness, honor, veracity, reliability, and uprightness.

Integrity is the expression of God's character revealed in us; and that character is the beauty of His perfection—His holiness. Holiness is the essence of His nature. It is not something He does or doesn't do. It is who He is. It is the same for us. We are holy because the nature of God is in us. It begins with a heart separated unto God and becomes evident in the Christ-nature expressed through us.

Creativity – a) The state or quality of being creative. b) The ability to transcend traditional ideas, rules, patterns, relationships, or the like, and to create meaningful new ideas, forms, methods, interpretations, etc.; originality, progressiveness, or imagination. c) The process by which one utilizes creative ability. *Synonyms*: originality, imagination, inspiration, ingenuity, inventiveness, resourcefulness, creativeness, and vision.

Creativity will not only be seen in a full restoration of the arts; it is the nature of His people, expressed in finding new and better ways to do things in any area of influence. It is a shame for the Church to fall into the rut of predictability and call it "tradition." We must reveal who our Father is through creative expression. We do not become culturally relevant when we become like the culture, but rather when we model what the culture hungers to become.

We are holy because the nature of God is in us.

2 Samuel 6:5—David and the whole house of Israel were celebrating with all their might before the Lord, with songs and with harps, lyres, tambourines, sistrums and cymbals.

BOOK QUOTE: *Dreaming With God* [Chapter 2]

WISDOM's nature is marked by three characteristics: integrity, creativity, and excellence. We looked at the first two in the last journal entry. Now we will consider excellence.

Excellence – a) The fact or state of excelling; superiority; eminence; b) An excellent quality or feature. *Synonyms:* fineness, brilliance, superiority, distinction, quality, and merit.

Excellence is the high standard set for personal achievement because of who we are in God, and who God is in us. It is not the same as perfectionism. Perfectionism is the cruel counterfeit of excellence, which flows from a religious spirit.

Excellence is impossible without passion. An excellent heart for God appears to be wasteful to those on the outside. In Matthew 26:8 Mary poured ointment upon Jesus that cost a full year's income. The disciples thought it should have been sold and the money given to the poor. Yet that move was so valuable to God that He said her story would be told wherever the Gospel is preached (see Matt. 26:13).

King David was extravagant when he took off his kingly garments and danced wildly before God, humbling himself before the people (see 2 Sam. 6:14-23). His wife, Michal, despised him for it. As a result she bore no children to the day of her death. Pride destroys fruitfulness, and attacks the heart of true excellence. Her biblical epitaph describes her as *Saul's daughter,* not David's wife. Her rejection of the generous heart toward God caused her to be listed with those God rejected.

David, on the other hand, was fruitful in all he put his hands to do. He was extravagant toward God. In pursuing this virtue, we are to live generously by *doing all to the glory of God, with all our might.* Such is the heart of excellence.

Excellence is impossible without passion.

1 Corinthians 12:7—*Now to each one the manifestation of the Spirit is given for the common good.*

BOOK QUOTE: *Dreaming With God* [Chapter 2]

MANY feel disqualified from creativity because they have narrowly confined it to the world of art and music. They fail to realize that everyone has some measure of creativity, which should be consistently expressed throughout life.

Today's Kingdom-oriented teachers must embrace the value of true wisdom, and develop children's creative skills outside the traditional box called "art." It is divine wisdom displayed in creativity that brings individuals to the forefront in his or her field of influence.

There are others who feel disqualified because they think that creativity always means we are to make something new or do something novel. In reality, most great ideas are actually the offspring of other concepts.

It is wisdom that can take something that is an everyday item or concept and build upon it creating something new and better. This is exactly what Solomon did. All kings of the day had cupbearers, servants, banqueting tables, and nice clothing for their servants. But there was something about his use of wisdom for everyday life that made him stand out above the rest. The queen of Sheba became speechless in response to Solomon's wisdom. It's time for the Church to display a wisdom that causes the world to become silent again.

There is a misconception that often exists in the artistic community; creativity must come from pain. There's no question but that some of the greatest works of art came from people who were troubled with life, or experienced some of the worst tragedies. The reality is this—it often takes trauma to launch a person into a place of seeing the true priorities for life. The believer doesn't need that experience. Having our old nature crucified with Christ is the only tragedy needed to launch us into our proper roles of creative influence.

. . . everyone has some measure of creativity, which should be consistently expressed throughout life.

Romans 8:19—*The creation waits in eager expectation for the sons of God to be revealed.*

BOOK QUOTE: *Dreaming With God* [Chapter 2]

THE Church has a clear assignment: we are to exhibit the multifaceted wisdom of God, now! It must permeate all we are and do. It is a part of the "witness" that turns people's heads. The spirit realm is watching, and more importantly, is affected by such a display. They must be reminded of their defeat, our victory, and the Father's eternal plan for the redeemed. It's our connection to wisdom that clearly manifests our eternal purpose of reigning with Christ. When we walk in wisdom, we mirror the reality of Heaven here on earth, and actually give Heaven a target for invasion. Agreement with God releases God to accomplish His purposes in and through us to the world around us. (If God is restricted in any way, it is a self-imposed restriction.) This is the reason He made humanity His delegated authority on this planet. (For more on this subject read Chapter Two of my book *When Heaven Invades Earth*.)

A reformation has begun. And at the heart of this great move of the Spirit is the total transformation of the people of God as they discover their true identity and purpose. Great purpose elicits great sacrifice. Up until this time, many of our agendas have failed. Our attempts to make the Gospel palatable have had a serious effect on the world around us. The world has longed for a message they could *experience*. Yet many believers have simply tried to make the good news more intellectually appealing. The natural mind *cannot* receive the things of the Spirit of God (see 1 Cor. 2:14). The wisdom of God is foolishness to men. It's time to be willing to appear foolish again, that we might provide the world with a message of power that delivers, transforms, and heals. This is true wisdom. It alone satisfies the cry of the human heart.

The list of heavenly answers is limitless. He looks for those who will ask.

When we walk in wisdom, we mirror the reality of Heaven here on earth, and actually give Heaven a target for invasion.

2 Corinthians 5:7—*We live by faith, not by sight.*

BOOK QUOTE: *Dreaming With God* [Chapter 2]

MANY are discouraged because their dreams have failed. In their pain and frustration they oppose the message that a believer has the right to dream. *"Hope deferred makes the heart sick..."* but the verse doesn't stop there and neither should we: *"...but desire fulfilled is a tree of life"* (Prov. 13:12 NASB).

When people pursue dreams but fail to see them fulfilled, they prepare the way for others who carry the same dream to eventually get the breakthrough that they were seeking. It is hard for many to take comfort in this thought, but that's because we usually think *it's all about us*. There is no failure in faith.

Often a tragic loss here on earth is viewed quite differently in Heaven. What is honored in Heaven is frequently pitied or mocked here on earth. When a person dies while trying to live out an expression of faith, people often criticize the foolishness of their decision. Few realize that their loss became the soil in which someone else could eventually realize their dream, because their loss actually paved the way to a breakthrough.

Those with failed dreams can take comfort in the fact that they prepared the way for others. It's a *John the Baptist* role. He prepared the way for the One to come. Countless times there have been those who never realized a fulfillment of their dreams. Many come to the end of their lives with the overwhelming conclusion that they failed. We have lived without the consciousness that a failed attempt at a dream often becomes the foundation of another person's success. Some water, others plant, and still others harvest. We all have an important role to set the stage for the King of kings to receive more glory. It's all about Him, not us.

Often a tragic loss here on earth is viewed quite differently in Heaven.

2 Peter 1:19—And we have the word of the prophets made more certain, and you will do well to pay attention to it, as to a light shining in a dark place, until the day dawns and the morning star rises in your hearts.

BOOK QUOTE: *Dreaming With God* [Chapter 2]

"These were all commended for their faith, yet none of them received what had been promised. God had planned something better for us so that only together with us would they be made perfect." (Hebrews 11:39-40 NIV)

In the 1920s, a man named Mallory led an expedition to be the first to climb Mount Everest. He attempted this feat on two separate occasions, but failed. He went back to work assembling the best team of climbers available, with the finest equipment in existence. They gave extra attention to the details of their assignment, especially focusing on the issues of safety. In spite of their efforts, tragedy struck. Many in the expedition were killed in an avalanche, including Mallory. Only a few survived.

When the team returned to England, a banquet was held in their honor. The leader of the survivors stood to acknowledge the applause of those in attendance. He looked at the pictures of his comrades that were displayed around the room. Choking back the tears he spoke to the mountain on behalf of Mallory and his friends. "I speak to you, Mount Everest, in the name of all brave men living, and those yet unborn. Mount Everest, you defeated us once, you defeated us twice, you defeated us three times. But Mount Everest, we shall someday defeat you, because you can't get any bigger, but we can!" Death and disappointment could have been the end of such a quest. But instead it became the foundation for future success. A seemingly tragic loss on Earth may be viewed quite differently in Heaven.

Death and disappointment. . .became the foundation for future success.

James 4:7—Submit yourselves, then, to God. Resist the devil, and he will flee from you.

BOOK QUOTE: *Dreaming With God* [Chapter 2]

THERE is a mountain of opposition against the purposes of God for this world. They are *principalities, powers, rulers of the darkness of this age, and spiritual hosts of wickedness in the heavenly places* (see Eph. 6:12). But the devil's dark realm is not getting any bigger. When he rebelled against God, he was removed from his life source. He walks about as a roaring lion, hoping to intimidate through noise. His noise, the constant report of bad news, is designed to give the illusion of greatness. But it is not so.

Hell is not the realm that satan rules from. It is not a place where he takes people and torments them for eternity. It is a place of eternal torment designed for him and his demons. Those who are slaves of the devil will suffer the same demise.

On another note, demons aren't being made anymore. There's the same number wandering around the planet today as there were in Jesus' day, yet the population of people has increased into the billions, with believers numbering in the hundreds of millions. On top of that, we all know from Scripture that there are two angels for every demon. And since Jesus has *all* authority, that leaves none for the devil. The "all" that Jesus possesses has been handed over to us. His great plan is not designed so He will have to come and rescue us from the devil. It's the gates of hell that *will not* prevail against the advancing church (see Matt. 16:18). Jesus' authority has been given to us to do great exploits. With the Moravians, let's declare, "Let us win for the Lamb, the reward of His suffering!"

Our commission to pursue divine wisdom comes with mystery.

. . . since Jesus has **all** *authority, that leaves none for the devil.*

Job 11:7—*Can you fathom the mysteries of God? Can you probe the limits of the Almighty?*

BOOK QUOTE: *Dreaming With God* [Chapter 3]

AN intellectual gospel is always in danger of creating a God that looks a lot like us; one that is our size. The quest for answers sometimes leads to a rejection of mystery. As a result mystery is often treated as something intolerable, instead of a real treasure. Living with mystery is the privilege of our walk with Christ. Its importance cannot be overrated. If I understand all that is going on in my Christian life, I have an inferior Christian life. The walk of faith is to live according to the revelation we have received, in the midst of the mysteries we can't explain. That's why Christianity is called *the faith*.

All too often believers abandon or dilute their call in order to feel better about the things they cannot explain. To allow what we cannot answer to downgrade what He has shown us is to be carnal minded. Too many only obey what they understand, thus subjecting God to their judgments. God is not on trial; we are. A true *Cross-walk* is obeying where we have revelation in spite of the apparent contradiction in what we cannot explain. To obey only when we see that there will be a favorable outcome is not obedience. Obedience is expensive. To embrace what He has shown us and to obey what He has commanded, often in the midst of unanswerable questions, is an honor beyond measure. It is a great privilege to be a believing believer in the midst of a culture of unbelief. We must embrace this privilege. No Christian should be unmoved by the Lord's question, "When I return, will I find faith on the earth?" (See Luke 18:8.) I have set my heart to be His pleasure by living in faith. God hides things *for* us, not *from* us.

The walk of faith is to live according to the revelation we have received, in the midst of the mysteries we can't explain.

Luke 4:23—*Jesus said to them, "Surely you will quote this proverb to me: 'Physician, heal yourself! Do here in your hometown what we have heard that you did in Capernaum.'"*

BOOK QUOTE: *Dreaming With God* [Chapter 3]

WHEN Jesus felt it was time to minister in His hometown of Nazareth, He went to the synagogue. As He began to teach the people, they were amazed at His wisdom. They were also very impressed with the healings they were seeing. When they realized they knew Him, having watched Him grow up, they were offended in their "reasonings." "It is Jesus. We know His brothers and sisters. He grew up here! How can He do this stuff? And where did He get this wisdom?" Their feelings were not hurt, nor were they caught up in bitterness. They simply could not put two and two together and arrive at the conclusion—*their Jesus was a miracle worker and a man of great wisdom.* It didn't fill them with wonder and awe. Instead it caused them to become hardhearted and reject Him. This unresolved question became the mental stumbling block that was strong enough to shut down Jesus' anointing to perform miracles and teach with power. To have questions is healthy; to hold God hostage to those questions is not. It sometimes creates an atmosphere that fulfills its own prophecy about the power of God not being for today. It shuts down the very anointing that would teach them otherwise.

Not understanding is OK. Restricting our spiritual life to what we understand is not. It is immaturity at best. Such a controlling spirit is destructive to the development of a Christ-like nature. God responds to faith but will not surrender to our demands for control. Maturity requires a heart-felt embrace of what we do not understand as an essential expression of faith.

A person's heart is more clearly seen by what they're willing to embrace without offense, than by their expression of faith only in what they already understand.

To have questions is healthy;
to hold God hostage to those questions is not.

2 Peter 1:4—Through these He has given us His very great and precious promises, to that through them you may participate in the divine nature...

BOOK QUOTE: *Dreaming With God* [Chapter 3]

MY oldest son, Eric, is 85-90 percent deaf in both ears. He has an amazing gift for life. He functions beautifully in the "hearing world" and has never had to learn sign language. His adjustments to life are miraculous, while his self-esteem is unaffected by this handicap. He is strong and Christ-centered. He is our Missions Pastor.

I was fasting and praying for his healing some years ago, and God spoke to me very clearly that He was going to heal him. It *has* happened in the atonement, and will be seen in my lifetime. We don't treat it as a *someday off in the future God will heal Him* kind of thing. We view it as a *right now* word. Yet he still can't hear without the assistance of a hearing aid.

It's interesting that the healing of deafness is one of the most common miracles I see in my meetings and in our church. Even more interesting to note is that in the last couple of months Eric has laid hands on two people who were deaf and God opened their ears. How could that happen without him being healed first? I don't know. But I do know that mental offense, stumbling over this apparent contradiction in our minds, will shut down this anointing. That is something we are not willing to do. Eric and I will continue to live in the understanding we have, and embrace the mystery we are required to live with, knowing that God is perfectly faithful and good beyond measure, all the time. He is worthy of our trust.

God is perfectly faithful and good beyond measure, all the time.

Luke 24:32—They asked each other, "Were not our hearts burning within us while He talked with us on the road and opened the Scriptures to us?"

BOOK QUOTE: *Dreaming With God* [Chapter 3]

GOD is not opposed to the mind; He created the mind to be a complement to all that He had made. He is opposed to the un-renewed mind. It is at war with God, being incapable of obeying Him (see Rom. 8:7). The believer who governs his Christian life through the mind is the carnal Christian that the apostle Paul warned about (see 1 Cor. 2–3). The soul can only lead us into religion, or form without power. The most common definition of the *soul* is the "mind, will, and emotions." It is what makes way for Ishmaels instead of Isaacs. (See Genesis 21:11-13. Ishmael was the son of Abraham's efforts, while Isaac was the son of God's promise.)

It's important to understand the learning process. Our spirit is where the Holy Spirit dwells. Our spirit is alive and well and is ready to receive great things from God. When I filter everything through my mind and remove what isn't immediately logical, I extract much of what I really need. Only what goes beyond my understanding is positioned to renew my mind (see Phil. 4:7). If we can learn more about the actual voice and presence of the Lord, we will stop being so paranoid about being deceived by the things we can't explain. Usually those who use the natural mind to protect themselves from deception are the most deceived. They've relied on their own finite logic and reason to keep them safe, which is in itself a deception.

Our hearts can embrace things that our heads can't. Our hearts will lead us where our logic would never dare to go. Courage rises up from within and influences the mind. In the same way, true faith affects the mind. Faith does not come from our understanding. It comes from the heart. We do not believe because we understand; we understand because we believe (see Heb. 11:6). We'll know when our mind is truly renewed, because the impossible will look logical.

Our hearts can embrace things that our heads can't.

1 Corinthians 4:1—*So then, men ought to regard us as servants of Christ and as those entrusted with the secret things of God.*

BOOK QUOTE: *Dreaming With God* [Chapter 3]

WHAT we don't understand is sometimes as important as what we do. It's one thing to obey when He has given us understanding about a matter, and quite another to obey while facing questions and circumstances that seem to contradict what we understand. So many fail at this point, and then bring the Bible down to their level of experience. Many do this to feel better about the fact that they are living in compromise—a compromise of their revelation from Scripture. Our challenge is instead to bring our lifestyle up to the standard of God's Word.

To embrace revelation4 with one hand, and embrace mystery with the other, forms a perfect cross. This is a cross that everyone who is hungry to do the works of Jesus will have to carry. God must violate our logic to invite us away from the deception of relying on our own reasoning.

When my children were small we hid Easter eggs for them to find. The measure of difficulty in the search was always determined by the age and capabilities of the child. When my children were two years old, we'd put the egg on a table, or on a chair. And as they got older we would make it more difficult, but never impossible. Parents delight in their child's curiosity, and love to see them enjoy the process of discovery. Children enjoy the pleasure of the search, and revel in the affirmation of their parent's delight in their searching and discovery. "*...Seek and you shall find...*" (Matt. 7:7). This curiosity and delight in discovery are meant to be a part of what it is to "*seek first the kingdom*" (Matt. 6:33) as well as to "*receive the kingdom of God as a little child*" (Luke 18:17).

> *What we don't understand is sometimes as important as what we do.*

Matthew 13:35—So was fulfilled what was spoken through the prophet: "I will open My mouth in parables, I will utter things hidden since the creation of the world."

BOOK QUOTE: *Dreaming With God* [Chapter 3]

PEOPLE wonder why God doesn't always speak in more open terms—audibly, with visible signs. The Bible indicates that *God receives more glory when He conceals*, rather than making things obvious. It is more glorious for Him to hide, and have us seek. In the introduction to the parable of the seed and the sower we find that Jesus did not merely use parables as illustrations, but at times to conceal truth so that only the hungry would understand (see Matt. 13:11,18-23). It is the mercy of God to withhold revelation from those who have no hunger for truth, because the chances are they won't obey it when they hear it. Revelation always brings responsibility, and hunger prepares our hearts to carry the weight of that responsibility. By keeping revelation from those without hunger, God protects them from certain failure to carry the responsibility it would lay on them. Yet, He doesn't conceal from us; He conceals *for* us!

But there's another part to this equation—*"it's the glory of kings to search out a matter"*(Proverbs 25:2). We are kings and priests to our God (see Rev. 1:6). Our royal identity never shines brighter than when we pursue hidden things with the confidence that we have legal access to such things. Mysteries are our inheritance. Our role in ruling and reigning with Christ, comes to the forefront when we seek Him for answers to the dilemmas of the world. It is important to note, *ruling* from God's perspective means "to be the servant of all." Too many have embraced wrong theology and have used it as an excuse to pursue ruling over others in the way Jesus warned against. Our strong suit has been, and always will be, serving.

Jesus answered them, *"To you it has been granted to know the mysteries of the kingdom of heaven, but to them it has not been granted"* (Matt. 13:11 NASB). We, as believers, have legal access to the realm of God's mysteries. The hidden things are placed in waiting for the believer to discover. They are ours by inheritance.

Our royal identity never shines brighter than when we pursue hidden things with the confidence that we have legal access to such things.

Philippians 1:23-24—I am torn between the two: I desire to depart and be with Christ, which is better by far; but it is more necessary for you that I remain in the body.

BOOK QUOTE: *Dreaming With God* [Chapter 3]

WHEN we believe that the darkness of world circumstances is the signal for Christ's return, we have a conflict that ultimately costs us a practical vision—to invade and transform the world system. Wrong assumptions about the unobvious can harden us to the obvious. One of the greatest errors in end-time theology comes from working to interpret types and symbols (the unobvious) until they redefine the clear commands of the Lord (the obvious). For example, many know much more about God and Magog, the ten-nation confederacy, the seven years of tribulation, the anti-Christ, etc. than they do about the simple command to pray "*on earth as it is in Heaven*" (Matt. 6:10). If we assume we know what certain types and shadows used in the prophets mean it can incorrectly influence our understanding of the clear commandments of the Lord. Wrongly interpreting when and how He is returning can undermine our approach to the Great Commission.

Jesus is returning for a spotless Bride, whose Body is in equal proportion to her Head. The Father alone knows when that moment will be. We don't. Our job is to do everything possible to bring about, "*Thy kingdom come, Thy will be done, on earth as it is in Heaven*" (Matt. 6:10). If my faith for His return has its anchor in the darkness of the world around me, then I will do little to change it. We will try to get converts, of course, but to bring answers to the issues of this planet will not be a priority. Yet this is the practical tool that turns the hearts of the kings of our day (see Prov. 22:29).

Our commission is clear: we are to disciple nations! And to insure that this seemingly impossible task would be possible, He caused the One called *the desire of the nations* to live within us. This revelation of Him is ultimately a revelation about us, for we are His Body. Being made in His image gives us the privilege and responsibility to reflect His greatness to the world around us. The nations are looking for a people who can bring the answers to the issues facing our world.

Being made in His image gives us the privilege and responsibility to reflect His greatness to the world around us.

Proverbs 20:21—*An inheritance gained hurriedly at the beginning will not be blessed in the end. NASB*

BOOK QUOTE: *Dreaming With God* [Chapter 3]

HANNAH'S was barren and without hope of bearing children apart from a miracle. God used this to bring her into her greatest success. In her barrenness she developed a desperate heart. The purpose of a promise is not to inspire us to strategize and make plans, but instead it works to make us desperate for God. Barrenness in any area is our invitation to excel. Hannah became a co-laborer in fulfilling her own destiny. Not everything comes to us easily, nor should it. The God who hides things for us also gives us His Kingdom as our inheritance. Israel was given the Promised Land, but was told it would come to them little by little so that the beasts wouldn't become too numerous for them. His promises cover everything—His promises are yes and *amen*! (See 2 Cor. 1:20.) All is covered by the redemptive work on the Cross, but it is gained little by little, sometimes through our co-laboring effort.

This became a great personal lesson in my quest for miracles. Twenty years ago, Mario Murillo encouraged me with one of the most powerful prophetic words of my life. In it the Lord spoke of His intent to make miracles a regular part of my life.

Mario, and his wife, Mechelle, recently came to our home for lunch. I showed him the prophetic word he spoke over me in 1988. I did so to express my thanks to him for being such an encouragement to me. He brought up the story of Hannah and her closed womb. He said that God has closed up the realm of the miraculous to me, not as punishment, but to draw me into the desperation needed to maintain it as a lifestyle once I received my breakthrough. I think I really understand.

The God who hides things for us also gives us His Kingdom as our inheritance.

Luke 1:29—*Mary was greatly troubled at His words and wondered what kind of greeting this might be.*

BOOK QUOTE: *Dreaming With God* [Chapter 3]

MARY, the mother of Jesus, lived with mystery in a most notable fashion. She carried revival better than anyone, since Jesus is revival personified. Mary was given the ultimate mystery—both in word and experience.

She pondered the things *spoken to her by God*, even though she didn't understand them. Her pondering gave place for the roots to be established and the word to grow until the promise became manifest. God's Word grows in the heart of the yielded believer.

Her encounter with mystery could be summarized as follows:

1. As a young girl Mary had an angelic encounter with Gabriel.

2. Gabriel gave Mary a word that was incomprehensible; she was to give birth to the Messiah while she remained a virgin—a biblically unprecedented experience.

3. She yielded to what was beyond understanding by saying, "*Be it unto me, according to Thy word*" (Luke 1:38).

4. Mary nearly lost Joseph, her fiancé, to the news that "God made me pregnant." An angel appeared to Joseph to convince him it was true, thus saving their marriage.

5. She began to "manifest" under the influence of the ultimate revival—Jesus. (You can only hide the reality of pregnancy/revival so long.)

6. Those who knew that her son was the Messiah would often speak to her of His greatness. She pondered the things they said in her heart, thus becoming pregnant again—this time with promise.

In essence, the glorious story of Mary is repeated every time we are impregnated with God's Word of promise. Christ is still being formed in His people. This spiritual reality is not to be thought inferior to the natural reality that Mary experienced. I want to increase respect for the work of the Spirit of God in every heart.

Christ is still being formed in His people.

Revalation 1:6—*...and has made us to be a kingdom and priests to serve His God and Father...*

BOOK QUOTE: *Dreaming With God* [Chapter 3]

WHEN I first heard this phrase, *the Kingdom now but not yet,* over 20 years ago, it was used as a statement of promise. It was helpful for me to realize that we have access to things right now that I had always thought were inaccessible. The phrase helped to bring into focus the reality that some things will be enjoyed in time, and some things only in eternity. But that same phrase has also been used to define limitations and restrictions, and not instill hope. It is used to ease people's dissatisfaction with unrealized promises now.

A full manifestation of the Kingdom of God is more than our physical bodies can endure. But when we are in Heaven we will still be able to say, *now, but not yet,* about the Kingdom, because there is no end to the increase of His government. Throughout eternity the Kingdom will be expanding, and we will always be advancing. I teach our people that if *now, but not yet* is used to define promise and potential, accept it. If it is spoken to build awareness of our limitations and restrictions, reject it. We don't need more people without authentic Kingdom experiences telling us what we can and cannot have in our lifetime. Those who walk out their faith with an experiential paradigm understand that we will always live in the tension of what we have seen and what we have yet to see, and that we are always moving on to *more* in God. This is an *understanding by experience* issue.

Very little of what exists today would exist at all if those who preceded us did not seek to surpass the boundaries experienced by their predecessors. And it is this adventure that we call *the normal Christian life.*

Very little of what exists today would exist at all if those who preceded us did not seek to surpass the boundaries experienced by their predecessors.

Psalm 20:4—*May He give you the desire of your heart and make all your plans succeed.*

BOOK QUOTE: *Dreaming With God* [Chapter 4]

As God draws us into a place of embracing the realm of His mysteries, He establishes the life of faith in us. Yet He longs to unlock the mysteries for those desiring to make a difference in the world around them. Hidden things are revealed to those who hunger for Him, and can recognize His voice.

A yielded imagination becomes a sanctified imagination; and it's the sanctified imagination that is positioned for visions and dreams. There is great paranoia over the use of the imagination in the Church of the Western world. As a result; unbelievers often lead the way in creative expression—through the arts and inventions. They have no bias against imagination. The imagination is like a canvas to a painter. If it's clean, the artist has much to work with. God would love to use our imagination to paint His impressions upon; He just looks for those who are yielded. However, those who are preoccupied with "not being worthy" are too self-centered to be trusted with much revelation. At some point it has to stop being about us long enough to utilize the benefits of being in Christ for the sake of those around us. Such a position gives us unlimited access to the mysteries of God that enable us to touch the needs of a dying world.

Jesus is the Word of God. It's hard for Him to not have something to say. Occasionally, we go through times when we feel God is not speaking to us. While that may be so, most of the time He has simply changed His language, and He expects us to adjust with Him.

God would love to use our imagination to paint His impressions upon; He just looks for those who are yielded.

John 12:28-29—*"Father, glorify Your name."* *Then a voice came from Heaven saying "I have both glorified it, and will glorify it again."* *Therefore the people who stood by and heard it said that it had thundered. Others said, "An angel has spoken to Him."*

BOOK QUOTE: *Dreaming With God* [Chapter 4]

THE audible voice of the Father came from Heaven while Jesus was speaking to a crowd. The people acknowledged hearing something, but none of them knew what it was. Not only did they fail to realize it was the voice of God, it never occurred to them that this unusual event had any meaning for their lives. Jesus responded to their unbelief by saying, *"This voice did not come because of Me, but for your sake"* (see John 12:27-30). In His mercy God spoke to provide a way out of the lifestyle of unbelief for every bystander. But their hardness of heart blocked their perception of what was said, who was speaking, and made what they heard unintelligible. We know that God spoke clearly (see 1 Cor. 14:9). Yet the people did not *understand* because of their predisposition toward unbelief (see John 12:37). Some thought it was thunder—an impersonal act of nature. Others thought it might have been an angel—spiritual, but just not for them. It is a true statement that it's the hungry heart that hears best.

The story of John 12 addresses one of my greatest concerns for the church in the Western world—the prevalence of unbelief. It has masqueraded long enough as wisdom and must be exposed for being the great sin that it is. Unbelief has the outward appearance of a conservative approach to life, but works to subject God Himself to the mind and control of people. It feeds off the opinion of others, all the while stroking itself for not falling into the extremes that others have stumbled into. What is seldom realized by those who live in such a religious trap is that an unbelieving mindset is completely unable to represent Jesus in His power and glory.

. . . it's the hungry heart that hears best.

Colossians 2:3-4—*in whom are hidden all the treasures of wisdom and knowledge. I tell you this so that no one may deceive you by fine-sounding arguments.*

BOOK QUOTE: *Dreaming With God* [Chapter 4]

IT is troubling to me that so many Christians need me to prove that God actually does what I say I've seen Him do—as though the Scriptures were not enough proof. What is even more astonishing is that when the miracles happen before their eyes, they still want doctors' reports, x-rays, etc. before they will give God any praise. I realize that charlatans exist. But the massive effort to protect ourselves from being fooled is more a sign of unbelief than it is of our wisdom keeping us from deception. Such a fear only exists where unbelief has reigned for a long time.

However, "*Love believes all things*" (1 Cor. 13:7 NASB). A deeper encounter with the love of God frees a person from the tendency to protect themselves out of fear through unreasonable caution. And considering that "*faith works through love*" (Gal. 5:6), it is reasonable to say that even the faith to believe God for miracles can come by experiencing His love. Overwhelming encounters with the extravagant love of our heavenly Father will do much to dismantle unbelief.

It is not wisdom that continually asks God to demonstrate Himself for us so that we might believe. While there is no question that exposure to the miraculous can help us grow in faith, such a demand is not a hunger for Him but is instead an effort to put God on trial. He is not on trial. We are. The un-renewed mind is at war with God and puts demands on Him to perform for us. That unhealthy attitude puts us in the role of a judge. Such arrogance is the father of unbelief. Jesus confronted these attitudes in his many encounters with the religious crowd.

The un-renewed mind is at war with God and puts demands on Him to perform for us.

Hebrews 10:9—Then he said, "Here I am, I have come to do your will."

BOOK QUOTE: *Dreaming With God* [Chapter 4]

THE heart of abiding faith "leans into God," anticipating His voice, looking for His next move. Like Jesus, we are to be able to say, "*My food is to do the will of Him who sent me*" (John 4:34 NASB). I am strengthened in hearing God speak. I am nourished through my own obedience to His voice. The situations of life take on meaning and purpose because of the abiding faith to follow Jesus. Hearing from God is the essential element of the Christian life, for "*man shall not live by bread alone, but by every word that proceeds from the mouth of God*" (Matt. 4:4). His voice is our life.

There are many tables to eat at in life. There is the table of *public opinion*. The food is sweet, but it sours in the stomach. There is the table of *personal achievement*. That's a power meal for sure, yet the crash is as rapid as the ascent. There's only one table with rich food that settles well and brings supernatural strength; it's the table of God's will.

The beauty of His will is lost for the person who does not know the language of the Spirit. It is vital to learn how God speaks. His first language is not English. In fact, it would be safe to say it's not Hebrew either. While He uses the languages of men to communicate with us, He is more inclined to speak through a myriad of other methods. We need to understand and experience the "languages of the Spirit." Go on your own adventure and discover His voice through the language of the Spirit.

There's only one table with rich food that settles well and brings supernatural strength; it's the table of God's will.

1 Corinthians 1:27—But God chose the foolish things of the world to shame the wise; God chose the weak things of the world to shame the strong.

BOOK QUOTE: *Dreaming With God* [Chapter 4]

WHEN I became the pastor of Bethel Church, in Redding, California, I came because of a cry for revival by the leadership of the church. The outpouring began almost immediately. Lives were changed, bodies were healed, divine encounters increased in amazing proportions—and approximately 1,000 people left the church. What was happening was outside their point of reference. Few things are more devastating to pastors than when people leave the church. Yet during this *exodus*, my wife and I were immune to the devastation, which is only possible if God gives a supernatural grace to joyfully live *opposite* of your circumstances.

It was the generosity of God that made this possible. Along with the increased manifestation of His presence, He made His will too obvious to ever miss. God often spoke to us in a dream, a vision, or a clear impression in our minds. There was never a question. The fruit of the increased measure of His presence, along with the bounty of transformed lives, was all we needed to smile in the face of such apparent loss. To this day, we've considered it a privilege to gain that kind of increase through such a loss.

Today we are growing fast. The miracles are increasing in astonishing ways. Yet I savor the moments of the initial outpouring when it was illogical to the natural mind to be so happy when so many things appeared to be so wrong. The opposition was fierce at times. The slander and rumors increased daily with a vengeance. For close to a year our denominational office received complaints and accusations about us every single day. Yet only God can make such a season so wonderful, because only His will is so completely nourishing. It has been, and continues to be, my favorite meal.

... God can make such a season so wonderful, because only His will is so completely nourishing.

Psalm 19:7—*The law of the Lord is perfect, reviving the soul. The statutes of the Lord are trustworthy, making wise the simple.*

BOOK QUOTE: *Dreaming With God* [Chapter 4]

THE Scriptures are the basis for all "hearing" from God. "Your word is a lamp to my feet and a light for my path" (Psalm 119:105). While God will not violate His Word, He often violates our understanding of His Word. Remember, God is bigger than His book. The Bible does not contain God; it *reveals* Him.

This truth can be represented by two Greek words for *word*, "logos" and "rhema."

Logos is often used to speak of the written Word, our Holy Bible. Bible reading is the most common way of receiving instruction and learning to recognize His voice. Page after page is filled with practical instructions for life. Learning the principles of God's Word helps us to learn to recognize His voice by establishing truth in our hearts. The Psalmist affirmed that purpose, saying, *"Your word I have treasured in my heart, that I may not sin against You"* (Ps. 119:11 NASB). This is where we find the Kingdom principles for life. They work for anyone who applies them.

Rhema is the freshly spoken word. It is always an expression of that which is *being uttered*. Therefore it carries an aspect of immediacy with it. Often times God breathes upon His Word and gives life to something written for "now." The spoken word is never to replace the written Word. The more of the written Word we have in our hearts, the greater capacity we have to hear the spoken word, because He speaks to that which has been deposited in our hearts and calls it forth.

The Bible does not contain God; it **reveals** *Him.*

Isaiah 30:21—*Whether you turn to the right or the left, your ears will hear a voice behind you, saying, "This is the way; walk in it."*

BOOK QUOTE: *Dreaming With God* [Chapter 4]

THE voice of the Lord is not an impression that we have to find language for. It is a direct word-for-word communication from God to us. The audible voice may come to the natural ear while we're awake or while we're asleep. It can also come to our spiritual ears. (The reason I make this distinction is that after it has happened, you can't always remember if it was out loud or internal. It is far more than an impression. It is as clear as hearing someone speak.)

On at least two occasions I have been awakened with the audible voice of the Lord. But in reflection I never thought that my wife would have heard it. She didn't. That's why I say it can come to the natural ear, as it did in John 12, or in our spirit. He once woke me, saying, "He watches over the watch of those who watch the Lord." That phrase then ran through my mind the rest of the night. It became apparent that He wanted my full attention so I could learn to watch Him only. In doing so He would watch over all that concerned me.

This is the quiet voice or impression of the heart. This is probably the most common way that people hear from God. It is sometimes thought to be our own "inner voice" in that it is our own thoughts and ideas. While we do have such a voice, it is wisdom to learn to recognize *His* still small voice. It is quiet. So we must become quiet to recognize it consistently. Someone gave me a helpful clue to discerning His voice; they said, "You know you've heard from God whenever you have an idea that's better than one you could think up yourself."

The voice of the Lord ... is a direct word-for-word communication from God to us.

Numbers 12:6—*He said, "Listen to My words: When a prophet of the Lord is among you, I reveal myself to him in visions, I speak to him in dreams.*

BOOK QUOTE: *Dreaming With God* [Chapter 4]

VISIONS come both to the natural eye and to the eyes of the heart. The second are the pictures in the mind, which are the visual equivalent of the still small voice—they are as easy to miss as they are to get. *Leaning into God* is what makes this one come into focus. This is a phrase I use to describe "anticipating God to act or speak at any time."

External—Many people refer to this as an "open vision." Though I have never had one, I have many friends who have, including my senior associate, Kris Vallotton. One such method that God has used with him is when something like a movie screen appears over a person's head, and God plays back portions of that person's life. Describing it to them get their attention, preparing the way for them to receive significant personal ministry.

Internal—On a ministry trip to Germany, preceding the evening healing meeting tends to, I was praying with the leadership of a remarkable ministry. I had a "snapshot" picture flash in my mind. In it I saw someone seated to my right, and then saw only their spine, as in an x-ray. I somehow knew it was arthritic. In this vision I pointed to them and said, "The Lord Jesus heals you!" This vision was a brief snapshot that I gave attention to. It was one that I could have easily missed. When it was my time to speak, I started by asking if there was anyone there with arthritis in the spine. A woman to my right raised her hand. After asking her to stand I declared, "The Lord Jesus heals you!" She began to tremble. When I asked her "where is your pain?" she responded with intense weeping, "It's impossible! It's impossible! It's gone!" She was healed through a declaration that was brought about by an internal vision.

Visions come both to the natural eye and to the eyes of the heart.

Acts 11:5—*I was in the city of Joppa praying, and in a trance I saw a vision.*

BOOK QUOTE: *Dreaming With God* [Chapter 4]

OBVIOUSLY, dreams mostly happen at night. But there is a form of dreaming that is similar to a *daydream*. They happen when you're awake and are more likely to be ignored because you think it's *your imagination*. In their more intense form they are more like a trance. Leaning into God brings this tool into a clearer perspective, giving us the needed discernment to recognize what is from God and what is actually our imagination.

I began to daydream about a prayer house. I could see four walls of windows to the north, south, east, and west. Over each window was the phrase from Isaiah, "*Say to the North, 'Give them back!'*" The same appeared over each of the windows facing their respective directions. In the carpet was the compass star, again pointing to the north, south, east, and west. In the center of the room was a fountain that flowed continuously. I knew it was to be called the Alabaster House. (An alabaster vial is what was used to contain the priceless ointment that the woman poured over Jesus as the ultimate expression of worship (see Mark 14:3). The disciples thought this woman *wasted* her perfume. Jesus had a different perspective; He called it worship.) I felt we were to build a place where people could *waste themselves on Jesus*! When I shared this experience with our church board, one of the members asked to meet with me. He was a contractor with plans he had drawn two years earlier of the very prayer house I had described. Needless to say, we built the Alabaster House, even though its construction was during the time when about 1,000 people were leaving the church. We built it with cash—another testimony of God's wonderful mercy and grace.

. . . there is a form of dreaming that is similar to a **daydream***.*

Matthew 2:13—*When they had gone, an angel of the Lord appeared to Joseph in a dream. "Get up," he said, "take the child and his mother and escape too Egypt. Stay there until I tell you, for Herod is going to search for the child to kill him."*

BOOK QUOTE: *Dreaming With God* [Chapter 4]

As I was preparing to come to Bethel Church, I had a dream warning me of the potential danger in the coming transition. In the dream I was taking an exit off of a freeway. I was then to cross over the roadway on an overpass, and get back on the freeway going in the opposite direction. When doing so I noticed that the road was icy and that I would need to be cautious as to how fast I made the turn or I would roll my vehicle off the embankment back onto the freeway. I woke up realizing that God just warned me not to make the needed changes too quickly. While some might have felt our transition happened rather fast, it was much slower than it would have been without that dream. Each step was preceded by a clear Word from God.

He let me know when that season of "cautious turning" was over through another dream. I saw the same freeway, but this time I was going the opposite direction. There was bright green grass on both sides of the road, and the pavement was wet from the melted ice. As strange as it may sound, the water didn't pose any danger but instead was a sign of His fresh outpouring. The ice, that made a quick transition dangerous and unwise, had melted. There were no other cars to slow down or impede our progress. In giving me this dream He spoke, saying, "It's time to pull out the stops." This second dream occurred around 18 months after the first one. The majority of the people had left that were going to leave and I was now given liberty to go at a pace more suitable to the increasing winds of change.

Each step was preceded by a clear Word from God.

Matthew 13:11—He replied, "The knowledge of the secrets of the kingdom of heaven has been given to you, but not to them.

BOOK QUOTE: *Dreaming With God* [Chapter 4]

GOD sometimes speaks to us by hiding truths in phrases, stories, riddles, and circumstances. The meaning is there for us to find. When we *lean into God*, anticipating His voice, it becomes easier to discern when those circumstances are from God, or are merely unusual events in life. This unique language from God is an invitation to enter His great adventure.

At my request, a member of our maintenance team took a dear prophet friend and me around our church's near 70 acres to find the corners of the property line. We drove stakes into the ground at the corners. Each stake had a different colored flag attached, representing a particular gift and calling upon our church. This was not something I had done before and found it to be a unique experience to walk the grounds and pray according to what the prophet sees. While it was different for me, I trusted him.

Upon driving the last stake into the ground, four geese flew by. The prophet told me the goose is the *watchdog* of the old world, and they represented the angels who stood at the four corners of the property guarding what God is doing there.

Jesus was teaching through the use of parables when He gave the disciples the promise that the Father has given us access to His mysteries (see Matt. 13:11). There are patterns of interpretation that can help us to find His intended message. For example, the number four represents the earth—the four corners of the earth; north, south, east, and west; etc. Understanding these things can help us to more clearly hear everything from simple words of affirmation to great words of revelation.

This unique language from God is an invitation to enter His great adventure.

Ezekiel 17:2—*Son of man, set forth an allegory* [riddle in KJV] *and tell the house of Israel a parable.*

BOOK QUOTE: *Dreaming With God* [Chapter 4]

GOD may speak to us at times by hiding truths in phrases, stories, circumstances, and riddles. I include this story in the *riddle* category because it needs an interpretation. Sometimes the Lord speaks in ways that can be researched through biblical principles of interpretation. For example, the number 50 means Jubilee. It comes from the Jubilee principle (forgiving all debt and releasing all slaves) that Israel was instructed to follow every 50 years. The following story could not be interpreted in that way. God alone could explain.

In October 2003, I woke up at 5:55 A.M. after running into those numbers several times in just a few days. While lying in bed I said out loud, "What are you trying to tell me?" Immediately, I was asleep as though someone knocked me out. He then spoke audibly saying, "The anointing for the day of the cancellation of debt is upon you." I instantly woke up realizing that I had been asleep for maybe three minutes. Since that day, all debt is gone from our lives, with the exception of our mortgage, which we believe is next. The numbers were like a puzzle that needed explanation from the manufacturer.

There are great books that give us principles of interpretation for numbers and symbols in the Bible and in life. However, I doubt that any of them would say that 555 means the cancellation of debt. I recommend people use those books as guides, but seek the Lord to see if there is something else He wants to say. Parables tend to be more symbolic, while riddles need divine explanation.

Parables tend to be more symbolic, while riddles need divine explanation.

Psalm 31:15—*My times are in your hands; deliver me from my enemies and from those who pursue me.*

BOOK QUOTE: *Dreaming With God* [Chapter 4]

WHILE it would be wrong to say that every coincidence has the voice of God in it, God is speaking through them more often than you might think.

He got my attention recently with the following chain of events. I checked into my hotel preparing for some meetings. The man behind the counter gave me room key #308. When I went to the next city I noticed I was again given a key for room #308. It seemed like a strange coincidence, but I can't say I felt it was anything but an unusual coincidence. Then I woke up at 3:08 in the morning. God finally had my attention. I asked, "What are you trying to tell me?" The answer didn't come for several days; while sitting at my desk in my office it hit me, about 18 years earlier I had been seeking the Lord whether or not I should attempt to write.

It had been in my heart, but I was never a great student, and had missed much of what I would need to know. But I had this desire that wouldn't go away. In response to my question about writing, He woke me in the middle of the night and said these words, "Isaiah thirty, verse eight." When I opened the Bible to see what it said I read, "*Now go, and write.*" Very soon afterward, I began to write small articles for our church bulletin. I made time for it in my regular schedule so that I could learn more of what I needed to know through experience.

Now 18 years later, I had written a fair amount, but I had filled my most recent schedule with conferences and other traveling engagements. Even the writing of this book is in response to that word.

While it would be wrong to say that every coincidence has the voice of God in it, God is speaking through them more often than you might think.

Exodus 3:4—When the Lord saw that he turned aside to look, God called to him from the midst of the bush and said, "Moses, Moses!" NASB

BOOK QUOTE: *Dreaming With God* [Chapter 4]

THE burning bush of Moses' experience is an unusual coincidences. These are highly unusual situations that usually seem to have no meaning. God brings those events into our lives to get our attention, hoping we will "turn aside" from our agendas and plans. When Moses turned aside, God spoke.

One night I was praying at church and a roadrunner with a lizard in its mouth, came to the window. He started to dance and jump. I got within 3 feet of him and thought, "This is too strange to not be prophetic." Minutes later he left. The time came for others to come to pray. Then the roadrunner returned. One of my staff members said, "Oh, the roadrunner's back." I asked him what he meant. He said, "Yeah. He was here last week."

For several months the roadrunner came to most every prayer meeting, usually with a lizard in its mouth. One day he got inside our church facility. Suddenly someone opened the door and startled the bird. He hit our plate glass window, and died instantly.

I decided we should raise it from the dead. With a sense of purpose and confidence we walked to the roadrunner. It made perfect sense to me that God would want the roadrunner, our prophetic message, alive. Strangely, I actually felt the anointing lift when I got 5 to 6 feet away from the bird. It was puzzling—God's presence was upon me until I got close. It was like He was saying my resolve was good, but my application and timing was not. The roadrunner was not raised from the dead. The Lord spoke, "What I am bringing into the house has to have a way of being released from the house, or it will die in the house."

God brings ... events into our lives to get our attention, hoping we will "turn aside" from our agendas and plans.

Romans 12:6—We have different gifts, according to the grace given us. If a man's gifts is prophesying, let him use it in proportion to his faith.

BOOK QUOTE: *Dreaming With God* [Chapter 4]

GOD has been very faithful to put prophetic people in my life at just the right times. As a result, we have a strong prophetic culture. To encourage risk on the part of prophetic people we emphasize the responsibility of the hearer to discern whether or not a word is from God. In the Old Testament the Spirit of God was upon the prophet alone, so he bore all the responsibility. Today the Spirit of the Lord is within every believer, so the responsibility is now given to the people of God to discern whether or not a specific word is from God. When it is from God, we respond according to the direction given in the Word. When it's not from God, we try to learn from it and sharpen our prophetic skills. (Kris Vallotton's Prophetic Manual, *A Call To War*, provides much practical instruction about this subject.)

Prophecy comes to us from another person. While this can be a very dangerous form of hearing from God, it can also be one of the most dramatic and faith-building. Once it is confirmed as having its origins from God, we must act accordingly.

One Sunday, I received a prophecy that God was going to support me publicly by bringing in the total amount of money needed to build our prayer house in one offering. This was the very day we were to present the project and receive an offering. In the natural this was the worst time to expect a large offering as this was when we had our lowest point in numbers. The amount needed to build the prayer house was an unheard of amount for our church to give in one offering, even when we had many members. But by the end of the service our CPA totaled the offering and had surpassed our goal by $8 and some change.

...we emphasize the responsibility of the hearer to discern whether or not a word is from God.

Revelation 19:10—*At this I fell at his feet to worship him. But he said to me, "Do not so it! I am a fellow servant with you and with your brothers who hold to the testimony Jesus. Worship God! For the testimony of Jesus is the spirit of prophecy."*

BOOK QUOTE: *Dreaming With God* [Chapter 4]

In the Old Testament the word testimony comes from the word, "do again." The implication is that God wants to repeat His wonderful works when we speak of what He has done. In the New Testament we have a confirmation of that principle in Revelation 19:10 (NASB): *"The testimony of Jesus is the spirit of prophecy."* This says that if God has done it once, He is ready to do it again. The spoken or written record of whatever Jesus has done carries the prophetic anointing to cause a change in events in the spirit realm so that the miracle spoken of can happen again. Indeed, a testimony often carries the actual voice of the Lord. Learning to recognize it will enable us to accommodate and cooperate with the move of His Spirit that was released in the testimony.

One Sunday morning I was teaching about the power of a testimony and telling the story of a little boy that was healed of clubfeet. A family was visiting from out of state. They had a little girl, almost 2 years old, whose feet turned inward so severely that she would trip over her feet when she ran. The mother heard the testimony about the little boy who was healed and said in her heart, "I'll take that for my daughter." When she picked up her little girl from our nursery, she noticed her feet were already perfectly straight! No one prayed for her. God spoke in the testimony, the mother heard, and the daughter was healed.

. . . God wants to repeat His wonderful works when we speak of what He has done.

Psalm 84:2—*My soul yearns, even faints for the courts of the Lord; my heart and my flesh cry out for the living God.*

BOOK QUOTE: *Dreaming With God* [Chapter 4]

OUR five senses are not only instruments that help us to enjoy life, they are tools that enable us to hear from God better. In the Psalms we are told that the songwriter's body actually hungered for God (see Ps. 84:2). In Hebrews, the writer states that the senses were to be *trained to discern good and evil* (see Heb. 5:14 NASB). In that passage, this ability is actually used as a mark of maturity—being able to use the senses to recognize God.

During a Sunday morning service, a young lady stood in front me. As people raised their hands or danced with joy, she made all kinds of different motions with her hands and arms. We have quite a number of people involved in the occult who come to our meetings—some come out of hunger, some come to disturb.

I was puzzled by her and tried to discern what was going on. It was as though my discernment was shut off. But I did notice that it got cold where I was standing. I remembered a demonic encounter that my brother had several years earlier where his office turned very cold and remained so for several hours. So I walked about 15 feet away and noticed the temperature was normal. I went to the leader of our prophetic dance ministry, and asked her to please go up on the stage and dance. I told her, "We need to break something." When she did, the young lady collapsed right in front of me. The demonic power that inspired her was broken through the prophetic act of the dance—*physical obedience brings spiritual release.* My wife knelt down next to her and brought deliverance to her and then led her to Christ.

Our five senses ... are tools that enable us to hear from God better.

Mark 10:45—*For even the Son of Man did not come to be served, but to serve, and to give His life as a ransom for many.*

BOOK QUOTE: *Dreaming With God* [Chapter 5]

WE were given authority over this planet in the commission God gave to mankind in Genesis (see Gen. 1:28-29) and was then restored to us by Jesus after His resurrection (see Matt. 28:18). But Kingdom authority is different than is typically understood by many believers. It is the authority to set people free from torment and disease, destroying the works of darkness. It is the authority to move the resources of Heaven through creative expression to meet human need. It is the authority to bring Heaven to earth. It is the authority to serve.

As with most Kingdom principles, the truths of humanity's dominion and authority are dangerous in the hands of those who desire to rule over others. These concepts seem to validate some people's selfishness. But when these truths are expressed through the humble servant, the world is rocked to its core. Becoming servants to this world is the key to open the doors of possibility that are generally thought of as closed or forbidden.

Jesus is the King of all kings, yet the Servant of all. This unique combination found in the Son of God is the call of the hour upon us. As truth is usually found in the tension of two conflicting realities, we have an issue to solve. Like our Master we are both royalty and servants (see Rev. 1:5; Mark 10:45). This is the essential combination that must be embraced by those longing to shape the course of history.

Royalty is my identity. Servanthood is my assignment. Intimacy with God is my life source. So, before God, I'm an intimate. Before people, I'm a servant. Before the powers of hell, I'm a ruler, with no tolerance for their influence. Wisdom knows which role to fulfill at the proper time.

Royalty is my identity.
Servanthood is my assignment.

Galatians 5:9—A little yeast works through the whole batch of dough.

BOOK QUOTE: *Dreaming With God* [Chapter 5]

THERE are seven realms of society that must come under the influence of the King and His Kingdom. For that to happen, we, as citizens of the Kingdom, must invade. The dominion of the Lord Jesus is manifest whenever the people of God go forth to serve by bringing the order and blessing of His world into this one.

The effort by many believers to simply obtain positions of leadership is putting the cart before the horse. Servanthood remains our strong suit, and it's through service that we can bring the benefits of His world into the reach of the common man.

The Kingdom is likened unto leaven (see Matt. 13:33). As yeast has an effect on the dough it is "worked into," so we will transform all the kingdoms of this world as we are worked into its systems. From there we must display His dominion and rule. As the people of God move into these realms of society to show forth the benefits and values of the Kingdom, His government expands.

For this invasion to work effectively, we must correct a few misconceptions. In doing so, it is equally important to establish the necessary Kingdom principles in their proper order.

There is no such thing as secular employment for the believer. Once we are born again, everything about us is redeemed for Kingdom purposes. It is all spiritual. It is either a legitimate Kingdom expression, or we shouldn't be involved at all.

Every believer is in full-time ministry—only a few have pulpits in sanctuaries. The rest have their pulpit in their areas of expertise and favor in the world system. Be sure to preach only good news. And when necessary, use words!

*There is no such thing as secular employment
for the believer.*

2 Corinthians 4:3—*And even if our gospel is veiled, it is veiled to those who are perishing.*

BOOK QUOTE: *Dreaming With God* [Chapter 5]

OUR church and ministry school is most often known for its overt ministry—outward and aggressive. We have seen hundreds of people healed and delivered in public places. We've even had words of knowledge given over the intercom of a local grocery store. The results were amazing. People responded by gathering around cash register number 10 and received the healing ministry of Jesus through one of our young men named Chad. Following God's merciful display of power, they were invited to give their lives to Christ. Many did.

Overt ministry is very common for us. Whether it's in the mall, neighborhoods, schools, or places of business, the Gospel is brought to those in need. But this is only half of the needed ministry equation. The other half is covert ministry. The word *covert* means "hiding place." This refers to ministry that is more subtle in nature. It is hidden not because of cowardice but rather out of wisdom. It works within the systems of this world to bring about change by reestablishing the proper norms of thought, beliefs, disciplines, and relational boundaries. In other words, we work to change the culture. This requires more time, as the goal is not a specific healing or conversion. The goal is the transformation of society itself by invading the systems of the city in order to serve. Serving for their benefit, not ours, is the key. As someone once said, "*We shouldn't try to be the best **in** the world. We should try to be the best **for** the world!*" When we set aside our religious agendas to make others a success, we have learned the Kingdom mindset, and have become a part of the transformation movement.

The goal is the transformation of society itself by invading the systems of the city in order to serve.

Matthew 20:28—*Just as the Son of Man did not come to be served, but to serve, and to give his life as a ransom for many.*

BOOK QUOTE: *Dreaming With God* [Chapter 5]

THE Church is sometimes known for its willingness to serve, but usually with well-meaning spiritual agendas as the ultimate goal. Serving simply to get people saved is a religious agenda. As pure and noble as it may seem to us, it is manipulative to the world, and is viewed as impure service. The world can smell it a mile away. We put them on the defensive when we carry such reasons for serving into their sphere of responsibility. But when we volunteer in our local school to help the principal succeed, then we've crossed the line into territory seldom visited by the Church. It is serving for the benefit of another. It's that kind of a servant that the world welcomes. The amazing bonus is you also influence the school in ways you never thought possible, including bringing people to Christ.

What would happen if parents volunteered in their local schools to help the teacher succeed? Generally teachers have an authentic interest in children succeeding in life. They invest themselves for the sake of another generation. They deserve honor for their commitment; and we can help them succeed.

Christians are notorious for trying to take over schools through political maneuvering. Being involved in the political process is not only acceptable for the believer, it is essential. We just cannot lower our standards by thinking that our strength is in the political process. Natural efforts in obedience to God bring spiritual release. His invasion is our strength. Political tactics may work from time to time, but this is not Kingdom. Nor is it long-lasting. There is a better way.

Interestingly enough, the fullness of the Spirit can also be seen in these two distinct approaches to ministry. To quote myself, the fullness of the Spirit makes way for "believers that walk in wisdom, making practical contributions to the needs of society, who also confront the impossibilities of life through the provisions of the Cross—solutions through supernatural display. Perhaps it is these two things working in tandem that should be considered *the balanced Christian life.*"

Serving simply to get people saved is a religious agenda.

Revelation 11:15—*The seventh angel sounded his trumpet, and there were loud voices in Heaven, which said: "The kingdom of the world has become the kingdom of our Lord and Christ, and He will reign for ever and ever."*

BOOK QUOTE: *Dreaming With God* [Chapter 5]

Both Dr. Bill Bright, founder of Campus Crusade for Christ, and Loren Cunningham, founder of Youth With A Mission, received the same revelation from God around the same period of time: there are seven major realms of influence in society that shape the way we live and think. These mountains of influence must be invaded by Kingdom-oriented people for the transformation of society to take place. These mountains are:

- Home.
- Church.
- Education.
- Media (Electronic and Print).
- Government & Politics.
- Performing Arts (including Entertainment and Sports).
- Commerce (including Science and Technology).

It is interesting to note that God gave this insight to two men who lead significant youth movements. It is obvious that God wants an entire generation to value their call regardless of what title it brings, teaching them how to invade a culture for its total and complete transformation. God fully intends for there to be a fulfillment of His Word about *"the kingdoms of this world have become the kingdoms of our Lord"* (Rev. 11:15).

The following list is a little different from the original. It does have a slightly different emphasis to more accurately represent our application of these principles. They are: *Business, Education, the Church, Family, Arts/Entertainment, Science & Medicine, and Government* (not listed in any order of importance).

Wisdom is the vital ingredient to be effective in this invasion. As a reminder, we've defined wisdom with these three words: Integrity, Creativity, and Excellence. It is the display of the mind of God, always in the context of integrity that brings forth the creative solutions for life while holding to the standards of excellence. These play a vital role in manifesting the Kingdom in ways that honor God and solve the issues of life for humankind.

Wisdom is the vital ingredient to be effective in this invasion.

3 John 2—*Dear friend, I pray that you may enjoy good health and all that may go well with you, even as your soul is getting along well.*

BOOK QUOTE: *Dreaming With God* [Chapter 5]

MANY Christians have tried to gain favor and position in the business world, but have failed miserably. It is hard to gain favor in that world without prosperity. Prosperity is a primary measure for success in that arena. With that in mind, the world is also full of stories of great financial success that were disasters in every other way. People instinctively want both—outward and inward success. The Kingdom businessperson has the chance to display a more complete picture of success by focusing not only on money. Their celebration of life, with all its many facets, will grab the attention of those hopelessly trapped in the "money is success" daily grind.

While there is room for overt ministry in every part of life, it is generally not the outward preaching of the Gospel that secures the place of favor in the eyes of the unbelieving businessperson. It is divine order (Kingdom) in the overall approach to life—to self, family, business, and community.

Even the world knows that money is not the only measure of true success. Most of those in business want much more than money for their labors. Simple things like joy, a happy home life, recognition, and meaningful friendships are an important part of the life of true prosperity. John, the Beloved, referred to this as "prosperity of soul" (see 3 John 2). Mixed into this quest is the cry for significance. The Kingdom businessperson is poised to illustrate that element by their approach to life. The extra efforts in world relief, along with the personal participation in helping the poor of our own cities as well as other projects requiring giving and sacrifice, help to give definition for the favor of God that is upon the Kingdom businessperson.

People instinctively want both—
outward and inward success.

Proverbs 22:29—*Do you see a man who excels in his work? He will stand before kings; He will not stand before unknown men.*

BOOK QUOTE: *Dreaming With God* [Chapter 5]

ONE of our men sold cars at a local used car lot owned by believers. When a woman came in to buy a car, he noticed that she was very troubled. Through the direction of the Holy Spirit, he was able to minister to her quite profoundly. She opened up to God and received major healing in her heart. When they were through he told her, "Because you have opened up your heart to me, I cannot sell you a car. It would be unfair for me to do so. Instead I will introduce you to another salesman who will help you find the kind of car you are looking for." He was unwilling to come close to the possibility of taking advantage of this woman by selling her something when she had become emotionally vulnerable to him.

Creativity is a necessary component for the Kingdom businessperson. It brings fresh ideas that keep adventure as a central part of their assignment. Witty inventions are going to increase in the Christian community, as God is using that expression of wisdom to bring about a transfer of wealth for Kingdom purposes.

Proverbs 22:29 tells us two things: One, the result of lives pursuing excellence; they will influence the influencers. Two, kings demand excellence. Many compromise in this area to make a quick buck, but it is excellence that provides wealth for the long term. It's a wealth that has no sorrow (see Prov. 10:22). Excellence is a Kingdom value, and is not to be confused with perfectionism, which is a counterfeit and comes from the religious spirit. One of the clearest paths of promotion is through excellence.

Creativity is a necessary component for the Kingdom businessperson.

Luke 19:13—*So he called ten of his servants and gave them ten minas. "Put this money to work," he said, "until I come back."*

BOOK QUOTE: *Dreaming With God* [Chapter 5]

O FTEN times the Church reacts to the abuses of the world system and creates an error equal in danger to one we've rejected. This was never truer than in the realm of education. The Western mindset, that values reason as the only proper measure of truth, has undermined the Gospel. This worldview, which Paul battled in First Corinthians, has been embraced by our educational culture. The supernatural then becomes subject to the evaluation of ignorant people. But the solution to this problem is not to reject education; the answer is to invade.

God is very secure in His understanding and arguments. He also backs up His insights with evidence that will bear up under scrutiny. Invading the educational system is essential as it's this mountain that greatly shapes the minds and expectations of the younger generation. While it could be argued that today entertainers have a greater role in shaping the minds of the young, it is the educators who generally shape the minds of the entertainers in their way of thinking.

Young people need to believe they live their entire lives on this earth, and plan accordingly. Get educated, married, have children, all with a Kingdom mindset. Too many generations who experience the outpouring of the Spirit forfeit their desires for training and education in order to do "the Lord's work." The desire for Heaven is right and healthy. But it must not replace our commission; "*Your kingdom come. Your will be done, on earth as it is in Heaven*" (Matt. 6:10 NASB). We were not commissioned to look into the clouds for His coming (see Acts 1:11). We were commanded to "occupy" until He comes   (Luke 19:13 KJV). *Occupy* is a military term. And according to Kingdom values, occupation is always for the purpose of advancement.

Get educated, married, have children,
all with a Kingdom mindset.

2 Timothy 3:14—*But as for you, continue in what you have learned and have become convinced of, because you know those from whom you learned it,*

BOOK QUOTE: *Dreaming With God* [Chapter 5]

OUR children must become educated, and become educators. But that goal is not complete without the Kingdom mindset. We are sending them into dangerous territory to get their training. Choose their schools carefully. Each teacher that trains your child is a delegated authority—delegated by you. The Bible does not give the authority for training children to the government, no matter how noble their intent. It rests upon your shoulders, so pray, pray, pray, and educate, educate, educate.

We would never send our child to a restaurant where only one in ten die of food poisoning. Yet we do that daily in our educational system, with odds that are much worse than one in ten. We often send them out, unguarded, into a system that works to undermine faith and ultimately their relationship with God. The answer is not to withdraw from society and move into the mountains to preserve the family unit. The answer is to train and invade. Our training is superior to theirs if it's authentic, because it is driven by a personal relationship with God, and includes transforming divine encounters.

As for the believers who are already in the educational system, bravo! Invade with a Kingdom mindset. Such a way of thinking provides the mooring needed to stay stable in storms and conflict. It also puts you in place to provide the answers to the dilemmas created by the inferior "Greek" mindset. Most bad ideas (including bad theology) are only one divine encounter away from oblivion. We owe people an encounter with God. And that is what you carry into that mountain of influence.

Our training is superior to theirs if it's authentic...

Isaiah 55:11—...so is My word that goes out from My mouth: It will not return to Me empty, but will accomplish what I desire and achieve the purpose for which I sent it.

BOOK QUOTE: *Dreaming With God* [Chapter 5]

Most people in our culture unknowingly live under the influence of a dark kingdom. Yet they suffer with problems that have their answer in the Kingdom of God and the believer. Both wisdom and power are available to us that we might provide solutions from another world that meet their needs.

At Bethel Church, we have a waiting list of schools wanting us to be part of their after-school program. Why? We have come alongside to serve, not take over. The liberty that is given to our teams is really quite amazing. Many believe that what we are doing is impossible. And as long as the Church maintains an adversarial relationship with the educational system, it will remain impossible.

Throughout Scripture we see that when God's people step forward to serve, God backs it up with power. The schools are asking for our help. They face problems on a daily basis that were unheard of 30 years ago. It is our hour to invade, serve, and shine for His glory!

Moral values are the basis for integrity. And moral values are rooted in the character of God. The supernatural educator has access to a realm of stability that others don't have. That is not to say one has to be a believer to have integrity. But the supernatural element available in the realm of character is reserved for those who have the Spirit of the resurrected Christ living in them. Young people need educators with integrity, but they also need those who believe in them. Calling out the treasure in a young person can mark them for good forever. Such an educator plants a seed that another person will harvest, but that is the joy of this Kingdom— no words return void. (See 1 Cor. 3:5-9 and Isa. 55:11.)

Both wisdom and power are available to us that we might provide solutions from another world that meet their needs.

Ephesians 5:8-9—*For you were once darkness, but now you are light in the Lord. Live as children of light (For the fruit of the light consists in all goodness, righteousness and truth).*

BOOK QUOTE: *Dreaming With God* [Chapter 5]

ENTERTAINMENT includes the arts, professional sports, and the media.

It wasn't too long ago that the world of entertainment was deemed so unholy that believers were forbidden to enter. The Church has often fallen to the notion that darkness is stronger than light. Entertainment is a mountain of influence that must be invaded. The indictment of that realm being 'unholy' was accurate, but unfortunately, it is also a self-fulfilling prophecy—anywhere we do not invade becomes darker in our absence. We are the "*light of the world*" (Matt. 5:14). The realms of society that we fail to invade are hopelessly lost to darkness. Invasion is the responsibility of light.

This is a realm which ought to have edification as a primary objective. When it is perverted, it steals and plunders. But in its primary function, it creates. Recreation comes from this—re-creation! It must not only be creative, it must create.

Heaven has what we want. Every creative dream is fulfilled in Heaven. The great news is that we have access to that realm through prayers of faith. For example: there are sounds in Heaven that earth has never heard. When a musician taps into that reality and communicates that sound here, Heaven will have found agreement and will invade. All art finds its origins in the person of God; more specifically, it's found in His holiness. The Scripture says, "*in the beauty of holiness*" (Ps. 29:2). It's tragic that holiness gets such poor treatment from the people of God. It is God's nature, His person. Beauty pours forth from that one attribute (see 2 Chron. 20:21).

No field is left untouched. God is planting His last days' army in these strategic places of influence.

Every creative dream is fulfilled in Heaven.

Psalm 89:15—*Blessed are those who have learned to acclaim you. Who walk in the light of your presence, O Lord.*

BOOK QUOTE: *Dreaming With God* [Chapter 5]

THERE'S such a vacuum in the area of integrity in this mountain that all true Kingdom people will quickly stand out. However, we can't be nonchalant about the pressure to conform to worldly standards that the believer will face. Being a stumbling block to others has been become an art form for many. People receive justification for their own immoral lifestyles by getting others to fall morally. But for those who have true foundations, the sky is the limit. In crisis, people will always turn to those who are stable. Integrity will be a beacon of light to those wandering through this land of disappointment and shame.

It might seem that creativity is where we have the biggest challenge in this mountain of influence. The opposite is true. Writers, designers, and the like have substituted sensuality for creativity. This has left a huge gap in the area of real originality. Anyone who has escaped the pressure to duplicate trash will automatically be positioned to create. Learning how to pray in the Spirit and soak in His presence will give great advantages to those wanting to invade this mountain. Heaven has what we're looking for. And you'll have to go there to get it. The best novels and plays have yet to be written. The most beautiful melodies to ever grace the human ear are yet to be discovered. Those with an ear for God, discovering the experience of "being seated in heavenly places" will have access to things no other generation has ever seen before.

In recent days, believers who have adopted the Kingdom mindset have caught up to, and in some cases surpassed, the world in the area of excellence and will continue to do so.

Integrity will be a beacon of light to those wandering through this land of disappointment and shame.

Galatians 6:10—*Therefore, as we have opportunity, let us do good to all people, especially to those who belong to the family of believers.*

BOOK QUOTE: *Dreaming With God* [Chapter 5]

ANY gospel that doesn't work in the marketplace doesn't work. Believers who have adopted the Kingdom mindset have caught up to, and in some cases surpassed, the world in the area of excellence and will continue to do so.

Jesus gave His disciples a warning about the potential influence of religion on the mind, saying, "*Beware of the leaven of the Pharisees and the leaven of Herod*" (Mark 8:15). The mentality of the Pharisee places God at the center of everything, but He's impersonal and powerless. Their God dwells mostly in the realm of theory and supposition. They excel at traditions that are convenient, and reverence that is self-serving. But there's not much in the religious community that is actually Kingdom. It has a wide-open door for people with a renewed mind.

Many in the religious community have a lot of sincerity. And when they see someone who actually practices the purity and power from the pages of Scripture, something comes alive in them. They hope it's true. They just lack examples. Kingdom-oriented people have great opportunities in the midst of great opposition. But the rewards are worth every risk.

Success is often measured by numbers of people attending services, copies of books or CDs sold, or how many watch their TV show. One of the most common fears in this world of influence is that "someone will steal my sheep." Being committed to another leader's success, with no personal agenda for gain, is essential for invasion into this mountain. Ignoring the external measurements of success will enable the leader in this realm to value what the King values—passion, purity, power, and people.

Kingdom-oriented people have great opportunities in the midst of great opposition.

Ephesians 4:32—Be kind and compassionate to one another, forgiving one another just as in Christ God forgave you.

BOOK QUOTE: *Dreaming With God* [Chapter 5]

Compassion is one of the greatest tools we possess to invade this mountain of influence.

The area of morality and integrity should be the area in which we have little problem. But that is not the case. While I don't believe the statistics that claim the Church (authentic believers) is equal to the world in divorce and immorality, the numbers are admittedly far too high. Divine encounters, accurate teaching from Scripture, and accountability to other members of the Body can help change this problem. Righteous people can provide a righteous peer pressure. When fellowship becomes valuable enough that it is sacrificial, then those in fellowship begin to walk in the light—openly, with integrity and accountability. (See Heb. 13:15-16.)

The Church is known for its ruts, not its new ideas. Thankfully a great transformation is taking place in that area. While change for change's sake is not always healthy, those resistant to change are usually resistant to the Holy Spirit. If anyone should be known for creativity, it should be those in whom the accurate image of the Creator has been formed—born-again believers. There are better ways of doing things. Always. And the Church is in the place of leading the way. Cultural relevance is rightfully the cry of the hour, but it must be relevance *with* power!

The Church has often taken the low road in the realm of excellence because of a misunderstanding of humility. But the choice of that road usually flows from low faith, and humility gets the blame. Excellence can and must be the expression of true humility as humility declares, "Our best, for His glory!" Most of the areas that can bring the greatest results have the greatest risk. This is no exception. Excellence is Kingdom. Perfectionism is religion. Poverty is demonic.

When fellowship becomes valuable enough that it is sacrificial, then those in fellowship begin to walk in the light...

1 Timothy 5:8—*If anyone does not provide for his relatives, and especially for his immediate family, he has denied the faith and is worse than an unbeliever.*

BOOK QUOTE: *Dreaming With God* [Chapter 5]

THE pressure being exerted on the family today makes this one of the easiest and most important areas to invade. Even those who seem to work overtime to destroy the family unit, instinctively hunger for healthy relationships, significance, and a legacy. All a family needs to do to have influence in this mountain is to be healthy, and not hidden. When relationships are good and the boundaries of godly disciplines are intact, there is no limit to the influence of the Christian home. The problem has often been a false standard of holiness wherein the Christian doesn't associate with the unbeliever, yet maintains similar values and habits to them. The opposite should be our goal—mingle and associate with the lost, but don't take on their values or habits. That way we, as both salt and light, have our proper effect of preserving and exposing in order to bring them into their destiny. Healthy families that are intentional, breed healthy families.

This is where an ounce of effort translates into a pound of impact. Few families actually purposely live the adventure of life together. Embracing such an adventure together is what gives place for creative expression to surface. My wife has been so good for our household in this area. She is adventurous by nature and tends to add joy to the things I might unintentionally crush by my intensity. My family is better…and I am better, because of her quest for creativity in the home.

This simply means that we always do things to the best of our ability. Sometimes money is tight. Excellence can't be measured in buying the finest car or the most expensive clothes. Rather it is displayed in our approach to life—all of us, for all of Him. It's a great deal!!

Healthy families that are intentional,
breed healthy families.

Psalm 90:17—*May the favor of the Lord our God rest upon us; establish the work of our hands for us—yes, establish the work of our hands.*

BOOK QUOTE: *Dreaming With God* [Chapter 5]

KNOWING that Jesus is the "desire of the nations" encourages us as we approach this mountain of influence. It means our simple task is to make the desired One visible.

Government usually lives in a crippled state because of the fear of voters. Noble people enter that world and end up loosing their dreams on the altar of intimidation. The *leaven of Herod* poisons many (see Mark 8:15). But there is a new breed being groomed for this hour who fears only God and lives with a wisdom that enables one to dance through the minefield of public opinion. Such is the price of working effectively in government.

Those who climb this mountain of influence must realize that it is necessary to increase "*in favor with God and men*" (Luke 2:52), just as Jesus did. Proverbs is probably the most practical book of instruction on this subject. Reading a chapter a day, will give leaders in this realm a compass bearing so that no issue arises that doesn't have a Kingdom solution.

One woman in our congregation was recently working in an Arab country for the U.S. State Department. She was invited to give input into the educational system. They had a problem with the discipline of high school boys, and though they rarely empower women in their country at that level, the favor upon her was larger than the cultural barrier. She addressed instructors and then wrote a paper, based on the principles we live by in our church—all Kingdom principles of discipline. Their educational leaders were so impressed that they adopted the report as the standard of discipline for their school system for the entire nation. The U.S. embassy responded in like manner, sending the report to their embassies around the world.

. . . our simple task is to make the desired One visible.

2 Corinthians 2:15—*For we are to God the aroma of Christ among those who are being saved and those who are perishing.*

BOOK QUOTE: *Dreaming With God* [Chapter 5]

> **Psalm 89:14**—*"Righteousness and justice are the foundation of your throne, love and faithfulness go before you."*
>
> **Psalm 33:5**— *"The Lord loves righteousness and justice; the earth is full of His unfailing love."*

IT is unfortunate that the words integrity and politician are considered an oxymoron. The Word of God remains true—*"when it goes well with the righteous, the city rejoices"* (Prov. 11:10). People instinctively want to be governed by people who are honest and righteous. They want leaders who are not self-serving, but will actually govern sacrificially for the benefit of the whole. Here again is where we need to embrace the standard of Jesus, which is to serve like a king and rule like a servant. It is His way.

It is sad to see believers who fall to the political tactics of unbelieving opponents because their popularity has declined in the public opinion polls. There are better ways of doing things, from running a campaign to surrounding oneself with people of wisdom for good decisions. All of these things are marks of a person committed to the wisdom of creativity.

Two of the most basic roles of government are to create a realm of safety and a realm of prosperity. When governmental leaders use their position for personal gain, it amounts to prostituting their charisma for themselves. Excellence is found in doing our best for the sake of others.

. . . our simple task is to make the desired One visible.

1 Corinthians 13:4—*Love is patient, love is kind. It does not envy, it does not boast, it is not proud.*

BOOK QUOTE: *Dreaming With God* [Chapter 5]

SCIENCE and medicine are becoming bigger influences in the world all the time. Diseases are on the increase, with little sign of cures. I believe in divine healing and have seen thousands healed through Jesus Christ, but I'm not opposed to medical intervention. The entire medical community is gaining power, credibility, and influence throughout our society.

One of our ministry targets is to pray for all those who are with the dying. That includes doctors and nurses, ambulance workers, convalescent hospital employees, police, firefighters, etc. We are praying that the righteous are assigned to those places of influence, because we want to make it nearly impossible to get to hell from our city.

We have a person in a place of authority in one of the convalescent hospitals in our area. It is written on the medical charts that the nurses must call her when anyone is dying so she can be with them. If necessary she will even remove the family members from that patient for a few minutes while she prays with them to receive Christ. We don't want people politely going to hell from our city. You've heard the saying; *there are no atheists in foxholes*—the same could be said of those on the edge of eternity. People are very receptive to the Truth when they are facing death. Authentic love and compassion for people, expressed by those planted within that system, brings forth a wonderful harvest. It's amazing what we are allowed to do when we go in low just to serve. People know the difference between authentic love and a person fulfilling their religious obligations. Real love has very few opponents.

Authentic love and compassion for people, expressed by those planted within that system, brings forth a wonderful harvest.

Galatians 5:13-14—...rather, serve one another in love. The entire law is summed up in a single command: "Love your neighbor as yourself."

BOOK QUOTE: *Dreaming With God* [Chapter 5]

CHRIST-LIKE character always puts others first. This highly respected industry has fallen on hard times due to the great number of doctors who make questionable decisions based on profit margins. Hospitals are often in the crosshairs of critics as they often operate without compassion. Yet that is not the norm. Most in this profession at least started out with sincere compassion to help others. Kingdom-oriented people will once again be easy to spot as the need is so great. If they believe in the power of God to heal, all the better. Miracles increasingly occur through the hands of medical professionals. The number of doctors attending our healing conferences is growing dramatically. It's beautiful when a whole segment of society can work in both the natural and the supernatural realms to bring about good health.

More and more Christian doctors are being trained by God to find answers to health issues. As wonderful as healing is, divine health is greater. Believers have been given access to the mysteries of the Kingdom regarding this subject. It would be tragic to come to the end of time and have the only generation to experience divine health be the Israelites. They lived under an inferior covenant and were in rebellion against God. Inferior covenants cannot make superior promises. Those in this mountain of influence have access to things that the entire world is aggressively asking for. Asking God for specific solutions will enable those involved in medicine to give true creative expression to a dying world.

This group of professionals has a head start in the area of excellence, as they are accustomed to paying a significant price for their role in society. If they can maintain passion and discipline, while embracing a humble heart, nothing will be impossible for them.

More and more Christian doctors are being trained by God to find answers to health issues.

Psalm 19:1-2—*The Heavens are telling of the glory of God; and their expanse is declaring the work of His hands. Day to day pours forth speech, and night to night reveals knowledge. NASB*

BOOK QUOTE: *Dreaming With God* [Chapter 6]

PERHAPS you've heard it said, *God is number one, the family is number two, and the Church is number three....* That unofficial list is important as it outlines a few of the priorities in a Christian's life that have become confused through the years. I know of many tragedies in pastor's families because they ignored these priorities of Kingdom living. Yet, as good as this list is, I don't believe it is technically accurate. When God is number one, there is no number two.

What may appear to be semantics for some has purpose for this reason: we must have a shift in thinking whereby we recognize that passion for God *gives birth* to a passion for other things. And it's those other things that are often to be pursued as *unto the Lord.* We shouldn't experience them as something in competition with, or separate from our devotion to God. Perhaps the best example of this in Scripture is found in First John 4:20. It says that if we love God it will be measurable by our love for people. This is such an absolute principle that God says if we don't love others, we don't actually love Him. The point is this: in the wake of our passion for God, passion for other things is created. It is often in giving ourselves to those things that we prove and manifest our love for God.

In my case my love of the outdoors is part of my devotion to Christ. While some worship nature, I worship the One it points to—the Creator. My love for my family, for hunting and fishing, the mountains and the ocean, fountain pens, and French roast coffee, are all part of the enjoyment of life for me; and that joy is born completely through a relationship with Him.

We shouldn't experience them as something in competition with, or separate from our devotion to God.

Psalm 98:1-2—*Sing to the Lord a new song, for He has done marvelous things; His right hand and His holy arm have worked salvation for Him. The Lord has made His salvation known, and revealed His righteousness to the nations.*

BOOK QUOTE: *Dreaming With God* [Chapter 6]

Psalm 18:1,2—*I love you, O Lord, my strength. The Lord is my rock, my fortress and my deliverer; my God is my rock, in whom I take refuge. He is my shield and the horn of my salvation, my stronghold.*

THROUGHOUT Scripture David is known as "the man after God's heart." His passion for God seems unparalleled in Scripture; yet he also illustrates a love for life that is without equal. In Psalms 137:6 (NASB), he says, "*May my tongue cling to the roof of my mouth if I do not remember you, if I do not exalt Jerusalem above my chief joy.*" In today's religious community this statement would probably not be accepted. How can Jerusalem, the community of the redeemed, be called his chief joy? Isn't God supposed to be his chief joy? The apparent paradox fits perfectly into the Jewish culture that looks for practical expression of spiritual truths. David's love for God needed expression, and Jerusalem was a perfect target.

When we live with genuine passion for God, it creates a passion for other things. *While it is possible to value other things above God, it is not possible to value God without valuing other things.* This is the key point confronting the religious mindset, which dismisses everything not considered sacred. The effort to accomplish the goal of loving God with no other passions has had to create a monastic lifestyle to survive. And while I admire many of the monastic believers in the past, it is not the model that Jesus gave us. The way we steward the rest of life becomes the litmus test that demonstrates an authentic love for God.

When we live with genuine passion for God, it creates a passion for other things.

1 Thessalonians 5:16-18—*Be joyful always; pray continually; give thanks in all circumstances for this is God's will for you in Christ Jesus.*

BOOK QUOTE: *Dreaming With God* [Chapter 6]

LIKE most people, I have a list of things I pray for. On the list are things which have obvious eternal significance—prayer for our cities, for the salvation of certain people we've ministered to, for healing breakthrough in tough cases, provision—both personal and the church. Following the urgent is the "it would be nice" section of the list. I've noticed that God sometimes bypasses the list and goes directly to the "I haven't even bothered to ask" part that dwells somewhere deep in my heart. It is a pleasant and sometimes offensive move.

Once a friend came up to me and said, "Hey, would you like a hunting dog?" I've always wanted to have a well-trained hunting dog, but never had the time or money for such a luxury. Just like that, I was to be the owner of a dog that wasn't on my prayer list. It wasn't even on the "it would be nice" part of my list. It was, however, a secret desire in my heart. God bypassed all that had eternal significance and went to something temporal and seemingly insignificant.

It offended me at first. Not that I wasn't thankful; I was. But it made no sense. I would have preferred He let me use that *trump card* for something that is more important to me.

It took awhile, but eventually I got it. My requests were important, but my view of Him was more important. I started to see that *if it matters to me, it matters to Him.* His bypassing my "urgent" prayer list, my "it would be nice" list, and entering the "secret desires of the heart" list told me more about my heavenly Father than answering all the other things I had been praying about.

My requests were important, but my view of Him was more important.

Romans 10:12—...*the same Lord is Lord of all and richly blesses all who call on Him.*

BOOK QUOTE: *Dreaming With God* [Chapter 6]

PEOPLE frequently come asking me to pray with them for someone else's healing. Sometimes they have an obvious physical need themselves, but will ask for their friend's healing instead. When I press them about their own condition, they usually say something like, "Oh, I'd rather have God heal them than me. They have cancer. I only have a ruptured disc in my back." Their compassion is wonderful because they are putting another person's need before their own. But their concept of God is wrong. Really wrong!

He doesn't have limited power. In other words, He won't run out of power after He heals their back. He'll still have enough power left to heal their friend's cancer. Also, you don't just get one wish and run out after the first one is used up. The desire for a friend is noble, but it's not an "either/or" situation. Besides that, His attention span is excellent; so good in fact that He can give His undivided attention to every human being on the planet, all at the same time. Neither does He view our prayers on the same priority scale that we do. Some would see it this way: "Of course God heals cancer. That's important. My ruptured disc is not as important. I have learned to live with it." We think of cancer being urgent (which it is) and everything else should be put on hold. In reality, it's often the blown disc that gets healed first. And the increase of faith in that one experience helps to bring about the faith needed for healing of the cancer. Our logic is not consistent with His, and He isn't going to change.

Neither does He view our prayers on the same priority scale that we do.

Genesis 12:2-3—...I will make your name great, and you will be a blessing, I will bless those who bless you...

BOOK QUOTE: *Dreaming With God* [Chapter 6]

O N a recent trip I stayed at an Embassy Suites Hotel. Leaning against my pillow was a laminated card that one of the hotel staff left. I've never seen anything so simple, yet so profound, which actually has the potential to bring great impact to a person or even a city. It represents the responsibility of Kingdom-oriented people to be a contributor to society for their good. We see that creative Kingdom influence can and must be demonstrated in all we do, big and small. It's called an *Ancient Prayer*—"The Stranger Within Our Gates."

Because this hotel is a human institution to serve people,
and not solely a money making organization,
we hope that God will grant you peace and rest
while you are under our roof.

May this room and hotel be your "second" home.
May those you love be near you in thoughts and dreams.
Even though we may not get to know you,
we hope that you will be comfortable and happy
as if you were in your own house.

May the business that brought you our way prosper.
May every call you make
and every message you receive
add to your joy.
When you leave, may your journey be safe.

We are all travelers. From "birth till death"
we travel between eternities.
May these days be pleasant for you,
profitable for society, helpful for those you meet,
and a joy to those who know and love you best.

How and what we communicate has the potential to change the atmosphere, creating the context for people to be released to their destiny. Therefore our communication skills must come under the influence of the Holy Spirit. Our words are able to release the presence of God into people's lives through the expressions of compassion and concern.

*How and what we communicate has the potential to change the atmosphere,
creating the context for people to be released to their destiny.*

Amos 4:13—*He who forms the mountains, creates the wind, and reveals his thoughts to man, he who turns dawn to darkness, and treads the high places of the earth—the Lord God Almighty is his name.*

BOOK QUOTE: *Dreaming With God* [Chapter 7]

THERE are many inventions, procedures and life-changing innovations that have been given through the revelation of God. To consistently bring these kinds of solutions to the forefront of society, we will have to learn how to access the realm of Heaven; for it is in Heaven where our answers lie. The spirit of revelation has been given to make this possible.

We thrive with the spirit of revelation, but we perish without it.

People who see what is unseen have the advantage over everyone else who desires a place of significance. Significance is a God-given desire. (Living to be famous is its counterfeit.) They are the ones who are able to *live from Heaven toward earth.* When we live conscious of Heaven and eternity, it changes the way we live and radically increases our measure of impact on society. It's really quite amazing that the ones who see Heaven most clearly have little desire for this world, yet they are the ones who have the greatest impact on the world around them.

Awareness of unseen things is a vital aspect of the Christian life. In fact, we are instructed: "*Set your mind on the things above, not on the things that are on earth. For you have died and your life is hidden with Christ in God*" (Col. 3:2-3). The abundant life that Jesus promised to His disciples is found in this unseen realm. The display of His dominion through miracles and various supernatural expressions are all rooted in this heavenly world. We must access His world to change this one.

When we live conscious of Heaven and eternity, it changes the way we live and radically increases our measure of impact on society.

Ephesians 2:10—*For are God's workmanship, created in Christ Jesus to do good works, which God prepared in advance for us to do.*

BOOK QUOTE: *Dreaming With God* [Chapter 7]

CHANGING the course of world history is our assignment. Yet we have gone as far as we can with what we presently know. (Martin Scott first said this.) We need signs to get where we want to go. Signs are realities that point to a greater reality—an exit sign is real, but it points to something greater—the exit. We don't need signs when we travel on familiar roads. But, if we're going to go where we've never gone before, we'll need signs to get there. These *signs* will restore the *wonder*.

To go any further we need to hear from God anew. We must see the things that are before our faces day after day, yet are presently hidden from our eyes. The ever present need to see and hear has never been greater. The key to staying current with the shifting seasons of God is the spirit of revelation.

Paul understood this as he prayed for the church at Ephesus. He asked the Father to give them the Spirit of wisdom and revelation (see Eph. 1:17). Many would consider the church in Ephesus to be the most significant church in the Bible. They were experiencing one of the greatest revivals in history; second perhaps only to Nineveh (see Jonah 3). There was a public confrontation with the occult, which resulted in satanic materials being destroyed by repentant citizens (see Acts 19:19). Some of the most notable miracles also happened there.

It is also the only church to receive a letter from the apostle Paul in which he gave no word of correction. In their letter he unveiled what is arguably the Bible's greatest revelation of spiritual warfare, husband and wife relationships/the Bride of Christ and Jesus, the fivefold ministry, the nature and function of the church, are a few examples.

We must see the things that are before our faces day after day, yet are presently hidden from our eyes.

Isaiah 5:13—*Therefore My people go into exile for their lack of knowledge; and their honorable men are famished, and their multitude is parched with thirst. NASB*

BOOK QUOTE: *Dreaming With God* [Chapter 7]

WHAT I know will help me. What I think I know will hurt me. It's the spirit of revelation that helps me know the difference.

The prophets warned us about what would happen to a people who did not increase in knowledge through revelation. All knowledge is useful, but can be general. But when God releases revelation, it releases knowledge that enables us to address specific issues at crucial moments. It often is the difference between life and death. It can be said that we thrive with revelation knowledge but perish without it.

*My people are **destroyed for lack of knowledge**. Because you have rejected knowledge, I also will reject you from being My priest. Since you have forgotten the law of your God, I also will forget your children* (Hosea 4:6 NASB).

The Old Testament prophets Hosea and Isaiah understood the challenge and spoke to the issues we would be facing. In the two passages there were two calamities mentioned. *Destroyed* means to "cease; to be completely cut off." Without revelation we are completely cut off from the purposes of God on the earth. It is possible to be busy about the Lord's work, yet still separated from His purposes. *Go into exile* is very similar in its meaning as it can also be translated as "remove." The picture here is of one who suffers an "official expulsion from a home, country or area as a punishment." Here we are exiled from His purposes, as we are unfit to carry the weightiness of such a responsibility apart from the spirit of revelation working in our lives. It is costly to have access to *sight*, and not use it (see Luke 12:56).

. . . when God releases revelation, it releases knowledge that enables us to address specific issues at crucial moments.

Proverbs 2:3-5—...*and if you call out for insight and cry aloud for understanding,...then you will understand the fear of the Lord and find the knowledge of God.*

BOOK QUOTE: *Dreaming With God* [Chapter 7]

*K*NOWLEDGE is more than mere concepts or theories; it is experiential. The word knowledge here comes from the word used in Genesis describing the experience of intimacy—"*And Adam knew Eve; and she conceived and bare Cain*" (Gen. 4:1 KJV).

It is foolish to think, "Because we have the Bible, the full revelation of God has already been given. We don't need anymore." First of all, while the Bible is complete (no more books are to be added) it is a closed book without the help of the Holy Spirit. We must have revelation to see what is already written. Secondly, we know so little of what God wants us to understand from His Word. Jesus said as much. He couldn't teach His disciples all that was in His heart (see John 16:12). This is the knowledge that comes from the Spirit of God as He breathes upon the pages of Scripture. It leads to divine encounters; truth experienced is never forgotten.

Another passage to examine in this line of thought is:

"*Where there is no vision, the people perish*"
(Proverbs 29:18 KJV).

The New King James Version says, "*Where there is no revelation, the people cast off restraint.*" That clarification is huge. Many have thought this passage was about goals and dreams. It's not! It's about the impact of the spirit of revelation upon a person's life, enabling them to joyfully restrain themselves from everything that works against the dream of God for us. As someone once said, *vision gives pain a purpose.*

> *... knowledge that comes from the Spirit of God*
> *...leads to divine encounters;*
> *truth experienced is never forgotten.*

1 Timothy 2:4—...*who wants all men to be saved and to come to a knowledge of the truth.*

BOOK QUOTE: *Dreaming With God* [Chapter 7]

Not all truth is equal. Truth is multidimensional—some things are true, and some things are truer. If you touched a leper in the Old Testament, you became unclean. A primary revelation of the Old Testament is the power of sin. In the New Testament you touch the leper and the leper becomes clean. A primary revelation of the New Testament is the power of God's love. Both statements are true (*sin is powerful* and *love is powerful*) but one is clearly superior.

The Holy Spirit has been given to lead us into all truth. But one of the things He is so clearly in charge of is taking us into the truths that the Father wants emphasized in a particular season. Peter understood this when he wrote:

> *For this reason I will not be negligent to remind you always of these things, though you know and are established in the* **present truth** *(2 Peter 1:12).*

Present truth implies truth that is at the forefront of God's thinking. It is a wise man who learns to recognize where the winds of Heaven are blowing. Life and ministry are so much easier when we involve ourselves in what God is already blessing.

One of the more offensive concepts that Jesus taught and believed is that children are more ready to enter the Kingdom than grown-ups. Many of us have adjusted to the concept for the most part, but still struggle with certain applications. The following is a case in point:

> *At that time Jesus answered and said, "I thank You, Father, Lord of heaven and earth, that You have hidden these things from the wise and prudent and have revealed them to babes (Matthew 11:25).*

> *... knowledge that comes from the Spirit of God*
> *...leads to divine encounters;*
> *truth experienced is never forgotten.*

Acts 16:10—After Paul had seen the vision, we got ready at once to leave for Macedonia, concluding that God had called us to preach the gospel to them.

BOOK QUOTE: *Dreaming With God* [Chapter 7]

MANY believers live with the concept that God will lead them when it's time for them to do something. And so they wait, sometimes for an entire lifetime, without any significant impact on the world around them. Their philosophy—I have a red light until God gives me a green one. The green light never comes.

The apostle Paul lived in the *green light district* of the Gospel. He didn't need signs in the heavens to convince him to obey the Scriptures. When Jesus said, "Go!" that was enough. But He still needed the Holy Spirit to show him what was at the forefront of the Father's mind concerning missions.

He had a burden for Asia, and tried to go there and preach. The Holy Spirit stopped him, which also means He didn't lead him. He then tried to go to Bithynia, but again, the Holy Spirit said no. He then had a dream of a man pleading with him to come to Macedonia. He woke up concluding that this was the direction he was looking for, and went to Macedonia to preach the Gospel. It's a wonderful story of God's leading (see Acts 16:6-10). But it's easy to miss the point; Paul was trying to obey what was on the pages of Scripture because he lived carrying the commandment *to go into all the world!* (See Matt. 28:19.) The old adage comes into play here; it's easier to steer the car when it's moving than when it's standing still. Paul's commitment to the lifestyle of *going* put him in the place to hear the specific directions God had for him in that season. It was the Holy Spirit who was trying to keep him from going to certain places in wrong seasons.

> *... He still needed the Holy Spirit to show him what was at the forefront of the Father's mind concerning missions.*

2 Corinthians 12:1—*I must go on boasting. Although there is nothing to be gained, I will go on to visions and revelations from the Lord.*

BOOK QUOTE: *Dreaming With God* [Chapter 7]

REVELATION is not poured out to make us smarter. Insight is a wonderful benefit of this encounter, but our intelligence is not God's primary concern. His focus in revelation is our *personal transformation*. Revelation leads to a God encounter, and that encounter forever changes us. The encounters can be stunning experiences, or the simple moments of being immersed in His peace; but they are markers along the journey of, "*Thy kingdom come….*" Without the encounter, revelation makes us proud. This was the nature of Paul's warning to the church at Corinth: "*Knowledge puffs up…*" (1 Cor. 8:1). The actual effect on our intelligence is according to the measure of transformation we've experienced. Revelation comes to *enlarge the playing field of our faith*. Insight without faith being released to have the truth realized through experience keeps truth unproven—only theory. It is the birthplace of religion. When God shows us that He wants people well, it is not to give us a theology on healing. It is so we will release our faith into the very area in which He's given us insight that we might experience the fruit of revelation—in this case, to heal people! Revelation means "to lift the veil" or "remove the cover." Revelation gives us access to the *realms of greater anointing available* to us to make that truth a personal experience and lifestyle. The greater the truth, the greater the anointing needed to demonstrate that truth to the world. Anointing must be pursued, not assumed (see 1 Cor. 14:1). The measure of anointing that we carry reveals the measure of revelation we actually live in.

Insight is a wonderful benefit of this encounter, but our intelligence is not God's primary concern.

Luke 10:21—*At that time Jesus, full of joy through the Holy Spirit, said, "I praise you, Father, Lord of Heaven and earth, because you have hidden these things from the wise and learned, and revealed them to little children. Yes, Father, for this was your good pleasure.*

BOOK QUOTE: *Dreaming With God* [Chapter 7]

CAN it be true that children are more open to revelation than adults? We tend to think that the weightier concepts are reserved for the mature. In part, that is true. But the really mature, from God's perspective, are those with a child's heart.

Many people ask me to pray for them to receive greater revelation from Scripture. While it's always an honor to bless someone with prayer, it is seldom understood how revelation comes, or to whom it comes. One of the greatest joys in life is hearing from God. There is no downside. But there is a cost that comes with the impartation.

The following is a list of practical suggestions for those wanting to grow in revelation from God.

Become childlike. Simplicity and humility of heart helps qualify a person to hear from God, while the desire to be profound is a wasted desire. What many discover after years of teaching is that the word that is simple is often the most profound. "*At that time Jesus answered and said, "I thank You, Father, Lord of Heaven and earth, that You have hidden these things from the wise and prudent and have revealed them to babes*" (Matt. 11:25).

Obey what you know. Jesus taught His followers, "*If anyone wills to do His will, he shall know concerning the doctrine, whether it is from God or whether I speak on My own authority*" (John 7:17). "*If anyone wills...he shall know*"—Clarity comes to the one willing to do the will of God. The willingness to obey attracts revelation, because God is the ultimate steward, investing His treasures into fertile ground—the surrendered heart.

Note: We will finish this list in the next journal entry.

. . . the really mature, from God's perspective, are those with a child's heart.

Psalm 77:6—I call to remembrance my song in the night; I will meditate within my heart, and my spirit makes diligent search. NKJV

Note: We are continuing our study from the last journal entry.

BOOK QUOTE: *Dreaming With God* [Chapter 7]

THE following is a list of practical suggestions for those wanting to grow in revelation from God.

Learn the biblical art of "meditation." Biblical meditation is a diligent search. Meditation has a quiet heart and a "directed" mind. Mulling a word over in our heart, with a pursuit that springs from the inquisitive child's heart, is meditation.

Live in faith. Living by faith in my present assignment makes me ready for more. Live with the understanding that God has already willed to give you His mysteries (see Matt. 13:11), and ask accordingly. Then thank Him in advance.

Acquire an understanding heart. Proper foundations attract the builder (revelator) to come and add to those foundations. "*But knowledge is easy to one who has understanding*" (Prov. 14:6 NASB). When fresh insights come, the understanding heart has a "slot to put it in."

Give God your nights. God loves to visit us in the night and give us instruction that we would have a hard time receiving during the day (see Job 33:15-16). Ask Him specifically to minister to you in the night through visions and dreams.

Give away what you have already received. Never underestimate what hungry people can "pull" from you while you minister the Word. Being in a place of continual giving is a sure way of getting more. He draws out of the deep places in our hearts things that are not yet a part of our conscious thought processes (see Prov. 20:5).

Become a friend of God. God shares His secrets with His friends (John 15:15). Listen as He speaks, but speak only what He gives you freedom to speak about. Some things are revealed only because we're friends, and are not to be shared with others.

He draws out of the deep places in our hearts things that are not yet a part of our conscious thought processes.

John 3:11-12—Truly, truly, I say to you, we speak of what we know and testify of what we have seen, and you do not accept our testimony. If I told you earthly things and you do not believe, how will you believe if I tell you Heavenly things? NASB

BOOK QUOTE: *Dreaming With God* [Chapter 7]

ONE of the fun parts of growing up was hearing stories of my family. It didn't matter if it was Grandpa talking about the Northern Pike he caught in Minnesota, or it was my dad talking about his days playing football in high school, they were the stories I loved to hear. And it didn't matter that we may have heard them last week. I wanted to hear them again and again, hoping each time I might get more detail. They were worth repeating, and are a part of my inheritance.

In this light, Jesus made some alarming statements (see John 3:12,12 above).

"We" refers to the Father, the Son, and the Holy Spirit. It is NOT a reference to Jesus and His disciples or even Jesus and the angels. Jesus said what He heard His Father say. The Spirit of God was upon Him, and made it possible for Him to succeed in hearing and seeing His Father clearly. God has a testimony, and is trying to pass on His story to anyone who would listen. He repeats His cry later in this chapter, "*What He has seen and heard, of that He testifies; and no one receives His testimony*" (John 3:32 NASB). Because it's our responsibility to "*loose here what is loosed in heaven*" (Matt. 16:19), we need to have a revelation of Heaven along with the heart to hear His testimony. That is the benefit of "*being seated in heavenly places in Christ.*" He desires to give us His testimony, but can't find anyone ready to hear it. He has spoken of earthy things (natural birth and the nature of wind; see John 3:1-8) and the people struggled—His desire is to speak to them of heavenly things, which have no earthly parallel.

. . . we need to have a revelation of Heaven along with the heart to hear His testimony.

John 16:12— *I have many more things to say to you, but you cannot bear them now. NASB*

BOOK QUOTE: *Dreaming With God* [Chapter 7]

JESUS couldn't teach His disciples all that was in His heart. He ached to give them more, but didn't because the weightiness of His words would crush them.

Their "weight-carrying capacity" was insufficient for what Jesus had to say. When God speaks, He creates. The realities created from what Jesus would have liked to declare were far too significant for them. And the realms of glory released over their lives would require a strength and stability that they did not yet possess.

While it's true that God does not give His glory to another, we're not *another*—we are members of His Body. The ability to carry more has to do with both character and faith. Character enables us to receive glorious promises of destiny without taking the glory to ourselves. And greater faith responds to the declarations with the great courage needed for fulfillment.

The Holy Spirit was given to prepare them for revelation at a whole new level. He would take them where Jesus couldn't. Perhaps this is part of the reason Jesus said, "*It is to your advantage that I go....*" The indwelling Holy Spirit enables us to bear more of the revelation of Jesus than was possible for the original twelve disciples.

But when He, the Spirit of truth, comes, He will guide you into all the truth; for He will not speak on His own initiative, but whatever He hears, He will speak; and He will disclose to you what is to come. He will glorify Me, for He will take of Mine and will disclose it to you. All things that the Father has are Mine; therefore I said that He takes of Mine and will disclose it to you (John 16:13-15 NASB).

The indwelling Holy Spirit enables us to bear more of the revelation of Jesus than was possible for the original twelve disciples.

John 16:13— *But when He, the Spirit of truth, comes, He will guide you into all the truth; for He will not speak on His own initiative, but whatever He hears, He will speak; and He will disclose to you what is to come. He will glorify Me, for He will take of Mine and will disclose it to you. NASB*

BOOK QUOTE: *Dreaming With God* [Chapter 7]

THE Holy Spirit is assigned to take us into *all truth*. The word *all* here is staggering, and should be. What makes this even more stunning is the realization that truth is to be experienced; the Holy Spirit is therefore leading us into experiencing *all truth*. He receives all of His instructions from the Father. It was the Holy Spirit upon Jesus that enabled Him to know what the Father was doing and saying. That same *gift* of the Spirit has been given to us for that *same purpose*.

One of the assignments of the Holy Spirit is to let us know what is to come. The warnings of difficulties are necessary as they help us keep our priorities straight. But it's the Father's good pleasure to give us the mysteries of the Kingdom.

He goes on to say, "*He will glorify Me, for He will take of Mine and will disclose it to you.*" A most touching thing takes place in this verse—Jesus inherits that which He previously gave up when He became a man and died in our place. It is also true that the Holy Spirit was given the task of not simply revealing all that Jesus possesses, but to actually "disclose" it to us. Disclose means to *declare*! There is an amazing transfer of resources taking place. All belongs to the Father—the Father gives everything to the Son— the Son gives everything to us through the Holy Spirit who transfers the resources of Heaven into our account through the declaration. This is astonishing! This is why hearing from God is so vital. He transfers Jesus' inheritance into our accounts every time He speaks. Every declared promise is a transfer of heavenly resources that enable us to fulfill the purpose of our commission.

All belongs to the Father—the Father gives everything to the Son—the Son gives everything to us through the Holy Spirit...

Colossians 1:12—*giving thanks to the Father, who has qualified you to share in the inheritance of the saints in the kingdom of light.*

BOOK QUOTE: *Dreaming With God* [Chapter 7]

ONE of the Holy Spirit's primary functions is to discover what lies in the depths of God's heart for us. Keeping passionate and encouraged is vital while we face the privilege of ascending mountains of influence. Passion wears out when it relies solely on self-motivation. God has fire in His eyes! Frequent encounters with Him will keep any flame in us burning. Our love for God affects our love for everything else. The Holy Spirit leads us into an understanding by experience to help us realize our inheritance.

For to us God revealed them through the Spirit; for the Spirit searches all things, even the depths of God. ...Now we have received, not the spirit of the world, but the Spirit who is from God, so that we may know the things freely given to us by God, which things we also speak, not in words taught by human wisdom, but in those taught by the Spirit, combining spiritual thoughts with spiritual words (1 Corinthians 2:10, 12-13 NASB).

This inheritance is freely given to us; it is the Holy Spirit who brings us into that *land of promise* that we might correctly navigate our way through life realizing the height, depth, length, and width of God's extravagant love for us. He unveils what is ours.

He is also the one who makes the Scriptures come alive; it is the *living* Word. Learning to recognize His presence, His ways, and His language will help us to succeed in our impossible assignment.

The Holy Spirit leads us into an understanding by experience to help us realize our inheritance.

Hebrews 4:12—For the word of God is living and active. Sharper than any double-edged sword, it penetrates even to dividing soul and spirit, joints and marrow; it judges the thoughts and attitudes of the heart.

BOOK QUOTE: *Dreaming With God* [Chapter 8]

THE ability to hear God, especially from His Word, is a mandatory skill if we are to enter divine purpose and true creative expression. It's as necessary as breathing. A yielded heart is impressionable as it studies Scripture and receives God's impressions easily. Within that sort of tender soil, the Lord plants the seeds of Kingdom perspective that grow into global transformation.

I believe the Bible to be the Word of God, inerrant, fully inspired by the Holy Spirit. It is without equal, not to be added to, nor subtracted from. I do not believe there will be any new revelation that has the same authoritative weight as Scripture. It alone stands as judge of all other wisdom, be it the wisdom of man or an insight or book purported to be revealed directly from God or given by an angel. God is still speaking but everything we hear must be consistent with what He has spoken to us in His Word. In light of these burning convictions, there are standards and traditions instituted by the church for our protection that practically suck the life and impact out of God's living Word. Though not the original intent, it has been an unintended result.

Being unaware of His presence has cost us dearly, especially as we approach Scripture. King David, who authored and sang songs of His love for God's Word, "set" the Lord before himself daily. He purposed to be regularly conscious of God's nearness and lived from that mindset. The sanctified imagination is a tool in God's hand that enables us to tap into true reality. My approach is this; since I can't imagine a place where He isn't, I might as well imagine Him with me. This is not vain imagination. Rather, it's vain to imagine otherwise.

The ability to hear God, especially from His Word, is a mandatory skill if we are to enter divine purpose and true creative expression.

1 Peter 1:23—*For you have been born again, not of perishable seed, but of imperishable, through the living and enduring word of God.*

BOOK QUOTE: *Dreaming With God* [Chapter 8]

THERE is a style of Scripture reading that is mainly concerned with finding and applying principles rather than enjoying His presence. This is good but limited. Kingdom principles are real and powerful. They can be taught to anyone. When they are applied to life, they bring forth fruit for the King. Even unbelievers will experience blessing when they live by His principles. My friend was having financial problems. He confided in a neighbor, who also happened to be a pastor, and the minister told him that his problems could be due to the fact that he wasn't honoring God with the tithe—10 percent of his income. He then challenged my friend to test God by tithing to see if his counsel was accurate. When my friend tithed in response to the challenge, blessing starting pouring into his life. He ended up giving his life to Christ because he saw and tasted God's love. But notice the Kingdom principle functioned even before his conversion. Finding and applying principles is something even an unbeliever can do.

I am not knocking the principles. The transformation of cities and nations depends on the receptivity of Kingdom principles. However, this is not the core of the Christian's experience with the Bible. Rather, more often than not, we should read to have a God-encounter.

I'm thankful I learned to hear God through the Scriptures before I found out what the rules were. It's like being told there are no miracles today. That laughable statement might have gotten my attention many years ago, but it's way too late now. I've seen thousands.

. . . we should read to have a God-encounter.

John 3:8—*The wind blows wherever it pleases. You hear its sound, but you cannot tell where it comes from or where it is going. So it is with everyone born of the Spirit.*

BOOK QUOTE: *Dreaming With God* [Chapter 8]

To value the Scriptures above the Holy Spirit is idolatry. It is not Father, Son, and Holy Bible; it's the Holy Spirit. The Bible reveals God, but is not God. It does not contain Him. God is bigger than His book. We are reliant on the Holy Spirit to reveal what is contained on the pages of Scripture, because without Him it is a closed book. Such dependency on the Holy Spirit must be more than a token prayer asking for guidance before a Bible study. It is a relationship with the third person of the Trinity that is continuous, ongoing, and affects every aspect of life. He is the wind that blows in uncertain directions, from unknown places (see John 3:8). He is the power of Heaven, and cannot be controlled, but must be yielded to. He eagerly reveals His mysteries to all who are hungry— truly hungry. He is so valued in Heaven that He comes with a warning. The Father and Son can be sinned against, but sinning against the Holy Spirit has unforgivable eternal consequences.

We are heirs of God, and the Holy Spirit is the down payment of our inheritance (see Eph. 1:13-14). Some teach that we should-n't talk much about the Spirit as the Holy Spirit doesn't speak of Himself. However, both the Father and Son have a lot to say about Him. It is wise to listen to them. God is to be praised, adored, boasted in, and interacted with—and the Holy Spirit is God.

The God who speaks through circumstances and unusual coincidences wants to talk to us again through the pages of His Word, even when it appears to be taken out of context or is not exactly in line with what appears to be the author's original intent.

We are reliant on the Holy Spirit to reveal what
is contained on the pages of Scripture...

Proverbs 26:4-5—*Do not answer a fool according to his folly, or you will also be like him. Answer a fool as his folly deserves, that he not be wise in his own eyes.*

BOOK QUOTE: *Dreaming With God* [Chapter 8]

THE Word of God is living and active. It contains divine energy, always moving and accomplishing His purposes. It is the surgeon's knife that cuts in order to heal. It is balm that brings comfort and healing. But the point I wish to stress is that it is multidimensional and unfolding in nature. For example, when Isaiah spoke a word, it applied to the people he spoke to—his contemporaries. Yet because it is alive, much of what he said then has its ultimate fulfillment in another day and time. Living words do that.

God said we were to choose whom we would serve, yet Jesus said He chose us; we didn't choose Him. We are predestined from before the foundation of the world, yet are told that *whosoever will* may come. Jesus said we had to sell all to follow Him, yet He instructs the wealthy to be rich in good works. The Holy Spirit knows what truth to breath on according to the particular season of our life.

A classic conflict to the Western rational mind is found in Proverbs 26:4-5 (see above) instruction on how to treat a fool. One verse says not to *answer a fool*, and it tells you why. Then it says to answer a fool, also giving us the reasons why. This is not a contradiction to the Hebrew mindset, which understands that truth is often held in the tension of two conflicting ideas.

The mindset that wants static, unmovable, tidy boundaries, and interpretations gets offended over the lines of reason and expectation that seem be in flux. Herein lies our great challenge—can we hear what He is saying now, for now? And can we accept that He may speak differently to each of us?

The Word of God ... contains divine energy, always moving and accomplishing His purposes.

1 John 4:6—We are from God, and whoever knows God listens to us; but whoever is not from God does not listen to us. This is how we recognize the Spirit of truth and the spirit of falsehood.

BOOK QUOTE: *Dreaming With God* [Chapter 8]

Truth is multidimensional. Some truths are superior to others. Lesser truths are often the foundation of greater truths. "I no longer call you servants, but friends." Friendship with God is built on the foundation of first being a servant. Truth is progressive in nature—line upon line, precept on precept.

Much division takes place in the church when people are devoted to different levels of truth. We tend to prefer static rules and boundaries, not things that flex and change. Preset boundaries are what keep us *obedience focused* instead of *relationship focused*. One is set on memorized rules and regulations. The other is entirely set on His voice and presence and the rules and regulations sit at a different level. When the woman caught in adultery was brought before Jesus, He decided to enforce His own rules and law in a way contrary to what the law demanded. And Jesus only did what He saw the Father doing. Obedience will always be important for us. But obedience out of love looks a lot different than obedience because of rules. Israel discovered they couldn't do it, and neither can we.

To say the Scripture changes is an uncomfortable concept. It doesn't change in the sense that it passes away or contradicts itself, but it does change in the same way a wineskin expands to reflect the ever-increasing move of the Spirit of God. In Deuteronomy 23:1 the Lord commands that an emasculated man "*shall not enter the assembly of the Lord.*" Yet in Isaiah 53:3-5, the eunuch who holds fast to the covenant will be given an everlasting name which will not be cut off. Finally, in Acts 8, Phillip converts a eunuch who becomes the very first evangelist to Ethiopia. Peter called this sort of movement "present truth."

*Preset boundaries are what keep us **obedience focused** instead of **relationship focused**.*

2 Timothy 3:16—All Scripture is God-breathed and is useful for teaching, rebuking, correcting and training in righteousness

BOOK QUOTE: *Dreaming With God* [Chapter 8]

In studying the Old Testament prophecies quoted in the New Testament, it doesn't take long to realize that Jesus and other writers of Scripture took many Old Testament passages out of context to prove their point. The common thought today is that the Holy Spirit worked that way for the Scriptures to be written, but it is unacceptable to do this today because the canon is complete. How could it be wrong to use the same principles used to write the Scriptures to interpret the Scriptures? That *rule* is designed to keep us from creating doctrine by experience and contradicting orthodox Christianity. While the reason is noble, the rule is not biblical.

The problem is not our tendency to incorrectly interpret Scripture; it's that after 2,000 years with the Holy Spirit being on the earth and in us, we still don't know Him! The rule is not the answer. Repentance for ignoring the third person of the Trinity is the beginning of the much-needed solution. That alone can take us into realms in God that have previously been thought impossible for an entire generation to experience.

How is it possible to set a rule of Bible interpretation that the Holy Spirit Himself did not follow in inspiring the Bible? And to say that it is no longer allowed because the canon is complete has little merit as the Holy Spirit is with us, and He knows what He meant when He wrote it. This is potentially dangerous because of the bent of some toward creating unholy and/or inaccurate doctrine, but it does not justify removing a necessary tool of the Spirit that He uses to speak to His people. There is danger, but there is also great treasure. This is the necessary tension.

How is it possible to set a rule of Bible interpretation that the Holy Spirit Himself did not follow in inspiring the Bible?

Titus 2:1—*You must teach what is in accord with sound doctrine.*

BOOK QUOTE: *Dreaming With God* [Chapter 8]

DOCTRINE must be a wineskin kept elastic by the oil of the Spirit. If it is rigid and unmoving, it will not yield to God's habit of opening up more of His Word to us. God loves to add to our knowledge. Too much rigidity bursts our doctrinal wineskins under the weight of ongoing revelation. The end result is the church becomes irrelevant and powerless to the world around them.

The Holy Spirit has to be free to speak to us about the things that are on His heart; especially to those things we have a natural resistance. We must be open to truth when it has a biblical basis and is accompanied by the breath of God making it come alive for a specific purpose. The error is building a theological monument around a particular point of view that conveniently excludes certain portions of Scripture to help us feel secure in a doctrinal bent.

Our most valued doctrines can be expanded under the inspiration of the Holy Spirit. We have the most difficulty when He begins to speak about what is, at first glance, a contradiction to what we have learned. The desire for rigid doctrine is in direct proportion to our inability to actually hear His voice. It's essential to be able to recognize His voice so we can embrace His revelation, even when it contradicts our traditional upbringing.

God is big enough to feed me from a particular verse everyday for the rest of my life. The Word of God is infinitely deep. When God reveals truth to us, it is always built on the foundation of previously revealed truth. The former is not discarded. It is what the fresh word is built upon. Again, it's the childlike heart that attracts revelation from God (see Matt. 11:25).

Our most valued doctrines can be expanded under the inspiration of the Holy Spirit.

Ephesians 1:17—*I keep asking that the God of our Lord Jesus Christ, the glorious Father, may give you the Spirit of wisdom and revelation, so that you may know Him better.*

BOOK QUOTE: *Dreaming With God* [Chapter 8]

THE one revelation that is about to change everything is the revelation of Jesus Christ. Paul declared as much when he said that there was something we would come to know by revelation (see Eph. 1:17.) that would bring us into the fullness of Christ, saying *"until we all attain to the unity of the faith, and of **the knowledge of the Son of God,** to a mature man, to the measure of the stature which belongs **to the fullness of Christ**"* (Eph 4:13). Coming into maturity is the result of gaining the knowledge of the Son of God. This revelation will completely change the church because as we see Him we become like Him. This will enable us to accurately represent Jesus.

Jesus Christ is perfect theology. He is the *"...exact representation of His nature..."* (Heb. 1:3 NASB), the ultimate portrayal of the Father. Questions that exist about God's nature in the Old Testament were clarified in the New Testament. Any understanding we have about the nature of God that can't be seen in the person of Jesus, must be questioned.

How many people came to Jesus for a miracle and left disappointed? None! He was 100 percent successful as a man dependant on God. Jesus also messed up every funeral He attended, including His own. When the disciples failed to bring deliverance to a child, He instructed them on how to get their breakthrough. He said it would come through *prayer and fasting* (Mark 9:29). It's time to respond to His counsel and discover for ourselves how to get the breakthrough that appears to be so elusive. He manifested the will of God. And we must not change it to fit our experience. It is time to manifest the will of God again.

Jesus Christ is perfect theology.

James 1:2-3—Consider it pure joy, my brothers, whenever you face trials of many kinds, because you know that the testing of your faith develops perseverance.

BOOK QUOTE: *Dreaming With God* [Chapter 8]

It is obvious and easy to assert that those who try to hear God from the pages of Scripture will not always hear clearly. Some of us will make huge mistakes and claim to have heard from God when it wasn't Him at all. Yet, to succeed, one must be willing to fail.

Early in the 20th century there was a gathering of believers who had tasted the power of God and were hungering for more. Many went to foreign countries to become missionaries but didn't bother learning the language because they knew that God would give it to them because they spoke in tongues. Great disappointment soon followed when they arrived and were unable to speak the national language. "*Hope deferred makes the heart sick,*" is a verse that was never truer than in those years of well-intentioned missionary efforts.

Many years ago a notable leader in the Body of Christ told me he had consciously gotten rid of the prophetic ministry in his church. He felt there was too much danger and too many potential problems. I respected him too much to voice my disagreement, but I quietly got excited in my heart because in the natural, counterfeiters don't make fake pennies; it's not worth the effort. I knew that if the enemy worked that hard to create a counterfeit, the original must have great value. Only things of eternal consequence are worth the devil's attention. For that reason I get encouraged when I see areas of danger, like the prophetic.

My solution is to find people of like mind to work with, realize the danger involved in our common pursuit, and stay humble and accountable in our pursuit of the authentic.

Only things of eternal consequence are worth the devil's attention.

Psalm 104:34—*May my meditation be pleasing to Him, as I rejoice in the Lord.*

BOOK QUOTE: *Dreaming With God* [Chapter 8]

BIBLICAL meditation is a completely different animal than what is encouraged in the New Age culture. Theirs is a counterfeit because it encourages us to empty our minds, making them vulnerable to any *angel of light* to enter, and eventually control. Unfortunately, there are many evil spirits looking for a vacancy. True meditation feasts on God's Word. That absolute foundation for thought sets a course of direction that is sure to take one on the journey of a lifetime. It is interaction with the Holy Spirit. It's a good start for obtaining the new wineskin of thought addressed in Scripture, by giving time for the seed to germinate in a person's heart. "*Tremble, and do not sin. Meditate in your heart upon your bed, and be still*" (Ps. 4:4 NASB).

God desires for us to bring forth His solutions for the difficulties and traumas of life on this planet. When we carry our concerns before the Lord, which come from our place of influence and authority on this earth, He begins to open up His mysteries that are concealed in His Word. For example, if there's a conflict on the job between two friends, God will give you specific insight through His Word about how to bring peace. If there is a need to expand your business, but you're not sure about how or when, He will speak from the pages of His Word. It is living, immediately applicable, and unlimited in its scope and power.

His Word comes to life. He breathes on the pages of His book, and something happens in our hearts. It comes to life! In the end it comes down to this: we will reproduce what we see as we come to the water of His Word.

True meditation feasts on God's Word.

Genesis 30:37-39—Then Jacob took fresh rods of poplar and almond and plane trees, and peeled white stripes in them, exposing the white which was in the rods. He set the rods which he had peeled in front of the flocks in the gutters, even in the watering troughs, where the flocks came to drink; and they mated when they came to drink. So the flocks mated by the rods, and the flocks brought forth striped, speckled, and spotted.

BOOK QUOTE: *Dreaming With God* [Chapter 8]

THERE is a very strange story in Genesis about Jacob and his deceitful father-in-law, Laban. He had worked for Laban, for what seemed like forever, and had been cheated over and over again. Jacob made a deal with Laban for a portion of the flocks to be given to him for his years of service. It would enable him to leave with something to start *life on his own*. They agreed that he would take all the spotted and speckled sheep and goats as his wages. Laban agreed to the terms knowing that spotted and speckled animals were an aberration.

As the animals came to drink, they would see spotted and speckled rods in the ground near their watering hole, which was also their breeding ground. As they came to the water and bred, they did so while looking upon the spotted rods. The result was that they reproduced spotted and speckled offspring.

When we come to God's Word, we will reproduce what we see. Even more interesting is this, which has become my personal experience—whatever my heart is set upon when I come to the Bible, will determine much of what I see in the Bible. That can be good or bad, depending on whether or not I have "*watched over my heart with all diligence*" (Prov. 4:23). Those with evil in their hearts can find the confirmation they are looking for through the misreading of Scripture. The problem is not the method or approach to the Bible; it is whether or not we are willing to stay humble, honest, and hungry before the Lord. Our desperation for truth makes us available for things that others seem to continually miss. Keeping a pure heart makes the journey to God's Word a journey where nothing is impossible.

When we come to God's Word,
we will reproduce what we see.

John 16:14—*He will take of what is mine and declare it to you.*

BOOK QUOTE: *Dreaming With God* [Chapter 9]

ADAM was given the unique responsibility of co-laboring with God in designing the nature of the world he was going to live in. We have been restored to that level of authority again. We have been given this amazing tool to fulfill our stewardship role; "*Death and life are in the power of the tongue...*" (Prov. 18:21 NASB). With our speech we design and alter our environment. Realities are created that didn't exist a moment earlier through simple proclamations. With this tool we can build up or tear down, edify or discourage, give life or destroy it. The declared word has the capacity to resource earth with Heaven's resources. As reformers we must first pay attention to what we say, realizing that we are actually building the world we have to live in. We have the ability to speak *from* God, revealing His world and His ways.

Jesus describes one of the primary roles of the Holy Spirit in John 16:14 (see above). He says this after revealing that all things belong to Him. Jesus is telling us how His inheritance (all things) would be transferred to our account. It would be done through the declaration. Every time God speaks to us, there is a transfer of heavenly resource from His account into ours. Hearing God is essential to the release and the discovery of the vastness of our inheritance in Christ. It is beyond comprehension. It is *all things* (1 Cor. 3:21).

The transfer of "*all things,*" our inheritance, begs this question, "Why would God give us all things?" Because *all things* will be necessary for us to fulfill the commission that God has given us. Our assignment from God will require the use of "all things" to be under our supervision to accomplish His purposes on earth.

Every time God speaks to us, there is a transfer of heavenly resource from His account into ours.

Luke 2:52—*And Jesus kept increasing in wisdom and stature, and in favor with God and men.*

BOOK QUOTE: *Dreaming With God* [Chapter 9]

I understand why Jesus needed to increase in favor with man, as it would give Him access and influence within society in ways He wouldn't have without favor. But how is it that the Son of God, who is perfect in every way, needs to increase in favor with God? I don't have an answer. But I do know this—if Jesus needed more favor from God to complete His assignment, how much more of an increase do I need!

As with most everything related to the Kingdom of God, we receive increase through generously giving away what we have. It is no different with favor—grace. "*Let no unwholesome word proceed from your mouth, but only such a word as is good for edification according to the need of the moment, so that it will give grace to those who hear*" (Eph. 4:29 NASB). In this passage we find that speaking words of edification brings grace into the life of the person we are speaking to. Grace is the favor of God; a highly valued heavenly commodity. This is a significant tool because it brings transformation through words of encouragement by attracting the favor of God to the one we choose to serve.

We get to choose who to encourage, realizing that God will extend to them the favor we have received from Him. It is an issue of stewardship. If we question whether believers have actually been given such a role of eternal consequences, I remind you that Jesus said, "*If you forgive the sins of any, their sins have been forgiven them*" (John 20:23 NASB).

. . . if Jesus needed more favor from God to complete His assignment, how much more of an increase do I need!

Isaiah 35:5-6—*Then the eyes of the blind shall be opened, and the ears of the deaf shall be unstopped. Then the lame shall leap like a deer, and the tongue of the dumb sing...*

BOOK QUOTE: *Dreaming With God* [Chapter 9]

ENCOURAGEMENT is the initial tool used to create what we call *a culture of honor*. We use honor to train believers to step into their destiny, to strengthen our community in righteousness, and even for evangelism. We have honored those in the various facets of our community with amazing results. The average unbeliever is not accustomed to Christians having something nice to say about them. Christianity is known more for what we don't like than for what we do like. In spite of our shortcomings, we have been given this wonderful gift to distinguish us from the rest—the grace to encourage. When we encourage, it is more than a *feel-good moment*; it actually releases the favor of God.

The truth that encouragement releases the supernatural activities of God into the environment, is a big issue in the Kingdom. In Isaiah 35:4, the people of God are told to minister to others with these words, *"Be strong, do not fear! Behold, your God will come with vengeance, with the recompense of God; He will come and save you."* That is encouragement founded upon the covenantal provision and promise of God. It is taking what is available by promise and declaring it into reality in a person's life. The angelic hosts recognize their assignment through the words spoken to insure they come to pass. (See Ps. 103:20). The amazing response from Heaven is noteworthy (see Isaiah 35:5-6 above). Impossibilities yield in the supernatural atmosphere of encouragement.

This atmosphere of honor creates a health from which we serve those around us with life. Instead of becoming the victim of our circumstances, our circumstances become our victims, bringing them under a covenantal purpose (see Rom. 8:28). We become the answer to the heartfelt cry of society.

. . . encouragement releases the supernatural activities of God into the environment. . .

Proverbs 4:23—*Watch over the heart with all diligence, for from it flows the issues of life.*

BOOK QUOTE: *Dreaming With God* [Chapter 9]

Contained in the realm of the Kingdom of God are all the answers to life's problems. It doesn't matter if it's the crisis with the ozone layer or a problem with a failing marriage or business; the realm of the King's dominion has the answer. That realm of dominion is the realm of the Holy Spirit manifesting the lordship is Jesus Christ, which is first realized in our hearts.

Israel was called upon to manifest the reign of God in their departure from Egypt and their entrance into the Promised Land. This journey should have only lasted a couple of weeks at most, yet it took Israel 40 years. They wandered through the wilderness for 40 years. In reality, they were only doing on the outside what they were experiencing on the inside. "*Therefore I was angry with this generation, and said, 'They always go astray in their hearts, and they did not know my ways'; as I swore in my wrath, 'they shall not enter my rest'*" (Heb. 3:10-11 NASB). The phrase go astray means "to wander." They wandered in their hearts first. What was going on inside of them defined and shaped the world around them. In other words, their internal realities became their external realities. What is going on inside of us affects what goes on around us. This principle affects health, relationships, success in our occupation, and our gifts and ministries. All things flow from the heart. Solomon realized this and taught this in Proverbs 4:23 (see above).

Stewardship of our heart is one of life's primary responsibilities. Successfully doing this guarantees success in other areas of life. When attitudes are properly guarded, godly conduct is insured. Careless attitudes give place to wrong thinking; and it's wrong thinking that gives way to sinful actions.

> *Stewardship of our heart is one of life's primary responsibilities.*

Mark 4:39—*He got up, rebuked the wind and said to the waves, "Quiet! Be still!" Then the wind died down and it was completely calm.*

BOOK QUOTE: *Dreaming With God* [Chapter 9]

IN Mark chapter 4 Jesus was in a life-threatening storm with the disciples. To their surprise, He was asleep. I think He slept because the world He was living in had no storms. Jesus was demonstrating what it was like to be *seated in heavenly places*. It is the exact application of what He meant when He said, that, "...*He who came down from Heaven, that is the Son of Man who is in heaven*" (John 3:13), even though He was clearly standing right in front of them on planet Earth.

They woke Him and said, "don't you care we are perishing?" which is an astounding question to ask the Savior of the world. He responded by speaking "peace" over the storm and the storm ended. The peace that enabled Him to rest in the middle of a conflict became the very substance He released that stilled the storm. In other words, His internal reality became His external reality. If it's in you, and it's genuine, it can be released through you. We have authority over any storm we can sleep in, as we can only give away what we've received.

This principle of the Kingdom affects all we are and do. It seems to be the heart behind "*Beloved, I pray that you may prosper in all things and be in health, just as your soul prospers*" (3 John 2). Once again we note that what is ruling on the inside of us affects the outside. Health in my emotions, mind, and will affects my physical well-being. It is also important to note that a prosperous soul attracts the blessing of the Lord materially and financially. This is the nature of life. The reality of the heart helps to define the nature of the world around us.

We have authority over any storm we can sleep in,
as we can only give away what we've received.

John 3:27—*To this John replied, "A man can receive only what is given him from heaven."*

BOOK QUOTE: *Dreaming With God* [Chapter 9]

A stumbling block for many children raised in Christian homes is the fact that Mom and Dad act differently in church than they do at home. Sometimes it's an issue of out-and-out hypocrisy. But most of the time it is well-meaning believers who never learn to watch over their hearts. When anxiety and unrest rule over a person's heart, they automatically create that atmosphere in their home. The joy that is sung about in the corporate gathering is foreign where it's needed most—in the home.

This is actually the source of much burnout for Christians. There is a pressure to produce on the outside what doesn't exist on the inside. It manifests in a works-oriented Gospel that tries to obtain favor through labor rather than working from the place of favor.

Sometimes we focus on merely changing our words knowing that they carry creative force. Still it's out of the heart that the mouth speaks. Changing the external without dealing with the heart is the way of religion. The push for miracles is the same. Trying to obtain a measure of Kingdom expression on the outside that is not manifest on the inside is the sign that the cruel taskmaster of religion is present. In the command to do the miraculous we find the key, *"Freely you have received, freely give"* (Matt. 10:8). We can give away *kingdom* in the measure we experience the *King's dominion* within us. What reigns on the inside rains on the outside. As it was with Peter's shadow, whatever overshadows me will be released through my shadow (see Acts 5:15). The heart is capable of all sorts of evil as well as all sorts of significant spiritual breakthrough. Stewardship of the heart is what determines what is produced there.

*We can give away **kingdom** in the measure we experience the **King's dominion** within us.*

Philippians 1:4-5—*In all my prayers for all of you, I always pray with joy because of your partnership in the gospel from the first day until now.*

BOOK QUOTE: *Dreaming With God* [Chapter 9]

THE soul that is bound by worry, jealousy, anger, resentment, and the like, is incapable of creativity on a consistent basis. It's impossible to thrive in that divine privilege because we are functioning separately from our design. Full potential is only found by carrying what God gave us to carry—"*my burden is light*" (Matt. 11:30). It is common knowledge that when a person's mind is not encumbered with these things, they are free for creative expression. Picture it like this—if I have an automobile with an eight-cylinder engine, I need all eight of them to reach full power. It is possible to run on only six cylinders, but it's not healthy. Nor is it the way the car was designed. People constantly learn to live with worry, fear, and other emotional pressures all the time and end up thinking their "motor" is running fine. The problem is that they've learned to define what is normal by their subnormal lifestyle. Holding on to resentment and the like actually drains power from our engine and disqualifies us from significant spiritual breakthrough. Repentance is the beginning of the answer. It brings us into forgiveness and into our purpose.

As His delegated authority on earth we have the responsibility to carry on the assignment that Jesus received from the Father—"*...destroy the works of the devil*" (1 John 3:8). The devil is defeated, but many of his works remain unchallenged. Before Jesus was taken to Heaven, He passed on the same commission to us that His Father gave to Him (see John 20:21). This is the overt ministry style of addressing those parts of people's lives that have been affected by the one who came to "*kill, steal, and destroy*" (John 10:10).

Full potential is only found by carrying what God gave us to carry...

Psalm 41:12—*In my integrity you uphold me and set me in your presence forever*

BOOK QUOTE: *Dreaming With God* [Chapter 9]

WE believe God has required us to have a 100-year vision for our church. In other words, we constantly make decisions with the knowledge they will affect a generation that we will never see. "*A good man leaves an inheritance to his children's children*" (Prov. 13:22). God's righteousness makes us good. And it's His righteousness that causes us to see the effect of our decisions today on the generations that follow.

This vision is possible only through the discovery of divine purpose. As we see the eternal purpose of God for His people, we are able to develop lifestyles that are consistent with such a purpose. The end result is that we make His purposes perceivable to the unbeliever.

We are first and foremost a people of God's presence. The Church is the eternal dwelling place of God. As such we are known for our ministry *to God*, which positions and equips us for more effective ministry *to people*. For example, evangelism in its purist form is simply an overflow of worship. If the glory of God could be seen on and within the house(s) of God in the Old Testament—though the hands of man built them—how much more is that glory witnessed in this house called the church; for God is building His Church (see Matt. 16:18).

We are to display the wisdom of God to be seen by all those in positions of power—including the principalities and powers in heavenly places. The creative expression that comes through wisdom is a reminder to all that exists that this company of believers is commissioned to bring heavenly answers to earthly problems. This will turn heads from the inferior wisdom of this world to the divine wisdom that answers the cry of the human heart.

The Church is the eternal dwelling place of God.

2 Kings 20:17-18—*"Behold, the days are coming when all that is in your house, and all that your fathers have laid up in store to this day will be carried to Babylon; nothing shall be left," says the Lord. "Some of your sons who shall issue from you, whom you will beget, will be taken away; and they will become officials in the palace of the king of Babylon."*

BOOK QUOTE: *Dreaming With God* [Chapter 9]

THERE are two basic mountains of opposition to the way of thinking that has us build for another generation to enjoy. The first is our own selfishness. It's easy to think in terms of what is best for us and lose sight of the ones that have to sleep in the bed we make. Hezekiah made such a mistake. He sinned by showing his complete treasury to foreigners. The Prophet rebuked him (see 2 Kings 20:17-18 above). It's hard to imagine how such a great reformer could have fallen so far but his shocking response is as follows, *"'The word of the Lord which you have spoken is good.' For he thought, 'Is it not so, if there will be peace and truth in my days?'"* (2 Kings 20:19 NASB). It's sad to see how one so great thought solely about himself in a time when he learned his family line would bear a curse because of his foolish choice. He was actually so happy that he would enjoy blessing in his day that he lost sight of being the one leaving a legacy of evil for his descendants. He left them with a curse instead of a blessing, which is a stunning end to a great revivalist's life.

The second problem is it's hard to occupy, as we were commanded, and pray for His dominion to be demonstrated when our hope is based entirely on life in Heaven. This is a difficult tension for the church that exists between supposedly conflicting truths; our *blessed hope* in Christ' return, and our delight in the privilege of praying and laboring for His Kingdom (the King's Dominion) to come—now! The promise of Christ's return does not give me permission to be irresponsible with Christ's command.

The promise of Christ's return does not give me permission to be irresponsible with Christ's command.

Matthew 25:32—*All the nations will be gathered before Him, and He will separate the people one from another as a shepherd separates the sheep from the goats.*

BOOK QUOTE: *Dreaming With God* [Chapter 9]

WE have the honor of living at a time when our lives make a dramatic difference in the outcome of world events. We were born for this hour. Our assignment is to live as though nothing were impossible. The command to disciple nations is not figurative. It was a literal command that has the backing of Heaven for those who embrace the assignment. This is a time when "sheep" and "goat" nations are being decided. Silence by the church, or unbelief concerning divine purpose, can cost us the privilege of fulfilling that part of our commission. It will end in disaster for many nations that could have had a significant outpouring of the Spirit.

Regardless of how and when you believe we are going to be taken to Heaven, we must rid ourselves of the idea that Jesus is coming to *rescue* His church. That lie has dislocated many generations of revolutionaries from their purpose in the same way a joint is pulled out of place. It has put the Church into a defensive posture of occupation to protect what we have instead of positioning ourselves for the purpose of increase. The strategy of occupation for the purpose of advancement and increase is an absolute Kingdom principle. Ask the man who buried his talent in order to protect it (see Matt. 25:24-28). He occupied (possessed) to protect (preserve) without increasing what he was given and suffered eternal consequences for his choice.

As we study God's Word, the heart of God is revealed. All that He has declared will come to pass. His Word will not return without bearing the fruit that He intended (see Isaiah 55:11). We have the privilege of saying what the Father is saying, and thereby learning how to shape our world through biblical declarations.

The strategy of occupation for the purpose of advancement and increase is an absolute Kingdom principle.

Isaiah 60:5—*Then you will look and be radiant, your heart will throb and swell with joy; the wealth on the seas will be brought to you, to you the riches of the nations will come.*

BOOK QUOTE: *Dreaming With God* [Chapter 10]

To resource the earth with Heaven's resources, our understanding of stewardship must grow. Many struggle whenever leaders teach about responsibly managing our gifts, time, relationships, and the world we live in. But the greatest honor bestowed on us as stewards is the responsibility to steward tomorrow, today.

Our role in shaping the world around us through creative expression is never more at the forefront than when we joyfully learn to pull tomorrow into today. God trains us for this role whenever He speaks to us, for in doing so He is working to awaken and establish our affections for His Kingdom. A people whose hearts are anchored in His world are best qualified to serve in this one. He establishes His eternal purpose in us whenever He speaks. His Word comes from eternity into time, giving us a track to ride on. It connects us with eternity, causing us to impact our world through the influence of His world.

The believer's inheritance is beyond human comprehension. To put the richness of that gift into the eternal future is to sell short the power of the Cross in the present. He gave us a gift beyond comprehension because we have an assignment beyond reason. Jesus gave us all things because we would need *all things* to fulfill our call. He intends to fill the earth with His glory, and His glorious Bride will play a role.

It is interesting to note that we have already inherited tomorrow—*things to come*. That makes us stewards of tomorrow in a profound way. God reveals coming events to us, and we steward the timing of those events. This amazing privilege is exemplified in Scripture and gives insight to passages that might otherwise be hard to understand.

. . . we have already inherited tomorrow—
things to come.

John 12:40—*He has blinded their eyes and He hardened their heart, so that they would not see with their eyes and perceive with their hearts, and be converted and I should heal them. NASB*

BOOK QUOTE: *Dreaming With God* [Chapter 10]

MANY times throughout the Scriptures we are faced with statements and principles that challenge our understanding of God.

Such a case is found in the Gospel of John (see above). At first glance it looks as though God has it in for Israel and that He hopes they don't repent because He doesn't want to heal them.

Yet the whole of Scripture gives us a different picture. We know God never hardens a tender heart. It's the tender heart that receives what God is saying and doing. Wherever people have truly sought God, He has welcomed them with much mercy and grace, as He is the restorer of broken lives. But a hard heart is a different story completely, as God will harden a hard heart.

Pharaoh is probably the best example of this (see Exod. 7). The Bible says that he hardened his heart against the Lord, and did so repeatedly. So God finally hardened his heart for him, making his condition permanent. If Pharaoh would not be used as an instrument of righteousness, then God would use his evil to display His wonders. God's intent was now to use him as a "chess piece" for His purposes.

Israel was similarly hardened and used for His purposes. While Nazareth was the only city we know of to resist because of unbelief, the others still didn't repent even though they saw extraordinary miracles (see Matt. 11:21). Seeing God display His wonders has a price tag—we can no longer live (think and act) the same way we did before. Miracles display God's dominion with a clarity that is seldom seen in the rest of life. To see and not change is to bring judgment upon ourselves. Such was the case for many of the cities of Israel.

Miracles display God's dominion with a clarity that is seldom seen in the rest of life.

Romans 11:11—*I say then, have they stumbled that they should fall? Certainly not! But through their fall, to provoke them to jealousy, salvation has come to the Gentiles. NKJV*

BOOK QUOTE: *Dreaming With God* [Chapter 10]

GOD is perfect in wisdom, and is able to use the worst that man can dish out for His glory. In His sovereignty, He chose to use this *season of rejection of the Gospel* as the time He would add the Gentiles to the faith. This is discussed more clearly in Romans 11 (see above).

Israel's rejection of Jesus provided the opportunity for the Gentiles to be grafted into the olive tree, the *Israel of God* (Gal. 6:16; Rom. 11:17-24). The entire story is a fascinating study about God's sovereign plan to save people from every tribe, tongue, and nation, but unpacking this is not the purpose of this chapter. Rather, tucked away in this wonderful story is a remarkable truth: if Israel would have seen what God had purposed for them within His Kingdom in the last days, and asked for it, God would have had to give it to them. He would have answered them even though it was not His correct time for that promise to be fulfilled. So He used their hardness of heart as the basis for blinding them to insure that His purposes would be accomplished on His timetable. Instead of just saying "No," He responded by hardening their already hard hearts so they would lose their ability to perceive Kingdom possibilities.

The implication of the story—if you see it, you can have it! Perhaps it would be better to say, if God lets you see future promises, it's because He's hoping they will hook you, and cause you to hunger for those things. It is through a desperate heart that you are able to bring the fulfillment of those promises into your day.

God is perfect in wisdom, and is able to use the worst that man can dish out for His glory.

John 14:26—But the Counselor, the Holy Spirit, whom the Father will send in My name, will teach you all things and will remind you of everything I have said to you.

BOOK QUOTE: *Dreaming With God* [Chapter 10]

JESUS and His mother, Mary, went to a wedding in John chapter 2. After they were there for a while, Mary noticed the wedding party was out of wine. She spoke to Jesus about their problem. Jesus' responded, *"Woman, what does that have to do with us? My hour has not yet come"* (John 2:4 NASB). Since Jesus only said and did what He picked up from His Father (see John 5:19), He let her know that this was not the right time to reveal Him as the miracle worker. Mary had been *pregnant* with God's promises about her son for 30 years, and found it difficult to wait much longer. She turned to the servants and told them to do whatever Jesus said. Jesus, who got all His direction from His heavenly Father, now perceived that this had become the right time. Amazing! God's timing changed! What was reserved for another day (revealing Jesus as the miracle worker) was pulled into her day through her desperation.

Another time, Jesus ministered to a Samaritan woman at the well. Jesus so profoundly impacted her that she was able to persuade the entire city to hear Him speak. They believed at first because of the woman's testimony, but ended up believing out of their personal contact with Him. Remember is that this was not supposed to be the time for the non-Jews to hear the Gospel. The disciples were not even allowed the chance to preach to them when they were commissioned in Matthew 10 as that new focus would come after the death and resurrection of Jesus. Yet in this story, the people of the city begged Jesus to stay two more days, which He did. They pulled a privilege into their day that was reserved for another time.

What was reserved for another day…was pulled into her day through her desperation.

1 Chronicles 15:3—David assembled all Israel in Jerusalem to bring up the ark of the Lord to the place he had prepared for it.

BOOK QUOTE: *Dreaming With God* [Chapter 10]

KING David takes the prize for having perhaps the greatest story which illustrates the principle of Biblical precedents.

David is known as the man after God's heart. He had a revelation of changes in their approach to God. This insight changed everything. He saw that the blood of bulls and goats did nothing to really touch the heart of God, and that He was really looking for the sacrifices of brokenness and contrition. Another radical change that would have been nearly unimaginable in that day was that every priest would be welcome into God's presence daily. And they didn't come with a basin of blood, but instead came offering sacrifices of thanksgiving and praise.

Preparations began. The musicians and singers were trained. Israel was getting herself ready for the presence of God to return to Jerusalem. Saul, Israel's former king, had little regard for the ark of the covenant. But David wanted God's presence more than anything. There were no sacrifices of animals before His presence in this tent. It was 100 percent worship.

It's important to note two things: One, what they did was forbidden by the law they lived under. And two, they were given a sneak preview of New Testament church life. Because of the blood of Jesus, each believer has access to the presence of God to minister to Him with thanksgiving, praise, and worship.

David was primarily a worshiper. As a young man he no doubt learned much about the presence and heart of God. He tasted of a lifestyle that was reserved for New Testament believers, yet hungered for that in his day. His hunger for what he saw became so strong that God let him have something in his day that was reserved for another day.

His hunger for what he saw became so strong that God let him have something in his day that was reserved for another day.

Micah 4:1-2—And it will come about in the last days…Many nations will come and say, 'Come and let us go up to the mountain of the Lord and to the house of the God of Jacob, that He may teach us about His ways and that we may walk in His paths…. NASB

BOOK QUOTE: *Dreaming With God* [Chapter 10]

WE have a bad habit of taking most of the good promises of the Bible and sweeping them under the mysterious rug called "the millennium." It is inconsistency to say the last days began with Pentecost in Acts 2, and say that the wonderful promises of the prophets about the last days refer to the millennium. A good example of this is Micah 4:1-2 (see above). The error is clearly realized in the fact that what is believed actually requires little or no faith to get what most of the Church is waiting for—the world to get worse, and the Church to get rescued. This is an irresponsible way to respond to great promise.

Had David lived with such a mindset, he would have had to live under the restraint of Old Testament law, and not provide us the testimony of a life of celebration and joy. He illustrated the New Testament believer before there ever was such a thing.

If ever there was a line to cross where it should have been impossible to bring something from a future era into a given time, it should have been during David's day. The barrier between the law and grace was so large that what David did would have been impossible to predict, were we on the other side of the Cross. Yet the desperation of a hungry heart brought about the impossible. It drew into their hour something that was not just for the future. Nor was it just reserved for another day; it was for another race of people. Believers are actually a new creation, a new race of people. (See 2 Corinthians 5:17 and 1 Peter 2:9.) Yet David brought this greatest of life's privileges across the greatest divide imaginable. He had daily access to the glory of His presence! This would be something that only the blood of Jesus could make possible.

It drew into their hour something that was not just for the future.

Romans 4:17—As it is written: "I have made you a father of many nations." He is our father in the sight of God, in whom he believed—the God who gives life to the dead and calls things that are not as though they were.

BOOK QUOTE: *Dreaming With God* [Chapter 10]

If it's true that the promises of restored cities and healed nations are actually millennium promises…and if the promise of God's glory being manifest all over the earth is far off into the future…and if in fact the people of God will not reach a place of true maturity, living like one mature man—then I must ask these questions: Is there anyone hungry enough for what He has shown us in the Scriptures that we will pull into our day something that is reserved for another? Is there anyone willing to lay themselves down to bring more of God's promises across another great divide? Or how about the promise that says everyone will know the Lord? (See Jer. 31:34.) Isn't that one worth pursuing for our cities?

If what I have shared is true, then no one can hide behind their eschatology. No one is exempt because of the doctrinal interpretation of the last days. No one is excused. If you can see the coming future promises, and He hasn't blinded your eyes to His intent, then He is hoping to hook you into the role of calling *"into being that which does not exist"* (Rom. 4:17 NASB). It is the role of the desperate heart of faith. We have the opportunity to affect the direction and flow of history through our prayers and intercessions. This is when we take hold of the future. This is why He wants to show us, *"things to come"* (John 16:13). The future is now, and it belongs to us.

We have the opportunity to affect the direction and flow of history through our prayers and intercessions.

Amos 9:13—*"The days are coming," declares the Lord, "when the reaper will be overtaken by the plowman and the planter by the one treading grapes. New wine will drip from the mountains and flow from all the hills."*

BOOK QUOTE: *Dreaming With God* [Chapter 10]

I T is my conviction that God is trying to get rid of our excuse concerning "seasons." Many have lived in a spiritual winter for most of their lives and called it *God's dealings*. The metaphor of the seasons has become an excuse for moodiness, unbelief, depression, inactivity, and the like. It must end. As the technological development has increased exponentially, so the development and maturity of this generation will increase.

Trees planted by God's river bear fruit 12 months of the year. They are the prophetic prototype of the last days' generation that has experienced the acceleration prophesied. How else do you think it's possible for the *"plowman to overtake the reaper?"* (Amos 9:13). This is an amazing prophetic picture of a time when planting and harvesting are done in one motion. How else can we come into the maturity talked about in Zechariah when the weakest among us is like David and the strongest is like God? (See Zech. 12:8.) These things are reserved for the hour directly ahead of us. Let's grab hold of tomorrow, today. We don't have time to waste and then blame God for it. It is the season to apprehend, because we see!

There's a message for us in the cursed fig tree. Jesus cursed it for not bearing fruit *out of season*. It died immediately. Was He unreasonable? Or was He showing us something about His expectations for our lives that we'd just as soon ignore? He has the right to expect the fruit of the impossible from those He has created for the impossible. The Spirit of the resurrected Christ living in me has disqualified me from the mundane and ordinary. I am qualified for the impossible, because I'm a believing believer. Faith qualifies me for the impossible.

The Spirit of the resurrected Christ living in me has disqualified me from the mundane and ordinary.

Jude 3—Dear friends, although I was very eager to write to you about the salvation we share, I felt I had to write and urge you to contend for the faith that was once for all entrusted to the saints.

BOOK QUOTE: *Dreaming With God* [Chapter 10]

Two years ago I sought for a breakthrough in my dad's healing. It never came, and he went home to be with Jesus—but that's a story for another day. Let's just say there are no deficiencies on God's side of the equation. It felt like I was pushing against a 1,000-pound rock that wouldn't budge. And although I pushed against that rock for months, it never moved. We celebrated his home-going and vowed to continue to push against those things which cut people's lives short.

It wasn't too long afterward that I realized that while I never moved that 1,000-pound boulder, I can now move the 500-pound rock right next to it. And I couldn't have moved this size rock before contending with the 1,000-pounder. Contending shapes us and makes us capable of carrying more than we've ever been able before, and opens up for us areas of anointing in ministry that were previously out of reach.

Often times God uses the fight to increase a person's experience in Him, far above all those around them. I call it a *spike in human experience.* In times past, people with that elevated position of experience and the extraordinary anointing and favor that goes with it, used it to draw people to themselves to receive from their gift. While that is always a part of the purpose of a gift, it falls short of God's intent entirely. The elevated experience is the position to equip the Body of Christ so that what was once the high point of breakthrough for an individual has become the new norm for the Church. Contending brings a breakthrough that must be shared. All must benefit from the price we pay to labor through the heat of the day. It's just His way.

Contending brings a breakthrough that must be shared.

Zephaniah 3:20—At that time I will gather you; at that time I will bring you home. I will give you honor and praise among all the peoples of the earth when I restore your fortunes before your very eyes.

BOOK QUOTE: *Dreaming With God* [Chapter 10]

GOD is using the hunger of His people to increase the momentum of the day, bringing about drastic changes in the pace of development. Brand-new believers are not waiting for the *mature* to tell them that something is possible. They've read the Book, and they know it's legal. This tattooed generation with their body piercings and little fear of death has locked into the possibility of significance. They have seen what prior generations have called impossible, and will settle for nothing less. I, for one, join myself with them in the quest for the authentic Gospel that has no walls, no impossibilities, with an absolute surrender to the King and His Kingdom.

God doesn't reveal coming events to make us strategists. He shows us the future to make us dissatisfied because hungry people move the resources of Heaven like no one else possibly could. It's the real reason the rich have such a hard time entering the Kingdom—there's so little hunger for what is real, what is unseen—their desperation has been numbed by an abundance of the inferior.

We are in a race. It's a race between what is and what could be. We are uniquely positioned with the richest inheritance of all time. It has been accumulating through several thousand years of humanity encountering God, and God encountering humanity. The righteous dead are watching. They fill the heavenly stands, and have been given the name, *"cloud of witnesses"* (Heb. 12:1). They realize that in a relay race, each runner receives a prize according to how the last runner finishes. They invested in us for this final leg of the race, and are now waiting to see what we will do with what we've been given.

God is using the hunger of His people to increase the momentum of the day...

Job 33:14-15—*For God does speak—now one way, now another—though man may not perceive it. In a dream, in a vision of the night, when deep sleep calls on men as they slumber in their beds,*

BOOK QUOTE: *Dreaming With God* [Chapter 10]

WE'VE been given the capacity to dream and, more importantly, to dream with God. His language continues to be unveiled, His heart is being imparted, and permission has been given to try to exaggerate His goodness. We have been given the right to surpass the accomplishments of previous generations using creativity through wisdom to solve the issues facing us. Their ceiling is our floor. This is our time to run.

I remember when I was a child and my parents would have guests come over to our house to visit. It was always exciting to be part of the food and the fun. But it was painful to have to go to bed while they were still there, sitting in our living room, talking and having fun. The laughter that echoed back into my room was just torture. It was impossible for me to sleep in that atmosphere. Sometimes, when I couldn't take it any longer, I would sneak quietly into the hallway, just to listen. I didn't want to miss anything. If my parents caught me they usually sent me back to bed. But there were a few times when they thought my curiosity was humorous enough to let me come out to be with them just a little longer. The risk was worth it!

I'm in the hallway again. And the thought of missing something that could have been the experience of my generation is pure torture. I can't possibly sleep in this atmosphere, because if I do, I know I'll miss the reason for which I was born.

We've been given the capacity to dream and, more importantly, to dream with God.